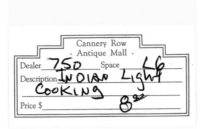

Indian Light Cooking

INDIAN LIGHT COOKING

Delicious and Healthy Food from
One of the World's Great Cuisines

RUTH LAW

DONALD I. FINE, INC.
NEW YORK

*To all of my Indian friends
without whom this book
would not have become a reality.*

CONTENTS

Acknowledgments

∾∾

I have always believed in destiny. During one of my many visits to Bali, Indonesia, I met Inder Sharma, then president-elect of the Pacific Asia Travel Association. Inder, always proud of his country, convinced me to visit India. That was just the beginning of many extraordinary culinary, cultural and travel experiences.

There are many people who have generously assisted with this book during all of its stages.

I would like to thank the Honorable Madhavrao Scindia, former Minister of Civil Aviation and Tourism, Government of India; B. K. Goswami, former Secretary, Ministry of Tourism, Government of India; Inder Sharma, Chairman, SITA World Travel (India), Pvt., Ltd.; and S. P. Dutt, retired manager Tourism and Public Relations, Air India, for planning and facilitating my trips.

A special recognition must go to Habib Rehman, President ITC-Welcomgroup Hotels, palaces and resorts, a supreme connoisseur of food, who had great faith in me. His group of talented and dedicated chefs and executives provided me with much to make my visits to India a delightful learning experience. They and the other chefs—and home cooks—who counseled me are credited throughout the book.

To The Oberoi Group of Hotels, the Taj Group of Hotels, their chefs and executives, the many government officials and the Institutes of Hotel Management, Catering Technology & Applied Nutrition in New Delhi, Jaipur, Bombay, Madras and Goa, where I both studied and lectured, and the many people who opened their homes to me, I am deeply obliged.

I would like to thank the hundreds of Indians both in India and in the United States who gave so unselfishly of their time, knowledge and hospitality. I have been able to formulate a strong bond with many new friends.

In the United States, I especially want to thank Mrs. Maya Ray, wife of His Excellency, the Honorable S.S. Ray, Ambassador of India; Kumud R. Sinha, Consul General of India, Chicago; Pyare Lal Santoshi, former Consul General of India, Chicago, presently His Excellency, Ambassador of India, Venezuela; Rabi Bohidar, former Regional Director of Tourism, Americas, Government of India and his successor Ram P. Chopra, Director of Tourism, Americas. A very special thanks goes to Andy Bhatia, District Sales Manager, Air India, Chicago, who became a close friend on whom I could always count.

To my son, Grant, and his wife, Mary, I extend special thanks for their support in my endeavors. And especially to Grant, who demonstrated extraordinary patience with his computer-inept mother.

Particular thanks should go to my right hand—and jack-of-all-trades—Tad Hillery, who assisted me, tested recipes and even managed to keep me organized—and to Joan Schuessler whose secretarial and culinary skills played such an important role.

Appreciation must also go to Mary Goodbody, my talented editor; Sarah Bush, her assistant; Jane Dystel, my literary agent; and to Vineeta Santoshi, who contributed her artistic talents by illustrating this book. Particular thanks go to Mary Ellen Druyan, whose vast knowledge about cooking as well as food science helped tremendously in the nutritional analysis of each recipe.

My many students and tour participants to Asia have been a strong motivational source. Their enthusiasm and joy of preparing and tasting the dishes in this book have been most inspirational.

I am extremely grateful to my loyal testers Lee Kellum, Dave and Mary Parta, Bob and Marsha Gordon, Richard and Melanie Gordon, Judy and Jerry Hirsch, Susan McGuire, Elizabeth Krainc, Cynthia Krainc, Sharon Cooke, Nancy Zubik, Valerie Prohammer, Marsha Boehm, Roseann Petrucci, Angie Bailey, Hugh Robinson, Cynthia Wills, and Lee Eichorn. Their previous limited exposure to Indian cuisine was a great asset as they approached each recipe as would an American home cook. Their excitement about the new taste experiences they were encountering and their suggestions to improve my writing skills to make the recipes more intelligible were a tremendous motivator.

Others who deserve acknowledgment for their advice, counsel and other contributions are J. Inder Singh Kalra, L. Edwin Brown, Executive Director, American Culinary Federation, Inc.; Gerald E. Piccolla, Senior Vice President—Marketing, Pacific Asia Travel Association; Bette Peters; Annette and Sam Cremin; Sue, Jim and Kim Nibeck; Bharti Patel, Prem Sharma, Florence and Jack Urhausen and Kiran Vohra.

* * *

My sincere gratitude to Kumud R. Sinha, Consul General of India, Chicago, and Ashok Sharma, Information Officer, India Tourist Office, New York, who read my manuscript and verified the information contained in the "Welcome to India" chapter and to Anjali Joshi Reddy for the Hindi translations throughout the book.

About the Nutritional Analysis of Recipes

‿∾‿

The recipes in this book were analyzed by Mary Ellen Druyan, PhD., MPH, R.D. The information is derived from calculation based on the Nutritionist IV computer program and the following:

Food for Fifty, 9th edition, Shugart, Grace and Molt, Mary, Macmillan Publishing Co., New York, 1993.

The Corinne T. Netzer Encyclopedia of Food Values, 1992 edition, Corinne T. Netzer, Dell Publishing, New York, 1992.

Bowes and Church's Food Values of Portions Commonly Used, 14th edition, revised by Jean A. T. Pennington and Helen Nichols Church, J. P. Lippincott Co., Philadelphia, 1985.

Agriculture Handbook No. 8, The U. S. Department of Agriculture, personal communication.

No warranty as to the accuracy of these results is expressed or implied.

The following applies to nutritional analysis of recipes:

- When an ingredient is listed as optional it is not included in the analysis.
- Ingredients added "to taste" are not included in the analysis with the exception of salt and pepper. Salt to taste is figured at 1/16 teaspoon per recipe. Pepper to taste is figured at 1/32 teaspoon per recipe. This is considered to be the average "pinch" of both ingredients.
- When a recipe yield of serving sizes is given, the recipe is analyzed for the larger serving. If a recipe yield is 6 to 8 servings, it is analyzed for 8 servings.

- The nutritional analysis of the following Indian ingredients are unavailable through the United States Department of Agriculture and have not been included in the nutritional analysis of the individual recipes.

Asafetida *hing*

Black cumin seed or
  royal cumin *shahi jeera*

Carom *ajwain*

Charoli seed *chironji*

Chat masala

Cocum *kokam*

Curry leaves

Fenugreek seed *methi*

Garam masala

Kalongi *nigella*

Kewra Essence

Mango powder *aamchoor*

Silver leaf *vark*

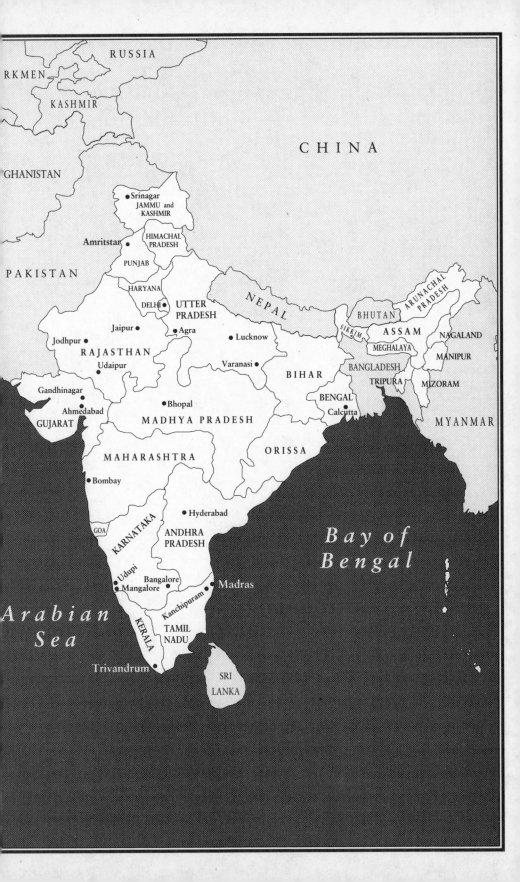

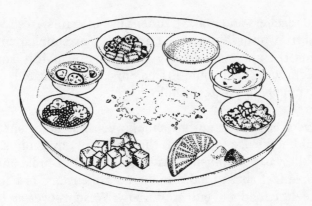

Introduction

~∾~

When I think of India, I think of quiet, generous hospitality, time-honored traditions, lively, colorful festivals, bustling streets and food that, for an untrained Western palate, defies description even as it entices and seduces. Nearly all Indian meals and certainly specific dishes are treated with great reverence and deeply ingrained spirituality.

I have traveled within India and throughout Asia for 15 years. Each journey reveals something new and unexpected and brings me face-to-face with cultures that differ so radically from my own that I quickly become immersed in them. I like to wander the streets of a city or stop over in a village I have never before visited, sample the food from vendors and take in the wonderful foreign aromas. I extend this exploration to the table, whether I am dining in a high-priced restaurant, a small cafe or a private home. In this book, I will introduce you to the marvelous foods of south India. Here, many cuisines are purely vegetarian and are as firmly rice-based as any I have encountered in Asia. Others include some meat and poultry, and more include a fascinating variety of seafood. I find this food light and refreshing and very much in tune with the way we, in the United States, eat today. I have also modified some dishes to conform to Western needs for light, low-fat cooking.

As you read through the following recipes you will notice I do not shy away from assertive use of herbs and exotic spices. No Indian cook I have ever met does, either! I also follow the lead of my Indian

1

friends and teachers and make frequent use of grains, fresh vegetables, yogurt and fruit-infused oils. Meat and fish play supplementary roles. By updating the ancient culinary traditions of mainly south India, through techniques and some ingredients, I have created a book like no other available to Western cooks.

Because every cookbook author should feel that he or she has some exceptional knowledge to bring to the reader, my mission is to convey a sense of the vast and mysterious subcontinent of India and how the Indian people feel about food. I make no pretensions of being Indian. Rather, I see the food and culture through Western eyes and present it in a way that I trust makes sense, educates and intrigues all at once.

I am fortunate to have met, at two different occasions, both Mother Teresa and Tenzin Gyatso, His Holiness the XIVth Dalai Lama of Tibet, who now lives in India. Both are Nobel Peace Prize laureates, but what they share far more deeply is tremendous inner strength and spirituality that translates into strong beliefs in peace, harmony, unity, love and hope for all humankind.

His Holiness The Dalai Lama explains Buddhism as being "not a religion, but a technique whose goal is final freedom." He continues by saying that the essence of any religion is "a good heart, then good use." Mother Teresa echoes this, using different words: "Make us worthy, Lord, to serve our fellow men throughout the world who live and die in poverty and hunger. Give them, through our hands, this day their daily bread; and by our understanding love, give peace and joy."

My exposure to these inspirational people has greatly influenced my view of India and helped me to understand the Indian people's reverence for harmony in life, which carries into their food. Needless to say, this has enlightened my own life, too.

The Indians' reverence for food starts in the kitchen. For example, before a southern Hindu housewife enters the kitchen, she must bathe and put on clean clothes, and then visit the *puja*, or shrine room. In some households, the kitchens are so immaculate that freshly purchased dried spices are washed and put out in the sun to dry before entering the house.

Practices such as these are steeped in ancient tradition. So are many of the dishes and methods of preparation. Centuries ago, dishes were created for wealthy rulers who prided themselves on their tremendous girth—a sign of great wealth. Their splendid, expensive, rich food was prepared by a multitude of servants, each specializing in a particular dish. On the other hand, the food of the wandering tribes and farmers was simple, hearty and combined high-cholesterol oils, animal fat and local ingredients that are filling and inexpensive.

Today, city life has changed how most Indians live and cook. While even today a noticeable waistline in a man might be considered a sign of prosperity, like most educated peoples, Indians are aware of health and nutrition. Today's Indian home diet concentrates on low fat, grains, vegetables, only a little meat and lots of freshly made yogurt. But this is not a *new* style of cooking for south Indians, who have long followed a diet rich in vegetables and rice. What is perhaps different nowadays from times gone by is the reduced use of animal fats and some oils and more reliance on modern cooking methods and utensils to make the job easier. I have concentrated on the vegetable- and rice-based dishes of the south, but have, when appropriate, included north Indian dishes, too.

Although many of the terms and ingredients are unfamiliar, Indian cooking is easy to master. You need very little special equipment or techniques, and most of the ingredients are easily obtainable in the supermarket. Main dishes can and should be prepared in advance of serving to allow their flavors time to mellow. This is great for today's busy lifestyles! To make it easier, many recipes do not need split-second timing or last-minute preparation. When they do, I indicate in the recipe exactly how to time the dishes.

When teaching these dishes to my students, I found most had not tasted south Indian food or north Indian home cooking. What most Westerners think of as Indian cooking is the restaurant cooking of the north, which, while it can be very good, tends to be heavy. With the exception of *tandoor* dishes, I do not recreate this familiar fare. My students delighted in the combinations of spices, fresh herbs and lentils I use to flavor the light, southern-style dishes and understood immediately how this food could become an integral part of many American meals.

Many of the recipes here are cherished family dishes that have been shared with me by home cooks; others are from the kitchens of famous Indian restaurant chefs. I am grateful that these generous cooks let me videotape them preparing food. By reviewing my tapes and listening to the verbal suggestions offered by the cooks as they worked, I believe I have been able to incorporate most of the special touches that make the ordinary extraordinary. It also gave me the unique opportunity to work in my own kitchen, video tape whirring, and capture the authenticity not possible when working from notes and memory only. Certainly, spices, herbs and other ingredients will vary in intensity, and ingredients grown and produced here will taste different from those grown and produced in India, but with these recipes you will be able to create light Indian food very similar in flavor and spirit to that prepared thousands of miles away.

Namaste!
Welcome to India!

∾◡◠

A greeting transformed into the spirit of hospitality. *Namaste*— I bow to thee and open the doors of my home to thee.

ATITHI DEVO BHAVA! The guest is truly your God! During my travels throughout India, these famous Sanskrit words were a dictum of the hospitality in the homes, the professional kitchens, the restaurants, the markets—everywhere! Gracious hospitality is but a small part of India's charm.

Other countries may enter your mind or even your heart, but India gets into your soul. There are many facets to India: the modern, bustling cities and the poor, rural areas where people live as they have for centuries, the intellectual India and the fast-paced, glamorous India of film stars. But the India that attracts me is old India with its long history, time-honored traditions, flamboyant dress, fabled architecture and astounding variety of food.

Indian cuisine is as diverse as the rest of the culture, with extraordinary variations to suit every taste. Its incredible variety lies as much in its geography as in its history. The subcontinent of well over one million square miles, or about one-third the size of the United States, is divided into 25 states, each with its own language, dress, customs and cuisine—all often influenced by age-old rituals and restrictions imposed by religious groups.

A RICH AND GLORIOUS CULINARY PAST

India can be very broadly viewed as having two major culinary divisions: the wheat-based north and the large rice culture of the central river basins and the south. These broad divisions are further split into eastern and western regions, with the major cities of Bombay and Calcutta claiming their own unique culinary heritages. The Hindu, Muslim and Buddhist religions together with other cultures and religious divisions, such as Brahmin, Parsi, Sikh, Jain and Christian, further fragment these divisions and dictate the style and form of cooking and eating as well as the content. Within each area, regional differences abound, but similarities exist as well. All share a richly textured past that contributes mightily to the present.

THE NORTHERN STATES

From the 16th century to India's independence in 1947, the maharajas of northern Rajasthan, who relished extensive hunting expeditions, gave rise to a royal cuisine that included generous amounts of wild boar and game birds. During the same period, the fame and splendor of the nizams from the city of Hyderabad, presently the capital of Andhra Pradesh, spread far and wide. Recognized as one of the richest states in India, there the royal household lived in a style that was lavish beyond words, entertaining guests with monumental, elaborate banquets that lasted for days. As a consequence, the chefs responsible for the banquets gained deserved prominence. Today, many of the descendants of these chefs are the "celebrity" chefs of the award-winning restaurants throughout India.

In the many ceremonial feasts still held in every state in India, the chef is a person with rare culinary skills passed from father to son from generation to generation. He is an artist obsessively and passionately involved with his art, one of the privileged few flag bearers of the great culinary traditions of the rich. Women cook too, but are more often found within the confines of the home kitchen. Their prowess, however, is no less impressive than that of a chef at a top restaurant.

THE SOUTHERN STATES

In sharp contrast to the north, where meat is considered part of everyone's diet but the very poor, is the vegetarian south. The most strongly entrenched culinary traditions in India exist here, and to travel through the southern states is to partake of meals as they have been served for time immemorial. Just as important as the vegetables are the different flavored rice dishes presented in a predetermined sequence at every meal that varies within each state and religion. Even for ceremonial occasions, the fresh, colorful food is served with understated elegance on glistening banana leaves. This custom gives rise to the term "banana-leaf meal," which I use frequently throughout the book to describe a meal served on a banana leaf during a special home gathering, a wedding banquet or in an eatery with no pretension beyond the desire to serve exquisitely prepared food.

Throughout India, specific dishes carry special ceremonial meaning. Each has its own tradition and for the gathering group or family brings to mind memories of momentous events, festivals, family celebrations and grand wedding feasts. It is said that the host should lay out *all* the food that he has before his guest. The guest, for his part, must reciprocate for this gesture by doing full justice to the meal— which regardless of its opulence or modesty is always partly viewed as ritual. It would a be sacrilege, for example, to use anything but the fingers of your right hand to devour the feast.

THE REGIONS

Rajasthan lies in the extreme northwest of the country, bordering Pakistan. The people of the cities of Jaipur, Jodhpur, Udaipur and others in the state lay claim to being the most colorfully dressed in India. The women wear dazzling saris and swinging multipaneled mirrored skirts of brilliant hues, boldly designed silver jewelry, bangles and bracelets of ivory and bone. The men wear magnificent bright red and yellow turbans, each tied in the distinctive style of their region.

Here, in the land that was once the home of warrior princes wealthy beyond all dreams, lies much of the romance of India. In days gone by, the princes (maharajas) continually sought to outshine one another through the splendor of their palaces. Today, colorful pageantry, forts, palaces and erstwhile maharajas combine with history and tradition to project the perfect image and charm of India.

The impressive turn-of-the century pink sandstone Umaid Bhawan Palace is still the royal residence for the former Maharaja of Jodhpur. One of the largest and grandest residences in the world, this architectural dream with its lavish exterior dominates that graceful city. While its exterior is lavish, it is really inside that the true grandeur of the palace can be seen. The lobby is embellished with black Italian marble, sweeping marble staircases and an impressive musical fountain made entirely of English crystal.

The palace is brimming with spoils from the glory days of the maharaja, including trophies such as stuffed leopards and bears from royal hunting safaris, polo prizes and equipment, an armory and an impressive collection of rare objets d'art from the precious royal collection.

I had the extreme pleasure of spending several splendid days at the palace. While sitting on the verandah overlooking exquisitely manicured, sprawling lawns and gardens, I enjoyed an English tea of thin cucumber and watercress sandwiches and wonderful miniature cakes and pastries. This pleasant custom immediately transported me back a century to the splendid days of the Raj when India was indeed considered "the jewel in the crown."

In the evening I enjoyed a traditional Rajasthani meal served from a large crested silver *thali* (a round tray containing numerous small bowls) placed before me by stewards outfitted in gray and black livery and intricately tied, brilliant red flowing turbans. The flavors and textures of the dishes were unfamiliar to me, but nonetheless delectable. *Ker, kumtia* and *sangria* (the beans of three desert shrubs) had a chewy, slightly nutty flavor. They were collected from the wild, dried for storage and then rehydrated when used. The bread made from *bajra* (millet flour) had an enjoyable robustness and when dotted with *ghee* (clarified butter) took on a seductive richness. Millet was also used in an unusual combination with mutton and spices in a dish called *Bajra ka Sohita.*

Other highlights of the feast were mutton cooked in yogurt with the beans of the three desert shrubs, and *Akha Murgh*, a whole chicken cooked in a combination of spices. The final sweet touch was *Dal ka Halva* made of lentils and *Ghewar*, a sugar basketlike base filled with a rich milk-and-sugar sweet. The finale was presented in a chased silver-and-gold ornamental *paan* box. Inside were *catechu* (lime paste), silver-coated betel nut slivers, whole betel nuts, fragrant cloves, fennel, cardamom, aniseed and rose hips wrapped in a betel leaf with a tissue-thin overlay of actual silver leaf. As the classic finish to an Indian meal, these morsels are considered to be great digestives.

Executive chef for the palace, G. Kumar Dey, explained that Rajasthani food was basically peasant food made special by the inclusion of distinctive ingredients and flavors. Palace chefs add more spices and rely more on meat-based dishes, especially those of wild game, than do ordinary home cooks. But essentially both peasant and royal food share the same roots.

The highly populated state of Utter Pradesh in north central India has both Hindu and Muslim elements. Lucknow, the predominantly

Muslim capital, is well known and respected for its cultural, artistic and culinary pleasures.

In 1784, after a year of great famine that affected both the rich and the poor, the ruler Asaf-ud-daula began the construction of the Great Imambara, an elaborate Muslim spiritual complex. Two distinct work forces were formed: the poor built by day and the rich destroyed by night. Obviously, this was not a forward-moving project; it was instead a form of welfare. The nawab (ruler) wanted to keep paying the poor and this was his method of extending employment. Further, he ordered that all laborers be fed. Enormous containers filled with rice, meat, vegetables and spices were placed on a fire and hot coals were heaped on top of the sealed containers. This slow cooking, called *dum pukht*, ensured that food was available day and night. *Dum* means to breathe in and *pukht* to cook.

Legend has it that one day the nawab passed by when the vessels were opened. Enticed by the intoxicating aromas, he ordered the royal kitchens to experiment with cooking some dishes in sealed vessels and slow baking others. Eventually, this technique became the one most often used in the royal kitchens and was considered the food of kings.

Some of my favorite dishes prepared in this fashion include *Raan e Dum Pukht*, succulent leg of lamb marinated in rum and stuffed with onions, cheese and mint; *Kachchi Gosht Biryani*, succulent *basmati* rice layered with lavishly spiced lamb and garnished with pistachios and mint with a final drizzle of saffron.

Happily, this superb cuisine can be savored at the Dum Pukht Restaurant in the Maurya Sheraton, New Delhi, where flamboyant superchef Mohammed Imtiaz Qureshi presides. Originally from Lucknow, his ancestors were accomplished cooks—and his two sons are now following their father's footsteps at Dum Pukht in the SeaRock Sheraton, Bombay. During visits to New Delhi and Bombay, Imtiaz shared his great talent with me. His Dum Pukht recipes appear throughout the book.

Calcutta, the throbbing nerve center of the eastern state of Bengal, assaults my senses as few other cities do. Extremes of wealth and poverty, good and bad, ugly and beautiful all are here: humanity in all its splendor and infirmity. I find Calcutta to be a very personal city that casts a bewitching spell over all who visit. To understand Calcutta is to begin to understand India.

A Bengali's first loves are intelligent reading, music and theater.

Good eating is a very close second. Bengali food is enticing, fragrant and subtly spiced. The food comes from the lush countryside where tea, rice, mustard plants and other crops are grown. The rivers and lakes are alive with fish.

As it is throughout all of India, food preparation in Bengal is steeped in ritual. For example, Bengali mothers-in-law judge a new daughter-in-law by her ability to cut up vegetables according to strict protocol: potatoes must be sliced into small squares for a dry vegetable dish, quartered for a meat curry and cut thin into half-moon shapes for serving with small, whole fish.

Shopping too is a fine art. Shoppers are assaulted on every side with gorgeous produce but this does not prevent them from being impeccably selective. In the orderly market stalls I passed sellers squatting or sitting cross-legged on tables among pyramids of luscious papayas, aromatic mangoes, golden-brown pineapples and juicy tart-sweet litchis, piles of green beans, aged dark brown tamarind pulp, purple eggplants and sweet limes. In the next alley I passed silver-gray garlic, golden knobs of turmeric and ginger, tiny hard betel nuts and gigantic mounds of chilies. A marvelous aroma filled the air as I came upon a staggering array of spices: cumin, mustard seeds, fennel, cloves, cinnamon and more.

Down another alley I was fascinated by the *paneer* maker who was preparing delicious, creamy unripened cheese and by the sweet maker putting the final touches on a magnificent spectrum of famous Bengali sweets, popular all over India. Almost every Bengali stops on his way home from work to purchase *Mishti Doi*, rich, sweet curd made from buffalo milk and sweetened with date syrup; *Sandesh*, a creamy cheese fudge; or *Gulab Jamun*, flavored with rosewater and soaking in a bath of simple syrup. Before leaving, I stopped by a tea cart for a refreshing spiced tea served in earthenware cups.

A Bengali housewife would not leave the market without a trip to the fishmonger, as no meal is complete without a fish or prawn dish. Nor would she leave without purchasing green mint, coriander, ginger and a full supply of fresh spices, especially mustard seeds, and mustard oil. Always used with a light hand, these spices, with their distinctive flavors, are the signature of Bengali cuisine. And if these spices are the hallmark, rice is the medium by which they are displayed.

I enjoyed many delicious meals in Calcutta. One of the most memorable was at the "super-posh" Victorian Oberoi Grand, which has a Shangri-la quality. It is moody, enchanting and romantic in its setting. Alphonso Gomes is the executive chef, who, in Indian tradition, learned his craft from his father. His *Doi Macchi*, an unforgettable curry of local river fish, yogurt, raisins and spices; *Bekti Tikka Ajwaini*, a delicious tandoori dish made from *bekti*, a local fish; *Paneer Shahi Tukra*, refreshing *paneer*, a sliced cheese stuffed with mint chutney and *chat masala*; and *Jhinga Pardanashin*, prawns cooked in a *masala*, then stuffed into a large gourd before sealing it with dough and cooking *dum pukht* style, were most impressive.

Dining in private homes is taken very seriously in Calcutta, as indeed it is throughout India. Guests are treasured and the food they are served is rarely similar to that prepared for restaurants. Travelers who do not have the privilege of being invited into an Indian home for a meal miss much of this country's magnificent cooking. I was fortunate to be a guest in many Indian homes and have recreated on the following pages recipes for what I consider to be the best, light food of India, most successfully created, perhaps, in home kitchens.

Amar and Sudha Mehrotra love to entertain in their Calcutta home. As we chatted in her kitchen, Sudha thoughtfully showed me how she prepares each dish and explained some of the customs still followed in the home. For instance, Sudha, always aware of the Bengali custom of being attentive to the needs of her guests, would not eat her own meal until everyone else had finished.

Among the evening's perfectly prepared dishes were *Jeera Aloo*, potatoes with cumin, chili, turmeric and coriander; *Saag Dal*, a marvelous, nutty-flavored spinach dish seasoned with *toor dal*; refreshingly spiced *Methi Murgh*, fenugreek chicken; fried prawns cooked in a delicate batter; perfectly seasoned *Ghughni*, a delicious chickpea *dal*; and, of course, rice. Next, came one of my favorite desserts, creamy *Mishti Doi*, but the grand finale was Sudha's favorite—a Western chocolate-covered vanilla ice cream bar!

Bombay, the capital of Maharashtra State is India's most cosmopolitan city. What fascinates me about Bombay is its intriguing mix of people who have gravitated there from all over India by the promise of upward mobility and opportunity. Its nine million inhabitants represent all languages, religions, costumes and foods of India.

Not surprisingly, this melting pot is home to a mouth-watering cuisine representing a multitude of cultures. People from every corner of India have brought their regional dishes with them and this alone serves to make Bombay one of the food capitals of India. Besides the Maharashtrians, Gujaratis, Parsis and Bohras, there are people from the far southwest and southeast coastal regions of Kerala and Madras; Christians from southern Goa, plus Jains, Sikhs and many other minorities from all parts of India. Even while borrowing from each other within the borders of this energetic city, the distinct cuisines maintain their own identity.

Nowhere is this diversity more apparent than at the bustling Crawford Market. Built in 1871, and boasting bas-reliefs designed by Rudyard Kipling's father, the market is home to the best food vendors in Bombay. The labyrinth of clean stalls contains everything from artistically arranged fresh fruits and vegetables to tasty fruit chutneys, fresh meats and poultry, Bombay duck (which is dried fish), the finest teas from Assam, Darjeeling and Ceylon, sensually aromatic fresh herbs, dried spices and an unbelievable array of sweets.

Draped in a traditional nine-yard sari of royal blue silk edged with navy and gold, Anjali Joshi, food editor for The Sunday *Observer* newspaper in Bombay, welcomed me into her home for a traditional *thali* from her state of Maharashtra.

A small individual one-inch platform decorated with a beautifully designed *rangoli*, a traditional design made with red, green and white powders, was set before us. In the center of the *rangoli* she placed a *thali* tray, a large silver plate of food. She explained how important the placement of the food on the *thali* was.

At precisely the twelve o'clock position was a tiny mound of coarse salt. Moving down the left-hand side was a wedge of lime, two fresh relishes; *Kachumbars*, a coconut and green chili chutney, *Raita*, a cucumber and yogurt salad and a tasty sweet and sour mango chutney. Next were savories: a *Pappadum* on which sat a few white sago crisps and *Bhajji*, vegetable fritters. In the center of the *thali* there was a small mounded mold of rice topped with a simple *toor dal*, very lightly seasoned with turmeric, asafetida and salt and drizzled with a touch of *ghee*. To the right of a small mound of salt was *Aloo Bhajji*, potatoes cooked with cumin seeds, coriander and lime juice, followed by a *katori* bowl of slightly spicy *toor dal*. The next course was a neat mold of *Masala Bhat*, a spicy fried rice flavored with cardamom, cumin, cinnamon, turmeric, curds and cashew nuts, garnished with coriander and coconut shreds. "On a Maharashtrian *thali*," explained Anjali, "the exact symmetry of placing the rice in the center would not be proper." Somewhat in from the rim was *Puran Poli*, a flatbread with sweet *dal* stuffing, and *Shrikhand*, a light, silky yogurt cheese sweetened and flavored with aromatic saffron and cardamom and garnished with pistachio slivers.

Ms. Joshi joined her palms before the *thali* to offer thanks to *Annadata*, the God of food, before we began eating. She explained that the meal was balanced in subtle ways to stimulate the appetite and help digestion. The people in this region eat sweets and desserts as part of the main meal, often along with a flatbread to balance the fat intake. My Maharashtrian *thali* concluded with buttermilk, also to aid digestion.

According to Anjali Joshi, the left-hand side of the *thali* is the test of the cook's creativity and imaginative juxtaposition of flavors. Maharashtrians are proud of the vast range of pickles, chutneys and *kachumbars*—always on the left side of the *thali*.

Paan was offered at the end of the meal. This is a bite-sized mixture of whole and shaved betel nuts, lime paste, almonds, cloves, cardamom, nutmeg and grated coconut wrapped in a betel leaf. For good fortune, my hostess placed a dot of red powder, *tikka*, on my forehead and then presented me with the auspicious coconut, a symbol of completeness and fertility.

My next culinary adventure in Bombay was at the tastefully decorated home of Mrs. Rashida Annes, a Muslim Bohri. There, standing in the elegant entrance hall, I was greeted by a life-size stuffed leopard, which, my hostess explained, had been shot by her mother-in-law.

Surrounded by exquisite antique Chinese furniture and porcelains, elegant antique English silver and a multitude of the family's sterling polo and riding trophies, Rashida described Bohra cuisine as being inspired by the sect's roots in Saudi Arabia, Egypt, Iraq, Syria and Iran. In India, the Gujaratis influence has played a significant role, too.

Bohra meals are served from a large, common brass *thali* set on a stand about seven inches high and laden with food that is distinctive to the community. The meal signifies brotherhood and is a time, she said, "when all the differences of the day are washed out and brings the family together."

The meal began with a pinch of salt, offered and consumed as a token of equality of all man. This was followed by rice cooked in sweetened milk and then a mix of light, healthy, elegantly spiced dishes including *Kuku Paka*, a delicate whole chicken in a soupy sauce. The main part of the meal consisted of trotters and goats feet with bite-sized *Rotis* in a slightly spicy sauce; a feisty cold *Baingan Bharta*, eggplant spiced with chilies and seasonings; cool, refreshing *Aloo Raita*, potatoes lightly seasoned with mustard and yogurt; Pineapple and Mango Relish; chickpeas cooked in spices and coriander; a mutton stew in mustard sauce served over the lightest flaked pastry and a round two-inch high baked *Naan*, quite unlike the familiar flatbread.

The traditional end to a Bohra meal is *Kud Bal Leda*, a mutton *biryani*, accompanied by a sweet yogurt, a dish that is also served to mark any auspicious occasion such as a wedding, birth, purchase of a house, etc. According to Muslim tradition, the *Kud Bal Leda* must be cooked after sundown on Thursday evening and served on Friday, the Muslim prayer day. We ended the meal with this dish and then I was served *Sheer Korma*, a favorite Bohra treat of sweet lightly fried fine vermicelli noodles, slivered almonds and pistachios, simmered in milk until slightly thickened and creamy, and Pineapple *Halva*, a sweet purée enhanced by pistachios, cardamom, cloves, nutmeg and cinnamon.

The Parsis or Zorastrians, a small ethnic and religious community that fled Muslim persecution in Persia in the eighth century, were given refuge and the right to practice their religion in India provided they conformed outwardly to the Indian way of life and adopted Indian dress. Although a small minority, their economic and cultural influence is considerable. Many of India's leading businessmen and philanthropists are Parsis. For example Zubin Mehta, the world-famous conductor of the New York Philharmonic Orchestra, is a Parsi.

Parsis love good food. Their mostly nonvegetarian cuisine is an exotic hybrid of both Persia and India—but ultimately not quite like either. The result is a variety of intriguing flavors and textures that are brought out through steaming, baking, barbecuing, frying and sautéing.

Mrs. Bakhtawar Tarapore, a Parsi, invited me to visit Sir Ratan Tata Institute, which was started during the great bubonic plague of 1903. I was told that during this time, so many men died and left their wives destitute that the Institute was started by six Parsi ladies as a way to teach the women to fend for themselves. They were first taught to make clothes and then later were instructed in the arts of cooking, confectionery and baking. Since the early part of the century the organization has grown considerably and still devotes itself to helping underprivileged women. In the city of Bombay there are ten popular Parsi specialty sweet shops, as well as the successful Landmark Restaurant, all run by graduates of the Institute.

Roshani Kerawalla, a Parsi friend, joined me for a lunch cooked by the women of the Institute at the Landmark Restaurant. How the food was positioned on a banana leaf and the order in which it was eaten was traditional Parsi. The starter was freshly made potato chips followed by *Patri ni Macchi*, pomfret, a flat fish, smothered with coriander, green chili and coconut paste and wrapped in banana leaves for steaming. This is one of the most traditional Parsi dishes. It was accompanied by thin griddle-baked whole wheat bread called *Chapatis* and an onion and tomato salad. This was followed by *Tamatar pur Inda*, tomatoes topped with eggs and seasoned with fresh coriander, and *Jerdaloo Sali Murgh*, sautéed chicken in gravy seasoned with spices, tomato purée, chilies, sugar and vinegar and garnished with crispy fried potato strings and apricots. *Lagan nu Custard*, garnished with cashews and almonds and quite similar to crème brulée, was served as a palate refresher.

I was thrilled to note that the next course was *Dhansak*, the recognized crowned prince of Parsi food that is admittedly heavy on the palate and the stomach. It appears to be a simple dish of mutton, *dal* and fried rice topped with fried onions, but the aggressive combination of fried *masala*, cinnamon, cloves, coriander, cumin and fenugreek combined with red chilies, make it an imposing dish of fire and spice. The dish is considered fairly ordinary in that it is served for Sunday lunch in Parsi homes and never served for holidays or other celebrations—although it is traditional to serve a meatless version four days after someone dies. We also ate servings of yogurt and sugar (a good luck sign) and drank a beverage called raspberry "soda," a typical Parsi drink tasting, to my palate, like sweet liquid jello.

To complete my Bombay experience, I traveled to Chowpatty Beach where Parsi millionaires, movie stars and even taxi drivers and day laborers gather to enjoy the evening sea breezes. Here vendors peddle Bombay's favorite snack, *Bhel-Poori*, which is a savory mixture of puffed rice, deep-fried vermicelli, chopped onions and potatoes seasoned with Mint-Coriander Chutney and thick Sweet-and-Sour Tamarind Chutney scooped onto little fried flatbreads about the size of a biscuit. A final taste delight in the city of Bombay!

Goa, about halfway down the west coast of the Indian peninsula, is a 1,350-square-mile state with easy-going, warm people and lush tropical groves of cashew, mango and coconut edged by some of the most beautiful beaches in the world. Paradise is influenced by the flamboyance of Portuguese exuberance set against the russet tones of Indian attitude and life.

The Portuguese, intent on controlling the spice route from the East, landed in Goa in 1510. By the turn of that century, they had captured the state to become chief spice traders and a powerful force in India. While the rest of India progressed toward independence and the 20th century, Goa remained a Portuguese colony until 1961 when the state was adopted into the Indian Union.

Goan food offers great variety influenced by the Hindus, Christians and Muslims and each style of cooking is as colorful and full of spirit as the state's inhabitants. The result is a luscious coconut and fish-based cuisine seasoned with such exotic spices as turmeric, cinnamon and tamarind plus healthy pinches of red chili. A dish of the same name may have entirely different sauces depending on its ethnic bent. For instance, the Christians use vinegar for tang, whereas the Hindus prefer the local fruit called *kokum*. Goan Christians like pork whereas the Muslims, whose religion does not allow them to eat pork, enjoy lamb. Both prefer fish to meat.

Fish is not only the food of choice, it is the subject of songs and dances and much local lore. Buying fish is never left to servants but is the sole responsibility of the woman of the house. It is eaten at every meal, although it takes second place to meat on special occasions. Approximately 180 varieties of fish swim in the local waters and apparently most make their way to the local markets at some point during the year.

In Goa, the main market is a lively, colorful sprawling affair with the extraordinary breadth and bustle that epitomizes an Asian bazaar. From local and regional crafts and clothes to fresh produce, spices and kitchen utensils, everything needed by the average household is available here. There is basket upon basket displaying spectacular fruits including pineapples, coconuts, golden-yellow cashew fruit (with the nuts attached), and small round green pickling mangoes. There are piles of neatly arranged aromatic spices used in most Goan dishes: brown, green and white cardamom, barklike cinnamon sticks, cloves, mace, whole nutmeg, bay leaf, cardamom, fennel, saffron and black salt. Deep into the stalls are straw baskets containing brownish tamarind and the small, sweet-sour fruit called *kokum*, as well as dried mango. These are used to give foods varying amounts of tartness. You can also find brownish-black coconut *jaggery*, unrefined sugar from sugarcane or palm, strands of the famous spicy Goan sausage (so reminiscent of Portuguese *chorizo*) and freshly baked Goan hard breads. Add to this an enviable array of cookware including jagged-topped coconut graters, ladles and other utensils made from coconut; shiny metal rice pots, water pots, tea kettles, clay pots, squatty round curry pots, covered drinking water pots, incense holders, round "piggy" banks, white, pink and yellow striped *puja* pots and drinking cups and small bowls that usually are discarded after every use.

Auntie Pauline de Sousa is the grandmotherly Goan chef for Cicade de Goa, a hotel modeled after one typical of a Portuguese hill town. She learned Goan cooking from her "mommy" and, as the hotels executive chef Alok Verma cautioned me when I watched Auntie cook, there is "no pad, no pencil allowed" when she prepares one of her famous twenty-two ingredient *masalas*—her closely kept secrets.

Happily for me, Auntie made an exception when she showed me how she prepared several of her family's favorite Goan dishes. These turned out to be complicated simply because they include her complex *masalas*, which she explained are hotter than most and make her sauces more fiery than the sauces made by the Portuguese. Among the recipes she shared were *Chicken Caffreal*, spicy roast chicken brought to Goa by Africans; *Pork Vindaloo*, a spicy pork stew native to Goa; and *Fish Amotik*, made with tamarind, cinnamon and black pepper and flavored with a liquor brewed from mildly hot *motyo* peppers that lend the dish a warm terra-cotta hue. Auntie also made prawn curry served with rice, a dish close to Goan's hearts, in which giant prawns simmer in a hearty red sauce made from coconut, hot red chilies, coriander, cumin, turmeric and onions.

Maria Fernandez, my local guide, said that the two ingredients considered essential for the characteristic Goan flavor are coconut toddy, a vinegar made with local coconut palm sap, and *ghatti mircha*, the hot and pungent local chilies. According to Maria and Auntie, there is no substitute for the distinct sweet-sour flavor and light effervescence of the Goan coconut vinegar.

A highlight of my Goan experience was dinner at Casa Portuguesa, a restaurant housed in a lovely old Portuguese-Goan home with whitewashed walls, vaulted ceilings, elegant dark-wood trim and hand-carved antique chairs. The restaurant's colorful owner, Francisco do Rosario e Sousa, presides painstakingly over the kitchen, insisting that all dishes be cooked in clay pots, as is typical in the villages and farms of India. His reasoning is that the porous pots absorb some of the smokiness imparted by the wood and coconut shell cooking fires give the food a slightly smoky flavor.

We dined that evening in the restaurant's peaceful garden on Vegetable-Stuffed Rolled *Papads*, spicy stuffed crab, and *Chonak*, a magnificent local grilled fish seasoned with garlic, Portuguese spices and coconut toddy, garnished with tomato slices, onions, orange slices and limes. The romantic ambiance of the garden was made even more delightful when Francisco picked up his guitar and serenaded us with Portuguese love songs.

The fame and splendor of primarily Muslim Hyderabad, the present capital of the state of Andhra Pradesh in south central India, was unequaled in Indian history. Before India's independence in 1947, Andhra Pradesh was India's largest and wealthiest state and was ruled by seven nizams, each in his own "kingdom."

The most famous of the nizams was Mahbub Ali Pasha, Nizam Asaf Jah IV, who ascended the throne in 1884 at the age of 17. Considered one of the richest men in the world, the nizam lived a lifestyle of pleasure, glittering extravagance and great luxury on a scale that exceeded any European monarch in any era—one only dreamed of, perhaps, in "Arabian Nights."

The nizams reveled in exotic food. Great feasts lasting several days were so commonplace that a cuisine called *nizami* developed to become one of the most outstanding culinary attractions of south India, particularly in Andhra Pradesh.

The food from this region is varied and fragrant, consisting of delicious *biryanis. Gosht Biryani Hyderabadi,* among the most famous dishes, is typical of the rich Muslim cooking you can expect to find here. *Basmati* rice is simmered with mutton, mace, screwpine essence and other seasonings and finished in a sealed dish with saffron and cardamom. The aroma and flavor is majestic.

The abundant crops grown in Andhra Pradesh include peanuts, lentils, rice, tobacco, cotton and the famous Guntur red chilies. So notable is the chili crop that it is jokingly said that no Andhra curry is complete without at least 40 chilies! It is therefore not surprising to find the sharp, hot Hyderabadi mango-based pickle at nearly every meal.

Because south Indians are for the most part rice eaters, Andhra Pradesh boasts a number of rice dishes. The best known here as well as in the southern states of Karnataka and Tamil Nadu are *Dosas,* paper-thin pancakes made from the paste of *urad dal* and rice, and *Idlis,* a steamed rice and *urad dal* combination. Both dishes are served with a fiery hot *Sambar,* a saucelike accompaniment that combines *toor dal* with vegetables, chilies, dried spices and chutney, mint, coriander and lime or fresh coconut.

To the west of Andhra Pradesh lies the state of Karnataka. It is the land of lush forests, beautiful silver-sand beaches, wandering rivers and large fields of rice, tobacco, sugarcane, sunflowers and pulses.

The seaport town of Mangalore is the center of the cashew and coffee trade. Situated on the Arabian sea, *Dosas* and *Idlis* are as important to the local diet as fresh seafood. But it is in Udupi, a town about 36 miles from Mangalore, where these two rice dishes reign supreme.

The famous 800-year-old Krishna temple can be found in Udupi, making the town one of the south's most important Hindu centers and the seat of Dwaita, a system of Hindu philosophy. There are also eight monasteries in town, and so the streets are always crowded with devout pilgrims.

The owners of Udupi restaurants, a style of eatery found throughout India, invariably hail from here. The restaurants are known for their inexpensive, strictly vegetarian food, with the *Dosas* and *Idlis* being foremost on the menus. These are the foods most often served to the pilgrims who travel to Udupi. Whether the restaurant is actually in Udupi or elsewhere in India does not matter. All are similar and have become the mainstay of India's fast-food business. If tandoori cooking is north India's contribution to the national food repertoire, *Dosas* and *Idlis* may well be considered the south's eloquent contribution. Today these treats are available not only throughout India, but in Indian restaurants the world over. Of course, they are best in the south of India!

A short distance from Udupi is the town of Manipal, a large educational township that to my mind is like none other in India. Dr. Tonse Madhava Ananta Pai, a physician and educational pioneer who believed that education lay at the root of all social progress, founded the Academy of General Education to sponsor a network of schools and colleges. The Kasturba Medical College and the Kasturba General Hospital are known all over the country as among the best in India.

With the India Tobacco Company (ITC)–Welcomgroup (Sheraton) hotels division, the T.M.A. Pai Foundation established the renowned Welcomgroup Graduate School for Hotel Administration, offering a Bachelor's Degree in Hotel Management and Food Service. When I dined in the school's private dining room with Dr. T. Ramesh U. Pai, Dr. Pai's nephew, I was able to visit with P.N. Raman, head of the food and beverage department. He explained that the foods of the Mangalore region are a combination of Portuguese-influenced Goan specialties and the traditional foods of the southern state of Kerala. Coconut, fresh seafood and rice play important parts in both these cuisines. Here, where nonvegetarian food is at its best, they use cinnamon, cardamom, cloves, tamarind and coconut for seasonings. Chicken *Shtew* served with *Sannas,* a form of *Idlis,* is a soothing dish that is cooked in coconut milk and seasoned with the spices indigenous to the area: black pepper, cloves and cinnamon.

The drive from Mangalore to Bangalore is a spectacular one with splendid natural forests, misty green slopes and impressive, manicured farms at every turn. I could not help envy the farmers simple lifestyle as I watched them begin work in their lovely fields. I felt as though I were in another world.

The agricultural center of this farming region is the village of Coorg, where large crops of rice, oranges, cardamom, pepper and coffee are grown. More than 25 percent of India's coffee crop is from plantations around Coorg. The area is also the home of the warrior Coorg or Kordagu people, who own many of the plantations. Tall and beautiful people with picturesque costumes, their warm, graceful manners belie a long martial tradition. Unlike most people in the vegetarian south, the Coorgs hunt and fish avidly and prepare game in all sorts of ways.

Bangalore, the capital of Karnataka, is an industrial city whose charm peeks through manicured tree-shaded gardens with beautiful flowers. As I drove around the city and the neighboring areas, it was obvious that everyone took great pride in keeping the city spotless, orderly and attractive.

Chitra Mughul, a Coorg, and her husband, a Parsi, took me to Coconut Grove, an upscale banana-leaf restaurant that serves specialties from Karnataka, Tamil Nadu, Goa and Kerala. While rice is central to the cuisine, the seasonings vary slightly from state to state. For our *thali*, we had *Kerala* Fish Curry, a creamy curry cooked in coconut milk, curry leaves and tart tamarind; *Shtew*; and *Sorpotel*, a Goan pork curry with a melange of flavors combining the heat of chilies with a touch of sweet onions and sour vinegar. Accompanying the meal was one of my favorite rice-based foods, *Appams* or Hoppers. These soft, pliable crepes with thin, crisp, lacy borders are customarily made in an open cooking area of the restaurant. The batter, made from ground rice and *urad dal*, fenugreek, coconut milk and yeast is poured into a shallow cast-iron, wok-like pan called a *chatty* and allowed to cook for a short period before the pan is covered. This process results in a thick, soft center with a delicate border.

Many Indians consider Mavalli Tiffin Rooms the best for Udupi food. Located on Lalbaugh Road, MTR (as it is known to locals) was established in 1924 and has had virtually the same menu ever since.

I was fortunate to visit the restaurant with chef P.N. Ramnath of the elegant Indo-Gothic Windsor Manor Hotel, one of the prettiest hotels in the south. As we approached, wealthy businessmen, government officials and many others were waiting in the breakfast queue, which begins forming at 6 a.m. every morning, to have what is said to be the best *Masala Dosas* in India.

Inside the crowded, immaculate restaurant we sat at marble-topped tables and, while cooled by lazy ceiling fans, sampled simple food. Perhaps this simplicity is the key to MTR's success. From 7 to 9 a.m. only three items are served: *Masala Dosas*, *Idlis* and *Karabat* or *Uppma*, a fluffy, molded version of Italian polenta. This is made from semolina, *urad* and *chana dal* and seasoned with coconut, mustard seeds, turmeric and chilies. It is served topped with a tomato slice. Promptly at 9 a.m., a fourth item becomes available: *Vadas*, a fried lentil-based doughnut that is brown on the outside but yellow on the inside due to the addition of turmeric. This is my favorite breakfast in all of India, made only better by the excellent regional coffee that my host said is the finest in India: "Even in the remotest villages, excellent filter brews are available." At 11 a.m., the tall, imposing wooden doors close until MTR opens again at 5:30 p.m. It is one of the few restaurants I know that serves breakfast and dinner but closes for lunch!

The small kitchen is nearly as crowded as the dining room, with cooks and waiters working frantically to prepare and serve the food. Still, it is a testament to cleanliness and organization. Every pot, pan, utensil, oven, grill—even the walls—look as if they have just been scrubbed and polished. Cooks on one side of the kitchen make *Masala Dosas* while snowy-white *Idlis* are steamed, twenty at a time, on the other side. As efficient as the system is, a quick look satisfied my curiosity as to why the menu politely asks customers in a hurry to "please order that item that is ready just at the moment."

A highlight of my sojourn in Bangalore was the Coorg wedding of Devika Appayya, daughter of Mr. and Mrs. Codanda Appayya. Mr. Appayya is a Director of India Tobacco Company, one of the largest holding companies in India. The marriage took place in the magnificent Bangalore Palace Compound, a fortified castle said to be modeled after Windsor Castle in England.

The bride was dressed in a richly woven, red and gold sari draped Coorgi style with the pleats in the back rather than the front. The custom derives from an ancient myth that explains that when the goddess Cauvery took the form of river, women who ventured into the holy waters were swept up by the goddess's powerful current and their saris were twisted around them so that the pleats faced backwards. Since then, women from the region have always worn their saris thus.

Mr. Appayya, father of the bride, was dressed in traditional style too, with a long black coat called *kupya*, a white turban trimmed with gold, a luxurious gold silk sash bordered in red, and the ritual sword tucked into it. This striking costume supports the theory that the Coorgs probably came from the Middle East centuries ago.

The food at a Coorgi wedding is as traditional as the other rituals. *Pandi Kari*, an absolutely gorgeous hot-and-sour, almost pickle-like pork stew that originally was made from wild boar is served with round rice balls called *Kadambuttu*. These are made from coarsely pounded rice combined with coconut milk and water and cooked to a very sticky dough-like consistency before being formed into tiny balls and steamed.

The wedding was an elaborate affair and all rituals were performed by members of the family and community elders rather than priests. For example, the custom called *balebirudu* required that a man from the bridegroom's family cut three plantain stumps with a single stroke of his sword to symbolize beheading any enemies (suitors) who might oppose the marriage. The bride displayed her stamina for hours during *ganga puja* when she was required to balance a flower-decorated water jug filled from the family well on her head while men from the bridegroom's family danced in front of her. Only after the dancing ended could she put the pitcher down and be accepted as a member of her groom's family.

The state of Tamil Nadu is situated by the deep blue waters of the Bay of Bengal on the southeastern side of the Indian peninsula. Incredibly rich in history and culture, the state glories in having some of India's most famous temples, which are built in the Dravidian style with characteristically ornate exteriors and soaring towers. Here the bells of the temples ring out over landscape of immense banana, coconut and sugarcane groves, fascinating narrow waterways and tropical green vistas.

Madras, the capital city of Tamil Nadu and the "Gateway to the South," is a city of writers, scholars, artists and movie stars. The warm, graceful people wear exquisite, brightly colored silk saris from the city of Kanchipuram (considered to be the best silk in the south) and have a lifestyle that is steeped in tradition.

Madras is known for its hospitality. A stranger is welcomed, a guest is fussed over and any occasion, sad or joyful, is reason for a feast. But the feast here is neither ostentatious nor lavish. It is an occasion for practically unlimited amounts of simple food cooked to perfection and for feelings of genuine congeniality.

Madras is the cradle of south Indian cuisine. Delightful savories— crisp brown *Masala Dosas*, doughnut-shaped *Vadas*, snow-white *Idlis* and *Sambar*, their spicy lentil accompaniment—are loved here as in all of south India. Other rice preparations of every taste are combined with vegetarian low-fat dishes. The basic spices are black pepper, red chilies, mustard seeds, fennel, cumin, turmeric and coriander. Hot fiery courses are usually followed by bland and soothing ones.

One beautiful, warm, sunny morning in Madras, Saroja Subbaraman invited me to watch her cook for a traditional Sunday family gathering. As I approached her immaculate white-washed home I knew I was going to have a rare treat. Saroja met me and, as in many Hindu homes, requested I leave my shoes by the door. She said her day had started in the usual Hindu tradition: after bathing, she had worshiped (as does each member of the family) in the *puja*, a private shrine room where members of the pantheon of gods are displayed in portrait and sculpture and the sacred lamp is lit.

Then, as in every Hindu home, Saroja had washed her front doorstep and traced ritual designs on it in intricate patterns. These *kolam* or *rangoli* are done with rice flour, but sometimes colored powders or flowers are used. She said that it is considered inauspicious for a Hindu to step out of the home before the *kolam* is drawn. When the ritual is completed and the gods are pleased, the family can go about the day.

She introduced me to her family, which included her husband, nephew, son and daughter. This Sunday was extra special, as her daughter-in-law, Padma Balakrishman, and Nithin, her beautiful eighteen-month-old grandson, were visiting from Muenster, Indiana. Padma's mother, who was visiting from nearby Kanchipuram, the home of beautiful silk, was dressed in a lovely Brahmin-style nine-yard silk saffron sari bordered with navy and gold. Everyone gathered, as they do every Sunday, over a banana leaf to experience traditional family oneness.

Saroja took me into her sparkling kitchen saying that before entering it she must have performed her daily Hindu rituals. Shoes are never worn anywhere in the home and most definitely never in the kitchen. Although in most traditional south Indian kitchens no one except the maid and the woman of the house are permitted in the kitchen, Saroja makes an exception by allowing her husband in to pour a cup of blended south Indian coffee. The rest of the family must go no further than the kitchen doorway.

The kitchen ceiling was very high and housed a loft for storing lentils, rice, tamarind and chilies, which she purchases when in season. In the same efficient mode, Saroja also buys limes and green mangoes when they are in season and pickles them for later use. The cabinets surrounding the gas stove held shiny jars of spices, lentils and flours, and those on the other side of the kitchen were stocked with china, glassware, shiny pots and pans and other kitchen utensils. Everything had a place and everything was in its place.

Saroja's kitchen had many modern appliances including two pressure cookers (constantly in use), a blender, warming oven, electric rice cooker, an iron press for making rice noodles for string hoppers, an intricate water purifier and heater, a coffee grinder and an elaborate coffee maker.

South Indians brew strong, filtered coffee that they mix with lots of milk and drink warm, not hot. To cool the coffee and give it a light, airy froth, they hold the tumbler of coffee high over a small bowl called a *dabara* and pour the coffee into it several times. This technique has given south Indian coffee the name "yard-long" coffee. Being fastidiously clean, Tamilian Hindus never touch their lips to the drinking vessel and instead pour the beverage (even coffee) into their mouths. This was a method I found difficult to master and credit any success I had to pure luck!

Continuing her explanation of how she organizes the kitchen, Saroja said that there is a special box for holding spices in every Indian kitchen called an *anjari*. Hers, typical of south India, contained mustard seeds, coriander, dried red chilies, fennel, fenugreek and *urad dal*. The choice of spices and their creative blending is the heart of south Indian cooking, and every day the maid, Lakshmi, prepares *masalas* by grinding whole spices on a flat grinding stone set on the floor of the kitchen. Because of this, the kitchen floor is kept scrupulously clean.

Also while sitting on the floor, Lakshmi cuts up vegetables on an *aruvalmanni*, an implement with a long, narrow wooden base and a sharp, rounded steel blade projecting from one end. At the very tip of the blade is a jagged edge used for grating coconut.

Saroja showed me how to prepare a lunch of palate-tickling *Avial*, a dish of shredded, mixed vegetables (green beans, plantains, carrots, snake gourd, yam, cucumber, bell pepper) and coconut seasoned with green chilies and a flavorful *masala*. This was accompanied by a fiery potato dish smothered with onions called *Aloo Pyaz*.

The meal was served family style with large containers or dishes set in the middle of the table. A freshly-washed, glistening banana leaf was placed before each person. Saroja explained that strict order is maintained when meals are served, with guests and men given food first, followed by children, younger women and, finally, grandmothers. Here the food is presented on a banana leaf for special occasions (*thalis* are for everyday use) and must be arranged in a precise way, just as it is on a *thali*. Everyone begins by eating a sweet to rid the mouth of acidity and stimulate the appetite. This is followed by two vegetable dishes, a yogurt dish (*raita* and yogurt rice) and, finally, another sweet. Once the food is placed on each individual's banana leaf it must never be offered to anyone else, since at this time it is considered *jutha*, or spoiled.

At the end of the meal, Lakshmi brought each of us a bowl of water to clean our hands. Although this meal is eaten entirely with the right hand and no other utensil, napkins are only to protect your clothes and not used to clean hands. Another servant immediately washed the dishes outside the house using a sink, dish drainer and other equipment set up for the purpose.

Both a banana tree and a jackfruit tree grew in the Subbaraman's yard, typical foliage for south India. Jackfruit is a large olive-green fruit with thick short spikes that Indians cook with spices and herbs and add to rice dishes. They also pickle it or serve it as a sweetmeat. After lunch Saroja offered me *supari,* a combination of crushed betel nuts, fennel, cumin and sweet sugar for digestion, and before I left, she proferred a platter containing a small round metal box of red powder called *kumkum.* She instructed me to dip a finger of my right hand into the powder and touch the center of my forehead with it to make a dot, a *pottu,* as a good omen. Finally, she gave me a coconut, banana, fresh turmeric, betel nut and betel leaves as a symbol of good hospitality, completeness and giving with a full heart. No visit to a south Indian home is complete without this gesture.

I ended my stay in Madras with a visit to my good friend Amelita Mullens, the principal of the Institute of Hotel Management, Catering Technology and Applied Nutrition. She is a marvelous person who is incredibly knowledgeable about Indian food and nutrition and who is responsible for making the government-owned college one of the best in India. I have lectured at many colleges throughout India and have always been most impressed by this one. I have been told that the curriculum is the same in all colleges, but the students and faculty here stand out. Perhaps they epitomize the southern traditions of friendliness, politeness and graciousness and seem truly unrestrained, open and curious about life.

Amelita took me to a market that she explained was exclusively for the elite segment of society. The fruits and vegetables neatly arranged in the stalls were the best available and throughout the day an incense man visited each stall with his burner to ensure all smelled nice. Here we visited stores that sold premixed *garam masalas, chat masalas, sambar masalas* and all sorts of prepared ingredients as well as individual dried spices, *dals,* dried fruits and sweets. As fascinated as I was with the food, the store I found the most impressive was that selling saris. At first I thought there was a sale in progress but soon realized the store was so crowded because Madras is a major silk center in India and attracts shoppers from all over seeking the finest quality.

Chettinad is a well-known cuisine of the area, reflecting the lifestyle of the Nattukotai Chettiars who come from one of the driest regions of south India. Theirs is an ancient merchant community that amassed great wealth by trading with Burma, Sri Lanka, Malaysia, Singapore and Indo-China. For centuries, the Chettiars have been famous for undertaking feasts that last for days and at which the food is as excessive as the event. Although independence brought the Chettiars home to India from foreign lands, they have maintained their spirit and love of opulent possessions and extravagant entertaining.

Modern feasts are prepared by teams of male cooks, who for generations have learned their skills from Chettiar women. Huge hearths are lit, massive metal pots and silver and brass dinner services are set out and the feast begins. This generosity is equally apparent in Chettiar homes when only a few guests are present.

Today, Chettiars are establishing "military" (meaning nonvegetarian) restaurants in Madras and other cities so that their cooking is becoming better known to a wide range of people. The food is obviously influenced by Southeast Asia, and so is quite distinct from other Indian food. It is served on a banana leaf with an assortment of small copper bowls for condiments and accompaniments. It is subtle and intriguing, but has an inherent sense of economy and a deep concern that the food should be both tasty and healthy. Often, it is topped with a boiled egg, which the Chettiars somehow consider essential for a proper meal.

The Raintree Restaurant in the Connemara Hotel in Madras is well known for its Chettinad cuisine, the chef having been a cook for one of the old Chettiar families. I dined there with Executive Chef K. Natarajan. On the highly polished brass *thali* lined with a banana leaf were dishes of *Meen Kozhambu*, a coconut-based fish curry, *Vera Varuval*, succulent, spicy fried prawns, and *Varuval Kola*, chicken cooked in spicy tamarind water. There also was *Gobhi Korma*, florets of cauliflower cooked with ground coconut, and my favorite, *Kodi Mellagu*, black pepper chicken with the nuances of black pepper and chilies combined with pungent spices and accompanied by *Rasam*, pickles and *Iddiappam*, freshly made rice noodles that are steamed and seasoned with coconut. The sweet, *Pal Paniharam*, made by soaking rice dumplings in cardamom-flavored milk, was followed by the traditional *paan*.

At the handsome south Indian Dakshin Restaurant in the Park Sheraton Hotel in Madras, *Dosas* and *Idlis* reach new heights when prepared by Paramasivam Iyer, or Sivam, as the chef prefers to be called. Sivam was born in Palghat, not far from Udupi, and since the age of fifteen has been working as a private cook and restaurant chef. At the hotel he interprets south Indian home cooking into elegant cuisine that manages to reflect all the states of the south.

During dinner with Amelita Mullens, I enjoyed *Kalyera Masala*, a rich creation of lobster cooked in a *masala* of chilies, coriander, tomatoes and *garam masala* from Tamil Nadu; *Pitta Roast*, a delicious preparation of quails roasted in a dry *masala* from Andhra Pradesh; *Meen Moilee*, the famous Kerala dish of fish simmered in a sauce of coconut milk, turmeric and green chilies; and from Karnataka, *Bisi Bele Hulianna*, an Udupi specialty of spiced rice and lentils, and

Rasavanghi, eggplant simmered with ginger and lentils accented with lime. A beautiful array of southern pickles was offered during the meal: Andhra pickles made from sour greens and loads of chilies, mashed mango pickles, gooseberry pickles, raw mango pickles, plus many, many more.

Throughout dinner Sivam was at his center-stage trolley preparing melt-in-your mouth Banana *Dosas;* Andhra *Pesarattus,* small crisp *dosas* packed with crisp fried onions; and *Appams,* the delicately thin rice and *urad dal* crepe. He walked from table to table, offering this selection to guests while extolling its virtues. Before we left, he insisted we end the meal with a south Indian coffee that he poured for us by the yard.

Delhi, both ancient and modern, constantly juxtaposes the old and new—not only in the remains of empires, but of social structures, too. There's Old Delhi with its Mughul architecture, the Red Fort, the mosques and tombs. There is the narrow maze of winding alleys in the old market section where vendors sell saris, jewelry, dried fruit and spices, and a favorite snack called *chat,* a spicy mixture of fruits, lentils or other treats. New Delhi, built earlier this century, is a city of magnificent buildings, elegant homes and wide tree-lined avenues ablaze with flowers.

The cuisine of Delhi has become a melting pot of Indian cooking and is now as cosmopolitan as that of New York or London. There is the food of the homes, where family traditions are passed down through generations; and the food of the restaurants, where a sophisticated new wave of food trends has emerged.

Knowing of my interest in Indian cuisine, Inder Sharma, a great humanitarian and president of Pacific Asia Travel Association and chairman of SITA World Travel in India (a highly respected national and international travel company), invited me to his elegant New Delhi home. Inder Sharma was the first and presently the only person to date to have been honored by the Indian government with one of the highest awards given by the government. A *PADMA SHRI* was presented to him by the President of India for his tremendous services to tourism.

For my visit he composed a menu of his best-liked dishes so that I might taste the nutritious cuisine served in his home. His wife, Dr. Aruna Sharma, a prominent New Delhi physician, shares her husband's commitment to healthy menus. Indian men are passionate about food. They can describe the exact ingredients, the method of cooking and the history of dishes—even though most do not cook.

Still, every Indian man believes that the food served in his home is the best in India—and Inder Sharma is no exception.

As we ate, he described each succulent dish in careful detail, including ingredients, nutritional value and history. We began the meal with delicately steamed fish wrapped in a banana leaf called *Patri ni Macchi* that was seasoned to perfection with ginger, garlic, green chilies, mint, coconut, spices, lime and sugar. The meal continued with Fenugreek Chicken, *Methi Murgh*, an exquisite dish flecked and flavored with fresh fenugreek; *Mash Dal*, superbly spiced *urad dal*; *paneer*, dumplings glazed with a tomato and coriander sauce; exquisitely spiced potatoes; and *Punjabi Kadhi*, chickpea dumplings bobbing in a tasty gravy of yogurt and chickpea flour; *besan* delicately seasoned with cumin, fennel, fenugreek, turmeric and chilies were accompanied by rice and freshly made hot *Chapatis*, delicate whole wheat flatbread.

A medley of sweets completed the evening and included captivating *Sooji Besan Halva*, a sweet made from semolina and chickpea flour flavored with warm aromatics such as saffron, fennel seeds and cassia leaves. Next was saffron-kissed *Kesari Kulfi*, which is a frozen dessert that seems a cross between ice cream and sherbet. The third sweet offered was the Bengali favorite *Mishti Doi*, a nutty yogurt custard sweetened with date palm sugar.

Ghulam Naqshband, managing director for SITA World Travel, lives in a Delhi home possessing subtle, old-world charm and reflecting the architectural design set by the British early in the century. The main hall is graced with imposing arches of Mughul design and hung with folk art paintings from the Kalamkaris and Pichwais as well as paintings from the Mughul, Rajput and Jaipur schools of art. More contemporary art is found in the rest of the rooms; particularly stunning are paintings by M.F. Hussain, Diren De and Ahmed, the earliest Indian abstract painters.

Ghulam and his cook also shared their knowledge of the art of cooking with me. We began the meal with *Badaam Shorba*, a rich almond soup, and then tried *Chooza-e-Nimbu*, a superbly flavored saffron chicken. Both dishes are typical of the royal cuisine of the nawabs of Avadh who in the 18th century ruled the kingdom that today is part of Bihar and Utter Pradesh. The next two dishes represented the cooking of the Muslims prior to their 1947 departure from Delhi for Pakistan: *Gosht Pasanda*, lamb seasoned with dried plums, chilies and *garam masala* and topped with almonds and coriander; and rich *Pullao Bhat*, fragrant *basmati* rice simmered with mutton and exquisite spices. The vibrant finale, introduced in India by the Mughuls who came to India in 1526 from Asia Minor, was *Gajar ka*

Halva, a delectable fusion of sweet carrots, cream, *ghee,* brown sugar, aromatic ground spices, almonds and currants served hot and garnished with silver leaf, almonds and cashews.

It is in New Delhi that the origins of the food revolution lie. After India's independence in 1947, the new administrative capital attracted immigrants from all over India, especially the Punjabis of the north, who dominated the hotel trade. They brought with them their hollow clay *tandoor* ovens and opened restaurants with dull rooms, flocked wallpaper and plush upholstery. Besides their *tandoori* chicken, they served sweet-and sour Chinese food and bland European fare, all cooked by the same chef! Rarely would you find a local eating in one of these restaurants. In the late 1970s, the five-star hotel groups, recognizing this void, consulted with Delhi chefs and began introducing authentic recipes in specialty restaurants in the hotels.

These restaurants specialized in a particular method of cooking *dum pukht,* in which food is very slowly cooked in a vessel sealed with flour paste and topped with hot coals to ensure even cooking. Some served food based on Portuguese-influenced Goan food, and others served the rice-based dishes of the south. The restaurants attracted Delhi residents who had up to this point eaten mainly at home, and the tradition of hotel dining, still very much alive in India, was born.

To sample excellent *tandoori* cooking that reflects the simple, robust fare of the Pakistanis from the northwest frontier, you need only go as far as the Maurya's Sheraton's award-winning Bukhara Restaurant where master chef Madan Lal Jaiswal practices his craft. Madan learned *tandoori* cooking in the frontier town of Lahore, Pakistan, from his father and grandfather, both recognized experts. Until his death at the reputed age of 120, his grandfather could be found at the oven—often with young Madan by his side.

The secret of *tandoori* cooking is the cut of meat, the authenticity of the spices and the marinade. It also depends on the ability of the cook to judge the heat and time necessary for success. As I watched Madan work, I noticed how precisely he monitored the grind and amount of spices added to each dish.

A *tandoor* is a hollow oven shaped like a large wine barrel and made of fine clay held together by animal hair and wheat husks. It is baked in the sun and then, when ready for use, fired by coal. Indians use *tandoor* ovens for barbecuing kebabs, baking breads called *Naans* and cooking meat, poultry and seafood. Meats and seafood are marinated generally in herbs and yogurt. The yogurt keeps the food moist. When done, *tandoor*-cooked foods are tender, succulent and boldly flavored. The reputation of any *tandoori* restaurant rests on two dishes: *Murgh Tikka* (chicken kebabs) and *Murgh Tandoori* (chicken tandoori). For both of these dishes, the chicken is marinated for several hours in a thick mixture of yogurt, Indian spices, crushed ginger and garlic, lime juice and salt. It is subjected to the intense heat of the *tandoor* (550°F. to 600°F.), cooked until it is crisp on the outside and moist near the bone. The other specialties include *Barah Kababs*, tender pieces of lamb strung on a skewer, *Seekh Kababs*, seasoned minced lamb finely ground together, and *Sikandari Raan*, whole leg of goat marinated in dark rum, braised in a conventional oven and finished in the *tandoor*.

The traditions of the cooking of Kashmir are carried out in a few Delhi restaurants, but nowhere more spectacularly than in the Chor Bazaar Restaurant. Kashmiri cooking reflects Persian, Afghan and Central Asian influences, all of which are apparent in an elaborate, traditional thirty-six course banquet called a *wazwan*. The term *waz* means the chef—someone with great culinary skills passed from generation to generation—while *wan* is a shop of abundant supplies of meats and delicacies. The head chef is assisted by *wazas*, the title grudgingly conferred on a chosen few only after years of apprenticeship.

My good friend Inder Sharma took me to Chor Bazaar so that I could experience this splendid feast. As soon as we sat down, we were given *tash-t-nari* to wash our hands, since it would be considered irreverent to use anything but fingers to eat this meal. Next, a large *thali* or *tarami* arrived heaped with rice and most of the courses: *Methi Maaz*, diced mutton lightly seasoned with fenugreek; *Tabak Maaz*, shallow-fried, tender spare ribs; *Gund Chatney*, onion rings with hot spices; and *Mutjan*, a magnificent pilaf prepared from Kashmiri rice with dried fruits. The crowning glory and grand finale of a *wazwan* is *Goshtaba*, which are velvety spheres of soft mutton flavored with cardamom and cooked over a slow fire in yogurt. No matter how sated you are at this point, refusing this delicacy would not only be bad manners but would hurt the feelings of the *wazas*. We ended the meal lingering over Kashmiri hyson green tea called *Kahwah*, which is flavored with cardamom, almonds and saffron served from a samovar.

Delhi, both old and new, is truly representative of all India, giving the adventuresome gourmet as wide a choice as there are cuisines on the subcontinent. Indeed, a tour of India would not be complete without a visit to this vibrant city—best, of course, if you also have a chance to visit other states and cities of India. *Namaste!* Welcome to India!

About
Light Indian Food
~~~

As in many Asian countries, rice is a mainstay of the south Indian diet. In north India, wheat (usually baked into bread) is the more common grain. I use rice in many dishes, appreciating its ability to enhance any number of foods. Despite some common misconceptions, rice is not fattening. It is a complex carbohydrate that provides needed fat-free calories and fiber.

When preparing these dishes, I reduced the amount of fat and eliminated *ghee* (clarified butter), cream and sweets traditionally found in Indian cuisine. Coconut milk, an ingredient in some south Indian dishes, has been eliminated because of its high-fat content. When a dish calls for grated coconut, I have substituted ground coconut, which even in small amounts provides stronger coconut flavor than grated coconut. I combine nonfat dry milk and skim milk for dishes calling for whole milk and cream along with many other substitutes for dairy products such as nonfat yogurt, cream cheese and cottage cheese. I find that the flavor is just as good as it is in the original Indian dishes.

In all recipes, salt is optional. I feel that because of the spices and other flavorings, rarely is there reason to add salt, unless you personally like it. However, Indians use salt very freely, and you may prefer to do so, too.

Indians love sweets. I chose to leave most sweets out of the book, deciding instead to end the meals with fresh fruit.

PLANNING AND SERVING INDIAN MEALS

In a typical Indian meal, knives and forks are not used—although they are showing up more and more in urban households. As in many Asian countries, the fingers of the right hand are used for eating, since the left hand is considered unclean and unfit for eating. Some would argue that food never tastes quite as good as when it's picked up with a small handful of rice and rolled into a compact morsel with some sauce or other accompaniment and eaten. In the north, where bread is the mainstay, a piece of bread is torn off and used as a scoop.

A typical Indian meal consists of about five or six dishes. Usually, all are served at the same time and consist of one rice dish, a *dal* or two, a vegetable or two and one major dish. In the north, breads usually accompany the food, and chutneys and pickles are always served for additional spicing. These should combine sweet, tart, salty and sour.

However, there are regional differences in the style of serving. For instance, in the south and in Maharashtra, a meal usually starts with a sweet where it is felt it stimulates the appetite. Most meals end with one or two sweets.

The food is arranged on a *thali*—a rimmed tray made of silver, brass, stainless steel or aluminum. On the *thali* are placed little *katoris*, or bowls, each filled with a different meat, vegetable, legume or yogurt-based preparation. A mound of rice is usually placed in the center of the *thali*, over which the contents from one or two of the *katoris* is poured. For special occasions, such as weddings, banquets, and family celebrations, the food is served on a banana leaf instead of the *thali*.

To Indians, eating is almost a ritual, and cooks are very concerned with how the food looks; aesthetic pleasure is as much a part of dining as the taste of the foods. The final essence of an Indian meal lies in the harmony of flavors, textures and colors.

BEVERAGES

Most people believe that beer, particularly Indian beer, is the beverage to drink with an Indian meal. While it does have its place, it is not the only choice.

Many of the Hindus, Muslims, Jains and Sikhs do not drink alcoholic beverages. For them, and for may other Indians, water is the drink of choice. There are also ample nonalcoholic beverages in the book, including *lassi*, a yogurt-based drink, fruit drinks and teas.

Indian wine is not the most desirable in the world, as the climate does not produce good grapes. However, wine can be delightful with a meal as long as it is not a delicate or fragile vintage that cannot stand up to spiciness and "heat." The wine should be strong in character and robust enough to hold its own.

The Indian Kitchen

ᨒᨑᨑᨑᨑ

$\mathcal{T}$he Indian kitchen is spotlessly clean. Traditionally, Indians regard cooking with great reverence. In many homes, only the women of the house and the cook are allowed in the kitchen and they must be properly bathed and attired in clean clothes prior to entering the kitchen. Shoes are not worn in the home and are left at the doorstep.

The most common cooking implements are neatly arranged along the wall. There is a *kadhi*, which is a form of a wok, a *tawa* or a slightly concave cast-iron pan to cook breads, and a *degchi*, a handleless pan made of heavy metal. The *sil batta*, a heavy stone slab with tiny grooves chipped into the surface used for grinding wet spices, and a *himam dasta*, a mortar and pestle for grinding dry spices, are the next most important pieces of equipment. A mini food processor, spice grinder or blender often takes its place in today's kitchen. In the north, often a *tandoor*, a clay oven, is tucked away in the corner. Most modern cooks have a gas or electric stove as well. And in the south, there are perforated steamers to make the light, rice flour dumplings called *idlis*.

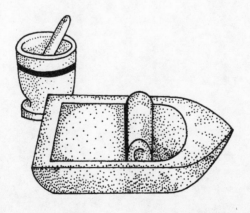

Although measurements for the recipes in this book are given for cups, teaspoons and tablespoons, these implements are rarely found in traditional kitchens. Most cooking is done without careful measurement, but by experience and estimation. A new bride does not take a cookbook to her new home, but rather brings with her what she has learned from her mother and aunts—how to tell by taste when a sauce is seasoned properly, how to tell if a pounded or ground mixture is correct by the feel of the ingredients in the mortar, how much water to use for new-crop rice or for older rice, and so on. I hope you will get into the true spirit of Indian cooking by adding a touch of this and a dab of that, using your own ingenuity until your dish reaches your highest expectations.

The menus are examples of traditional and contemporary Indian meals. Do not feel you have to try a whole menu your first time. Instead, try a single main dish, along with rice or bread, and complete the meal with some familiar dishes. As you gain experience with these dishes, you will be ready to serve a complete meal of the delectable, light, healthy foods of India.

Cooking Utensils

∾∾∾

Equipment for the Indian "light" kitchen is quite simple: mortar and pestle, mini-food processor, blender, spice or coffee grinder and good quality non-stick pans. A larger food processor is convenient, but not an essential.

For many Indian recipes, the mortar and pestle is nice to have. It is used for pulverizing spices into a powder and pounding aromatics into seasoning pastes. Its major advantage is that it can handle small quantities and that the ingredients are mashed into a smooth paste rather than chopped, producing a wonderfully fragrant blend that releases the flavors more effectively than a machine.

With today's limited time, I have found processing the small amounts for paste mixtures in a mini food processor or in a blender produces satisfying results. When preparing a paste mixture in the mini food processor, chop the harder ingredients by hand first and then add them to the mini food processor. If necessary, you may have to add a little water to produce a smooth paste. A mini food processor is also very handy for chopping and puréeing small amounts of food.

A spice grinder or coffee grinder reserved especially for spices is nice to have. If you use your coffee grinder for coffee beans, the spices will take on the flavor and aroma of the coffee beans.

A larger food processor is convenient for slicing and mixing and kneading dough for Indian breads. For small quantities of wet or dry ingredients used in individual recipes, I find it is too large to effectively grind and purée.

I prefer high quality non-stick pans, which allow you to cut down significantly on the amount of oil. Since no recipe in this book calls for deep frying, you will not have use for the usual Indian wok called a *kadhi*. It is handy to have a non-stick stir-fry pan, although I have found for most recipes, non-stick frying pans are just as useful for stir-frying. A steaming basket or steamer is convenient, and pressure cookers are extremely useful, since they reduce the cooking time needed for legumes and long-simmered dishes. Almost every home kitchen in India has at least one or two pressure cookers.

Cutting Techniques

~~~

Shredding or Julienne Cutting

The terms shredding and julienne are interchangeable. In Asian cuisine, the term shredding is most common.

To shred, cut the food into slices of the desired length. Stack the slices and slice down through the layers into sticks, which are square in cross section. Shreds are usually very fine, about 1/8 to 1/16 inch in diameter.

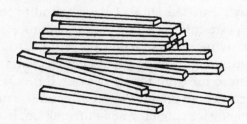

Dicing, Chopping and Cubing

Cut the food into slices. Stack the slices on top of each other and cut them lengthwise into strips, as in shredding. Stack the strips and cut crosswise into evenly sized cubes or dice. Uniform cubes are unnecessary when the chopped food is to be used for making pastes in the mini-food processor. The machine will work more efficiently if the ingredients are chopped prior to their addition to the processor.

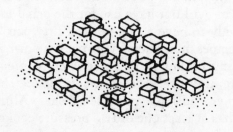

Mincing

To mince an ingredient means to cut it into very small pieces, about 1/16 inch.

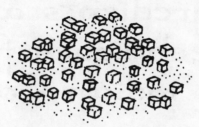

Smashing, Crushing and Bruising

Many ingredients are crushed before cooking to bring out their full flavor and aroma. Place the pieces on a board and hit them sharply with a knife or other implement. This can also be done prior to mincing an ingredient, making the process much easier.

Ingredients and Techniques for Light Indian Cooking

⤛⤜

SPICES

You can find most Indian spices in the grocery store or supermarket. However, there are a few used in Mughlai dishes that can only be found in an Indian grocery store. You will find that most Western spices—cloves, cinnamon, fennel, nutmeg to name a few—are much less expensive in an Indian grocery store. It is best when shopping in an Indian store to take both the English and Hindi name with you because you may have a communication problem. You will find both in the glossary of ingredients on page 349.

Most spices have to be cooked in hot oil to release their true essence, which is why most recipes start with cooking the spices and many end with the same technique. All spices release more aroma

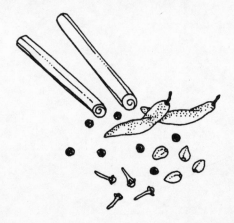

when slightly crushed first and then cooked in oil. When spices are cooked in oil to complete a dish, this is a uniquely Indian technique often referred to as tempering.

It is best to purchase spices whole, and to grind them to a powder in a coffee or spice grinder when needed. Freshly ground spices are always more aromatic and potent. If you find this impractical, store ground spices in airtight containers in a cool dry place. They can be kept for up to 3 to 4 months. Whole spices will keep up to one year.

ROASTING AND GRINDING OF SPICES

TO ROAST SPICES: Heat a heavy dry pan over medium heat. Add one spice and roast over medium heat, shaking and stirring the pan constantly. When the spice starts to brown, be very careful not to burn. When browned, remove spice from the pan immediately and place in a heatproof bowl to cool. Repeat with other spices.

TO GRIND SPICES: Grind the spices together to a fine powder in a coffee grinder reserved for spices, a spice grinder or an electric blender. A mortar and pestle is best for grinding very small amounts of spices. If you do not have a mortar and pestle, place the spices on waxed paper or plastic wrap. Cover the spices with another layer of waxed paper or plastic wrap and roll them with a rolling pin or pound them with a kitchen mallet. The ground spices may be stored in an airtight container for about three months.

CRUSHING SPICES

Crush the spices in a mortar and pestle or between the palms of your hands or between your finger and thumb. Crushing spices should be done shortly before cooking because they loose their flavor and aroma.

FRYING OF SPICES

Cooking spices in a little hot oil is the essence of Indian cooking. It removes the raw flavor of the spices while releasing their flavors and aromas. In some recipes, I refer to this technique as "tempering" when the seasoned oil is poured over cooked foods such as legumes and vegetables. This technique takes a little practice especially for light cooking where you use less oil than normal for the process. When using a non-stick pan, heat the oil over moderate heat. Add the spices and cook, stirring constantly, until they begin to crackle or pop. If cooking whole and powdered spices, always cook the whole spices first and then add the powdered spices. Exact timing is tricky to determine, since every pan and burner varies. It is also important to have the next batch of ingredients, such as meat or vegetables, ready to add immediately to the fried spices to stop their cooking process so that they will not burn. Black mustard seeds must be added first and fried until they crackle, otherwise they will be bitter. This is specified in each recipe.

HERBS AND SEASONINGS

Fresh basil, coriander leaves, mint leaves, curry leaves, garlic, ginger root, onions and shallots are essential to create aromatic and flavorful dishes. I prefer not to use basil, coriander, mint or curry leaves in the dry form and do not suggest them as a substitute.

Masalas

Many people think of "curry" as typical Indian food. However, curry powder as we know it does not exist in India. The term *masala*, which is a blending of any number of spice, herb and seasoning combinations that may or may not be combined with "wet" ingredients such as ginger, garlic, hot chilies, fresh lime juice or tamarind, is the key to an Indian curry. The *masala* is crucial to the individuality and flavor of each dish. Each individual entrée in the book has its own *masala*, or spice mixture, necessary for that dish.

The following are the most commonly used *masalas*:

Garam Masala

꙳ꙮ꙳

This aromatic mixture of spices is best when freshly ground, as it is more flavorful. However, it may be kept in an airtight container for about 1 month.

2 tablespoons black cardamom
   seeds
2-inch cinnamon stick, crushed

2 teaspoons whole cloves
4 teaspoons black peppercorns

Dry roast the spices separately in a skillet over moderate heat until aromatic. Grind to a fine powder in a spice grinder. Store in an airtight container for about 3 months.

YIELD: approximately 6 tablespoons.

Garam Masala, Bengali Style

꙳ꙮ꙳

2 tablespoons cloves
1-inch cinnamon stick

2 tablespoons black cardamom
   seeds

Dry roast the spices separately in a skillet over moderate heat until aromatic. Grind to a fine powder in a spice grinder. Store in an airtight container for about 1 to 2 months.

YIELD: approximately 6 tablespoons.

SOUTH INDIAN CURRY POWDER
KARI PODI

∼ତ୍ୟଙ

3/4 cup coriander seeds
1/3 cup split *toor dal*
1/4 cup *chana dal*
2 teaspoons canola oil

1/3 cup dried red chilies
1 teaspoon ground asafetida, *hing*
(optional)

Dry roast the coriander seeds, *toor dal* and *chana dal* separately in a skillet over moderate heat until aromatic. Grind to a powder in a spice grinder. Add 1 tablespoon oil to the skillet. Add the red chilies and cook, stirring, until lightly browned. Add the chilies to the spice grinder. Grind to a powder. Add the asafetida. Mix well. Store in an airtight container for about 1 to 2 months.

YIELD: approximately 1-1/4 cups.

CHAT MASALA

∼ତ୍ୟଙ

Chat masala is a sand-colored spice blend that is traditionally sprinkled on fresh fruit and other snacks. It is quite potent and a little goes a long way. Ready-made *chat masala* from India may be purchased in Indian grocery stores and is quite acceptable.

2 tablespoons cumin seeds
2 teaspoons fennel seeds
2 teaspoons dried mint leaves
1 tablespoon *garam masala*
1 tablespoon mango powder

1 tablespoon black salt
1 teaspoon ground red pepper
1/8 teaspoon ground asafetida
(optional)
1/4 teaspoon ground ginger

Dry roast the cumin and fennel seeds in a skillet over moderate heat until aromatic. Grind the cumin, fennel and dried mint leaves to a powder in a spice grinder. Add the *garam masala*, mango powder, black salt, ground red pepper, asafetida and ground ginger. Mix well. Store in an airtight container for about 3 months.

YIELD: approximately 6 tablespoons.

SOUTH INDIAN SUMBAR POWDER
SAMBAR MASALA

∞∾∾

Sambar masala is very popular in the south. It is similar to *garam masala*, but much spicier, in accordance with southern Indian tastes.

1 cup coriander seeds	1/4 cup split *urad dal*
1 cup dried red chilies	1 teaspoon poppy seeds
1/8 cup black peppercorns	2-inch cinnamon stick
1/8 cup cumin seeds	20 curry leaves
1 teaspoon fenugreek seeds	1 teaspoon ground turmeric
1 teaspoon mustard seeds	

Dry roast the coriander seeds, red chilies, peppercorns, cumin seeds, fenugreek seeds, mustard seeds, *urad dal*, poppy seeds, cinnamon stick and curry leaves separately over moderate heat until aromatic. Grind to a fine powder in a spice grinder. Add turmeric and mix well. Store in an airtight container for about 3 months.

YIELD: approximately 2-1/4 cups.

COOK'S TIP: This mixture is very hot. Use sparingly or according to recipe directions.

OIL

I cook with vegetable oil, usually canola or olive oil, and have used the smallest quantity possible throughout the book. I have found that by lightly misting a non-stick pan with a spray that I have been able to significantly reduce the amount of oil.

With the use of the new high-quality non-stick pans and wonderful Indian seasonings, I can produce dishes that are delicious but not as heavy as many I sampled during my travels. Instead of using the usual *ghee* (clarified butter) to finish a dish, I spray cooked rice dishes, steamed vegetables and other dishes with a perfumed mist of canola or extra-virgin olive oil prior to serving. Oil cannot be eliminated when cooking raw spices as this is the essence of Indian cuisine and brings out their aromas and fragrances as no other cooking method can.

When a recipe calls for mustard oil, which is intensely pungent, it is important to heat it to the smoking point for a moment. Remove the pan from the heat until it stops smoking before starting to cook. This will soften the harsh mustard flavor, making it pleasantly flavored. Look for "pure" mustard oil, which can be purchased in an Indian grocery story. Mustard oil is often used in Bengali cooking.

An important tip to remember is that when you double a recipe, you do not double the amount of oil.

You will find additional tips for lowering fat throughout the book.

BROWNING AND FRYING ONIONS

Usually, when an Indian recipe calls for golden brown or caramelized onions, the onions are browned in a fairly large amount of oil. I have developed a method requiring very little oil using a non-stick pan.

Slice the onions into very thin, even slices or chop the onions into small uniform pieces. Heat about 1 tablespoon oil over moderate heat. The amount of oil depends upon the amount of onions to be cooked. Stir the onions for 2 minutes. Reduce the heat to low. Add about 2 tablespoons of water and continue cooking, stirring constantly. If cooking large quantities, add additional water 1 tablespoon at a time if the onions begin sticking to the pan or fry too rapidly. This allows the natural moisture of the onions to be coaxed out while browning. Continue frying until the onions are golden brown. This process can take about 20 minutes. When simmered slowly, the onions add a rich dimension and melt into the sauce, thickening it as well. Brown fried onions can be prepared in large quantities and refrigerated or frozen and defrosted when needed. Once defrosted, they cannot be refrozen. It is best to package them in small quantities.

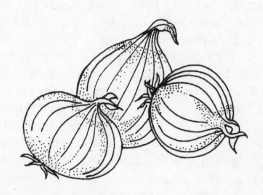

GINGER AND GARLIC PASTE

~~ε∽

10 cloves garlic, peeled and chopped	1 piece of fresh ginger about 3 inches long by 1-1/2 inch thick, peeled and chopped

Blend the garlic and ginger with a little water in a mini-food processor, food grinder or blender to a paste. The paste will keep in a tightly sealed jar in the refrigerator for about 1 week.

YIELD: approximately 1/2 cup.

COOK'S TIP: If preparing a large quantity of Indian food, process peeled, chopped ginger and garlic separately into a paste in a mini food processor, food grinder or blender, adding a little water to make a smooth paste. Store pastes separately in airtight glass containers in the refrigerator for several days.

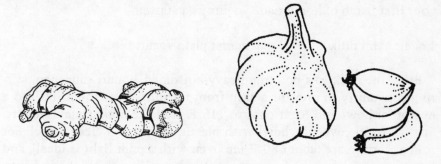

MILK PRODUCTS

Yogurt *Dahi*

Yogurt might be considered India's secret ingredient. It is a staple that is made daily in Indian households. Yogurt is one of the few foods common to all of the diverse regional cuisines and appears both on the vegetarian and nonvegetarian table. I have also used yogurt in combination with other ingredients throughout the book as a substitute for high-calorie dairy products.

Yogurt is enjoyed by itself and with vegetables or fruits in a salad called *raita*. Yogurt may also be combined with ginger and garlic and seasonings to flavor and tenderize meat, fish and poultry dishes prior to cooking and to impart both flavor and body to sauces for many dishes. Incorporated into dough, it becomes a leavening agent. When used in mint or other dips, it becomes a delicious accompaniment to grilled meats and kebabs. Not to be overlooked is its use in desserts such as Yogurt with Saffron (page 312). Its uses are so varied it would be impossible to mention them all here.

One note of caution when cooking with yogurt: bring it to room temperature first if possible. Always whisk the yogurt lightly before adding it to a dish. Add the yogurt over low heat a little at a time. This will prevent it from curdling.

Yogurt is very simple to make. With a commercial yogurt maker, you can easily make yogurt at home following the manufacturer's directions. Or you can make it by following these directions.

Preparation of Nonfat Yogurt: The preparation of your first yogurt is crucial to future batches. Always purchase nonfat yogurt with the latest expiration date, which will be the freshest. It is best to use store-bought nonfat yogurt as a starter without added ingredients such as gelatin. Once you have made your own yogurt, you can use some of your first batch of homemade yogurt as a starter.

1 quart skim milk   1/4 cup nonfat plain yogurt

Bring the milk to a boil in a heavy-bottomed 3 quart saucepan, stirring constantly to prevent a skin from forming. Pour the milk into a heatproof bowl and let it cool to 115°F. Add the nonfat plain yogurt. Stir well and cover the bowl with plastic wrap and a clean towel. Set it in a warm place, about 80°F. (an oven with a pilot light is ideal), and let it rest for about 8 hours or until the milk has thickened into yogurt. Refrigerate, covered. The yogurt will keep for several days in the refrigerator.

Indian Cheese

Homemade Indian cheese is similar to ricotta or farmer's cheese. In curd form it is called *chenna* and when compressed into a cake, it is called *paneer*. This natural cheese does not keep for a long time and is best when used within several days.

INDIAN COTTAGE CHEESE
CHENNA

∼∾⌒∽

2 quarts 2 percent milk   4 tablespoons fresh lemon juice

Bring the milk slowly to a boil in a large, deep-sided, heavy non-stick saucepan over medium-high heat, stirring often to prevent sticking. When the milk comes to a boil, reduce the heat and add the lemon juice. Stir gently until a white curd forms and separates into soft, moist curds. This should take about 10 to 20 seconds. When the curd begins to form, the mixture should be stirred very slowly and carefully in order to prevent the freshly formed curds from disintegrating into small pieces. The curd should be in lumps. Remove immediately from the heat.

Line a strainer with several layers of cheesecloth. Pour the cheese mixture into the lined strainer and let the liquid (whey) drain into a bowl. Hold the cheesecloth under a medium stream of running water for about 10 to 20 seconds to remove the lemon smell. Gather up the sides of the cheesecloth and secure the top by tying the cheesecloth together. Gently squeeze the cheesecloth to remove any excess moisture. Hang the cheesecloth over a bowl for about 1-1/2 hours. This drained, slightly moist cheese is *chenna*.

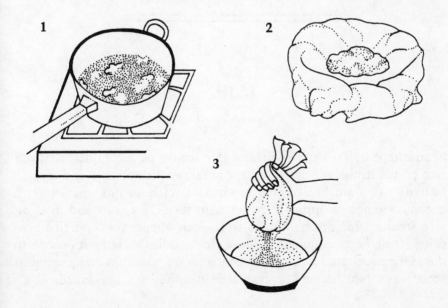

INDIAN CHEESE CAKES
PANEER

～⌒～

Prepare Indian Cottage Cheese (*chenna*) as above. Place the cheese, still wrapped in the cheesecloth, on a clean flat surface such as a large plate. Place a heavy weight, such as a cast-iron skillet or a large pan filled with water, over the entire top of the cheesecloth for about 1 hour or until it becomes firm and all the moisture has been extruded. The cheese must be firm enough to be cut with a knife. Cut the cheese into rectangles or according to your recipe. *Paneer* will keep refrigerated for about 4 days.

COOK'S TIP: If the curd does not form after adding all of the lemon juice, you may have to add more lemon juice gradually until lumps of curd form and the whey separates.

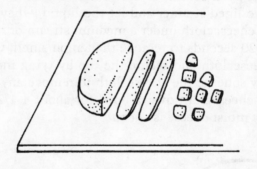

Rice
Chawal

In southern India, a meal without rice would be incomplete. Rice or rice preparations are devoured for breakfast, lunch, tea and dinner. Indians eat plain boiled rice or cook it with onions, mix it with coconut, lemon or lime. They eat it in pilafs, *biryanis* and in light, airy steamed *idlis* (page 70), as well as in *hoppers*, a light rice pancake; string *hoppers*, long strands of rice noodles mixed with coconut; *dosas*, rice and *urad dal*–stuffed pancakes; in puddings and numerous other ways. Northerners eat less rice since their staple is bread.

When rice is served, it is painstakingly prepared with fragrant spices and can include vegetables and meat. Mughlai *biryanis* and pilafs can be so exquisite that they often surpass the main course.

Long-grain *basmati* rice is the preferred rice and was used in testing all recipes for this book. However, if this is not available, you may use any long-grain rice. The best *basmati* rice grows in the foothills of the Himalaya Mountains. The grains are slender, delicate, and naturally perfumed. There are many grades of rice, and it is best to purchase the best quality available in your Indian grocery store, which is *Dehradun basmati.* It is also available in Middle Eastern and specialty stores. Unlike regular long-grain rice, *basmati* rice must be soaked in water prior to cooking.

Preparation of *Basmati* Rice for Cooking

SORTING: Often the *basmati* has a few unhulled rice grains, pieces of stones and sticks. It should be picked over prior to soaking. Place the rice on a large cookie sheet or other flat surface and pick over the rice, discarding all the foreign matter.

WASHING: Place the rice in a large bowl. Cover with water. With your hands, swish the water around to remove the starch coating on the rice grains. Let the rice sit for a few seconds to allow any husks to float to the top for removal. Drain the rice and continue this process until the water is no longer milky in color and is clear and clean.

SOAKING: It is essential to soak *basmati* rice before cooking. Place the rice in a bowl. Add enough warm water to cover the rice by at least 1 inch. Soak the rice for at least 20 minutes to allow the grains to absorb moisture and relax prior to cooking. This allows the rice to expand into long thin grains that will not break during cooking. Drain the rice, saving the water to use as cooking water after the rice has been soaked. This preserves the nutrients from the rice. (You may use fresh water if desired.)

STEAMED *BASMATI* RICE
OBLA CHAWAL

∽◡∾

Rice is cooked painstakingly, for each grain has to be fully cooked and separate. Rice that sticks together is not desirable.

1 cup *basmati* rice	1-2/3–2 cups of water, preferably that used to soak rice

Bring the water to a boil in a heavy-bottomed, preferably non-stick saucepan. The amount of water used will vary depending upon the strain and age of the rice and the depth and weight of the pan. Therefore, the measurements given are approximate.

Add the soaked rice and stir carefully. Bring the rice to a second boil, stirring gently. Reduce the heat to low, and simmer, partially covered, until most of the water is absorbed and the surface of the rice is full of little craters, about 10 to 15 minutes.

Cover the pan with a tight lid. If you do not have a tight-fitting lid, cover your pan with aluminum foil and place the lid on top of the foil to achieve a tight seal. Steam until fully cooked.

Steaming of the rice can be achieved in two ways:

1. Reduce the heat to the lowest setting. Place a pair of metal tongs or a Chinese wok ring over the burner and place the pot on it. The rice should be about 1 inch above the source of heat. Steam the rice for about 10 minutes.

or

2. Place the tightly covered pan with the rice on the center shelf of a 300°F. preheated oven for 25 minutes.

Let the rice rest, covered, undisturbed for 5 minutes before serving. Fluff the rice with a fork just before serving. Cooked rice will stay warm for about 20 minutes, covered. As a general rule, 1 cup uncooked rice yields approximately 3 cups cooked rice.

Cooking Long-Grain Rice

It is not necessary to wash and soak regular long-grain rice.

1/2–3/4 cup long-grain rice
  per person
2 cups water for the first measured
  cup of rice

1-1/2 cups water for each
  additional cup of rice

Select a saucepan with a tight-fitting lid. Bring the water to a boil. Add the rice and bring to a boil. Cover the pan with the lid. Reduce the heat and simmer until all the water is absorbed, about 18 to 20 minutes. Do not lift the cover during this time. At the end of this period, open the cover long enough to check to see that all the water has been absorbed. Cover again. Turn off the heat and let the rice rest for at least 5 minutes. Fluff the rice with a fork. Serve warm.

GROUND COCONUT

Indian grocery stores sell coconut in powdered form. By using unsweetened ground coconut, you will be able to use less coconut in your cooking yet get more coconut flavor. If you cannot obtain ground coconut, purchase unsweetened desiccated coconut and grind it to a powder in a food processor or blender.

TAMARIND

Tamarind produces the tart flavor in many dishes. It is the thick flesh inside the pods of the tamarind tree. Available in Indian and Southeast Asian grocery stores as tamarind pulp, it is the peeled, pitted, and compressed tamarind.

It is also available as tamarind concentrate. When the amount needed in a recipe is small, I have used prepared tamarind concentrate. For recipes calling for a large amount of tamarind, I have chosen to use tamarind purée as it has a more herbal flavor and a richer taste.

TAMARIND LIQUID

∾≎∾

1 2-1/2 × 1 × 1 inch piece of   1/2 cup hot water
    tamarind pulp

Place the tamarind pulp in a small container and add the hot water. Let the tamarind soak for 20 to 30 minutes, squeezing the pulp with your fingers or a spoon to break it apart and separate the seeds and strings. Strain the tamarind liquid through a fine sieve, forcing the pulp against the strainer, reserving the liquid. Discard the pulp. Use immediately, or store tightly covered in a glass container for several days.

YIELD: approximately 1/2 cup.

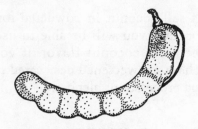

BANANA LEAVES

Banana leaves give a subtle aroma to cooked foods and are frequently used for steaming and grilling. Frozen banana leaves are available in Asian grocery stores. If unavailable, aluminum foil may be substituted; however, the pleasant fragrance of the banana leaf will be missing.

To wrap food in a banana leaf, pour boiling water over the leaf to make it pliable. Start with a 12 inch–square leaf. With the leaf fibers horizontal, place the food in the center of the leaf, allowing 4 inches on all sides. Fold the far and near edges over the food, making a neat parcel. Secure the package with a metal skewer, string or a toothpick. Banana leaves are fragile and split easily, but you can patch the leaf with another leaf.

Many chefs wrap the banana leaf with aluminum foil outside the leaves if splitting occurs. The fragrance of the banana leaf will be imparted, and the aromatic seasonings will not be lost during cooking.

Legumes
Dals

Legumes can be grouped into three categories: lentils, beans and peas, all of which are called *dal* in Hindi. Most *dals* are available whole, split without skins or ground into flour. They are an inexpensive source of protein, have no cholesterol and only a trace of fat. They are also high in carbohydrates, fiber, B vitamins and minerals. These highly nutritious vegetables are extremely popular all over India, either as side dishes or the ever-present *dals*, which are basically spiced lentils, either puréed or served whole. Whether served with rice or one of the tasty breads, this delicious preparation is present at every meal. "No wonder there is an old Hindi proverb, "Rice is good, but *dals* are my life!"

CLEANING AND WASHING *DALS*: All legumes should be picked over carefully before washing to remove kernels that have become too hard and for foreign matter such as dried leaves, stems and stones. Spread a handful of the *dal* on a large cookie sheet and pick through them, discarding any foreign matter.

Put them in a fine-mesh sieve and lower it into a bowl full of water. Rub the *dal* between your hands. Remove and discard the water. Repeat the process until the water is clear. Drain or soak as directed in each individual recipe.

COOKING *DALS*: The *dals* may be cooked in a heavy pan with the suggested amount of water and seasoning as directed in each recipe. Bring to a boil over high heat. Reduce the heat to moderate, removing any residue that may come to the top during cooking. Cover with a tight-fitting lid and gently boil according to the recipe until the *dal* is thoroughly softened. The cooking time varies for each type of *dal* and the age of the *dal*. An old *dal* may take twice as long as a new *dal*.

A pressure cooker is ideal for cooking *dal* as it reduces the cooking time by about one-third. Be sure to follow your manufacturers directions. For medium to thick *dal* purées and sauces, it is best to use a saucepan as the *dal* might clog the vent of the pressure cooker.

TYPES OF *DAL*

CHANA DAL: This is very much like the yellow split pea although it is smaller in size and sweeter in flavor. It is pale buff to bright yellow and is sold split without the skin. Yellow split peas may be used as a substitute.

KABULI CHANA: Also known as chickpeas or garbanzo beans. Chickpeas are pale to light brown and are sold whole, without the skins.

KALA CHANA: Kala chana is related to the chickpea, but is somewhat smaller and darker brown than chickpeas. *Kala chana* and chickpeas are not interchangeable as they have different flavors.

MASSOR DAL: A hulled, salmon-colored split pea, this is also known as red split lentils. If buying from an Indian shop, make sure you buy the skinned variety.

MUNG DAL: Also known as mung beans or *green gram*. Split mung *dal* is sold both whole with skins (*sabat moong*), without skins (*mung dal*) and split (*mung dal*) with skins.

TOOR DAL: Also known as *toorvar dal* and *arhar dal*. Pale yellow to gold in color, these lentils are sold split without the skins. They have quite a dark, earthy flavor. Some stores carry oily *toor dal*. This *dal* has been rubbed with castor oil which acts as a preservative. The oil needs to be washed before the *dal* can be used. None of my recipes call for the oily dal.

URAD DAL: Also known as *black gram bean.* It is sold whole with skins (*sabat urad*), split without skins (*urad dal*), and split with skins (*chilke urad dal*). For this book, most recipes call for the split without skins variety (*urad dal*).

Starters, Snacks
and Savories

Indians love snacks! They are devoured at any time of the day, especially in the morning or mid-afternoon and are usually accompanied by a light relish or chutney that provides a lively contrast. A beverage such as a spiced tea or a fruit drink is served as well.

Many snacks are based on *dals* such as Spiced Chickpea and Potato Snack (page 63). Also immensely popular is *sevian*, a durum wheat flour dough that is pressed through a mold to make a threadlike vermicelli that is then cooked. For elaborate savories, the fine *sevian* noodle strands are combined with vivacious ingredients as in Spiced Vermicelli, Chickpeas and Tomatoes (page 74). Semolina is also used in savories such as Semolina with Mixed Vegetables (page 77). These snacks also make excellent light luncheons or suppers.

Until recently, appetizers as known in the Western world were not part of the Indian meal. Today, Indians are serving dishes such as Chicken Kebabs (page 143) and other kebabs from their traditional main meal repertoire as an appetizer or first course. You will find many appropriate dishes throughout the book that may be served as appetizers.

If offering a "snack" as a starter, serve just enough to whet the appetite for the delectable meal to follow.

Tomato Cocktail TAMATAR KA THANDA SHORBA
Spiced Chickpea and Potato Snack KALA CHANA ALOO CHAT
Savory Chickpeas KABULI CHANA CHAT
Spiced Potato Chat ALOO CHAT
Potato Patties ALOO TIKKI
Spicy Potato Crisps ALOO BHAJIA
Yam Chips CHENAIKIZHANGU VARUVAL
Steamed Rice and Urad Dal Dumplings IDLIS
Lemon-Flavored Rice Noodles ELUMBUCHAPAYAM SEVAI
Savory Vermicelli SEVIYA UPPMA
Spiced Vermicelli, Chickpeas and Tomatoes
SULTANA SEVIAN
Semolina with Mixed Vegetables SOOJI UPPMA
Spicy Chicken Salad MURGH CHAT
Pineapple Sesame ANANNAS SASME
Spiced Fruit Salad CHAT
Fruit Chat CHAT
Lentil Wafers PAPPADUMS
Sago Wafers PHUL BADI

Tomato Cocktail

TAMATAR KA THANDA SHORBA

When red-ripe garden tomatoes are in season, this burst of flavor is outstanding.

5 large ripe tomatoes
1–2 teaspoons hot red pepper
   sauce

4 teaspoons sugar, or to taste
2 teaspoons fresh lemon juice
Salt to taste

GARNISH:

2 tablespoons finely chopped
tomatoes

2 tablespoons chopped fresh
mint leaves

Bring water to a boil in a large saucepan. Submerge the tomatoes in batches in the water for 15 to 30 seconds. Remove the tomatoes from the water, let them cool or plunge them into cold water. Remove the skins with a sharp knife. Cut each tomato in half. Gently squeeze out all the seeds.

Purée the tomatoes in a food processor or blender. Add the red pepper sauce, sugar to taste, lemon juice and salt to taste. Process until blended. Chill in the refrigerator.

Serve in glasses garnished with chopped tomatoes and mint leaves.

YIELD: 6 servings.

ADVANCE PREPARATION: Prepare 1 day ahead. Garnish when serving.

VARIATION: Substitute a good quality low sodium tomato juice for the tomatoes. Omit the sugar.

34 Calories per serving:
1 G Protein   46 MG Sodium
0 G Fat   0 MG Cholesterol
8 G Carbohydrate

Spiced Chickpea and Potato Snack

KALA CHANA ALOO CHAT

∽⌢∾

This simply prepared tangy salad is delightfully refreshing as an appetizer, snack or as a side dish. In India, the street vendors ladle it onto a "plate" made of dried leaves and top it with a flatbread.

The *chat* is more flavorful and has a marvelous texture when prepared with dried *kala chana* (brown-skinned dried chickpeas found in Indian grocery stores). However, you can save time by using drained canned chickpeas.

1-1/2 cups dried chickpeas,
kala chana

1 medium potato, boiled in
the skin and cooled

1–2 teaspoons fresh minced
green chilies

2 teaspoons chopped red onion

1 teaspoon *chat masala* (page 44)

1/4 teaspoon salt, or to taste

1/4 cup chopped fresh mint leaves

1/4 cup chopped fresh coriander
leaves

1 teaspoon peeled, chopped
fresh ginger

1-1/2 tablespoons fresh lemon juice

Lemon slices to garnish

Sort and wash the chickpeas as described on page 55. Place the
chickpeas in a bowl with enough water to cover. Soak for 8 hours or
overnight. Drain. Place the chickpeas in a large, heavy saucepan. Add
enough water to cover by 2 inches. Bring to a boil, reduce heat, cover
and simmer for 1-1/2 to 2 hours or until the chickpeas are tender to
the bite. Drain the chickpeas and place in a bowl. Peel the potato and
cut into 1/4-inch cubes. Add to the chickpeas with the chilies, red
onion, chat masala and salt. Set aside.

In a mini-food processor or blender, process the mint, coriander,
ginger and lemon juice to a paste. Add the paste to the chickpea mixture and toss to coat. Serve chilled or at room temperature.

Yield: 4 servings as a snack.

Variations:

1. Substitute 1-1/2 cups drained, canned chickpeas for the *kala
chana*. The chickpeas must not be mushy.
2. For an interesting variation, wrap the chickpea mixture in a
Boston or romaine lettuce leaf and serve as a lettuce package.

Advance Preparation: Prepare 1 day ahead. Refrigerate. Serve chilled
or at room temperature.

305 Calories per serving:
16 G Protein
4 G Fat
52 G Carbohydrate
151 MG Sodium
5 MG Cholesterol

Inspired by G. Sultan Mohideen, Executive Chef, Rajputana Palace, Jaipur

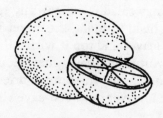

Savory Chickpeas

KABULI CHANA CHAT

~⦿~

This popular north Indian dish is both tart and hot. It is served as a snack with Indian bread or as an accompaniment to a light luncheon. For contrast, crispy raw vegetables are often served too.

1 cup dried chickpeas, *kabuli chana*
1 teaspoon ground turmeric
1 teaspoon ground cumin

1/2 teaspoon red pepper powder
Salt to taste
Fresh lime juice to taste

Sort and wash the chickpeas as described on page 55. Place the chickpeas in a bowl with enough water to cover. Soak for 8 hours or overnight. Drain. Place the chickpeas in a large, heavy saucepan. Add enough water to cover by 2 inches. Bring to a boil. Add the turmeric. Cover and simmer for 1-1/2 to 2 hours, or until chickpeas are tender to the bite.

Drain the chickpeas while hot. In a bowl combine the chickpeas, cumin, red pepper powder and lime juice to taste. Add salt if desired.

YIELD: 1 cup.

ADVANCE PREPARATION: Prepare 1 day ahead. Refrigerate. Serve at room temperature.

203 Calories per serving:
11 G Protein
3 G Fat
33 G Carbohydrate

42 MG Sodium
4 MG Cholesterol

Spiced Potato Chat

ALOO CHAT

∽ఎ⌒

Here is an easily prepared potato snack with a flicker of fire.

4 medium potatoes, boiled in the
  skins and cooled
1/2–1 fresh green chili, seeded and
  chopped
1/4–1/2 teaspoon red pepper powder

1/2 teaspoon salt or to taste
2 teaspoons fresh lemon juice
2 tablespoons chopped fresh
  coriander leaves

Peel the potatoes and cut into 1/2-inch cubes. Place in a bowl and add the chili, red pepper, salt, lemon juice and coriander. Toss well to mix. Serve at room temperature with Tamarind Chutney (page 286).

YIELD: 6 servings as a snack.

81 Calories per serving:
  2 G Protein
  0 G Fat
 .19 G Carbohydrate

196 MG Sodium
  0 MG Cholesterol

Inspired by Suman Sood, Registered Dietitian, President, Club of Indian Women, Chicago, formerly from New Delhi.

Potato Patties

ALOO TIKKI

∽ఎ⌒

Potato patties stuffed with peas, punctuated with Indian spices and a hint of red pepper powder, make an excellent appetizer or picnic snack. Serve hot or at room temperature with Mint-Coriander Chutney (page 285).

2 pounds potatoes, boiled in the
  skins and cooled
2 tablespoons cornstarch
Salt to taste
1 teaspoon canola oil
1 teaspoon cumin seeds

1 cup frozen peas, defrosted
1 tablespoon ground coriander
1/2–1 teaspoon red pepper
  powder
Olive oil spray

Peel and grate the potatoes. Put the grated potatoes in a bowl. Add the cornstarch and salt to taste. Mix well. Divide the mixture into 12 equal portions and shape into balls. Set aside.

Heat the 1 teaspoon of oil in a non-stick skillet. Add the cumin seeds and stir until they begin to crackle. Add the peas and cook, stirring occasionally, until the peas are cooked. Add the coriander and red pepper. Cook, stirring for 1 minute. Remove from the heat and mash the mixture. Divide the mixture into 12 equal portions.

Flatten each potato ball between the palms of your hands. Place a portion of the pea mixture in the middle. Reform the balls and flatten them into 3/4-inch thick patties. Mist a heated non-stick skillet very lightly with olive oil spray. Place the potato patties in the skillet and cook over moderate heat until crisp and golden on both sides. Press with a spatula and remove. Serve with Mint-Coriander Chutney (page 285).

YIELD: 12 servings.

ADVANCE PREPARATION: The patties may be cooked and refrigerated 1 day ahead or they may be frozen. Defrost prior to reheating. Reheat in a moderate oven prior to serving.

86 Calories per serving:
  2 G Protein   113 MG Sodium
  1 G Fat   0 MG Cholesterol
 18 G Carbohydrate

Spicy Potato Crisps

ALOO BHAJIA

∽∾∾

The fragrant hint of turmeric, cumin, coriander and red pepper powder adds a delectable touch to these crispy oven-fried potatoes. They are delicious as part of a meal or as a snack and are a favorite Indian treat.

2 pounds potatoes, peeled
2 teaspoons olive oil
1/4 teaspoon ground turmeric
1/2 teaspoon ground cumin

1/2 teaspoon ground coriander
1/2 teaspoon red pepper powder
1/4 teaspoon salt (optional)
Freshly ground pepper (optional)

Preheat oven to 425°F. Slice the potatoes lengthwise into 1/2-inch slices. Cut the slices lengthwise into 1/2-inch wide fries. Soak the potatoes in cold water for 5 minutes. Drain the potatoes and dry thoroughly between dish towels.

In a bowl, combine the oil, turmeric, cumin, coriander and red pepper powder. Add the potatoes and toss to coat. Arrange the potatoes in a single layer on a non-stick baking sheet. Bake in the oven for 20 minutes or until the potatoes start to brown. Remove the baking sheet from the oven. Turn the potatoes over and bake them for 15 to 20 minutes more or until the potatoes are cooked and have a deep golden-brown crust. Remove from oven. Sprinkle with salt and black pepper, if desired. Serve immediately.

YIELD: 8 appetizer servings or 4 main course servings.

95 Calories per serving:
  2 G Protein
  1 G Fat
19 G Carbohydrate
          8 MG Sodium
          0 MG Cholesterol

Yam Chips

CHENAIKIZHANGU VARUVAL

~~~

Here is a South Indian snack food that is consumed like potato chips. Although usually deep-fat fried, oven roasting provides an excellent alternative.

1 pound yams, peeled
4 teaspoons ground turmeric
1 tablespoon olive oil

1 teaspoon ground asafetida, *hing*
2–4 teaspoons red pepper
    powder

Cut the yams into 1/8-inch thick slices. In a bowl combine the turmeric and 6 cups of water. Add the yams and soak for 30 minutes. Drain the yams and pat dry between dish cloths. Spread the yams on a dry cloth for about 10 minutes. Preheat the oven to 425°F.

Place the yams in a large bowl. Add the olive oil and toss to coat. Arrange the yams in a single layer on a large non-stick baking sheet. Bake in the oven about 10 to 15 minutes or until beginning to brown. Remove from oven. Turn the yams over and bake for 5 minutes more or until lightly browned and fairly dry.

Remove the yams from oven. Combine the asafetida and red pepper. Sprinkle the mixture over the yams. Serve immediately.

YIELD: 4 servings.

ADVANCE PREPARATION: Prepare ahead completely. After cooking, cool completely and store in a tightly covered container for about 1 to 2 weeks. Serve at room temperature.

135 Calories per serving:
  2 G Protein   29 MG Sodium
  4 G Fat   0 MG Cholesterol
24 G Carbohydrate

Steamed Rice and Urad Dal Dumplings

IDLIS

~~~

While traveling in India, I always look forward to *idlis*, one of my favorite breakfast or luncheon snacks, which, along with *dosas* are unquestionably south India's most popular breakfast and "tiffin" treat.

A combination of steamed rice and *urad dal*, the spongy and slightly moist dumplings are accompanied by a fiery hot spicy vegetable and lentil stew, *Sambar* (page 261). The *sambar* combines *toor dal* cooked with vegetables (possibly onions, okra, tomatoes and a type of long bean called drumsticks), chilies and a variety of Indian spices. It is served with a chutney or two; possibly mango, mint or fresh coconut ground with chilies, ginger, onion and tamarind. In each part of the south, the *dals*, vegetables and spicing for the *sambar* vary, adding a most intriguing touch. This start to the day is a very simple, nourishing low-calorie breakfast with contrasting textures and dynamic taste juxtapositions combining the rather bland *idlis* with the vivid tastes of the *Sambar* and the diversity of flavors of accompanying chutneys.

The basic *idli* batter is made from two parts ground rice to one part split *urad dal*. The rice forms a satiny paste; the *dal*, a light foamy one. They are combined, fermented overnight, allowing the batter to expand. It is said that this process increases the nutritive value and eases digestion.

They are then steamed in a special steamer containing many round individual molds, which are deep in the center. This produces an *idli* that is thick in the middle and tapered on the edge. I have included instructions for using Pyrex custard cups or muffin tins at the end of the recipe if you do not have an *idili* steamer. Serve with *Sambar* (page 261) or Mint-Coriander Chutney (page 285).

1 cup *basmati* or other long-grain rice	1/4 teaspoon salt, or to taste
1/2 cup split *urad dal*	1/4 teaspoon baking soda
1 cup warm water	Canola oil or spray for brushing the molds

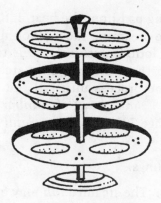

If you are using *basmati* rice, sort and wash the rice in several changes of water until the water runs clear. Drain and set aside. Sort, wash and drain the *dal* in the same manner. Set aside in a separate bowl. Add about 3 cups water to each bowl. (Both the rice and the *dal* should be covered by 2 inches.) Soak them for 8 hours or overnight. Drain and rinse the rice and the *dal* separately.

Put the rice in a food processor or blender and grind to a coarse powder, similar to cornmeal. Add 1/2 cup of the warm water and process for about 4 minutes or until the rice is a satiny purée. Transfer the mixture to a large bowl.

Put the *dal* in the food processor. Add the remaining 1/2 cup of warm water and process about 3 to 4 minutes or until *dal* is a light, fluffy purée. Mix the two purées together, add the salt and mix. Cover the bowl with plastic wrap and leave in a warm place for 12 to 14 hours to allow the batter to ferment. (If the room is cold, it may have to ferment for as long as 36 hours.) The batter is ready when it has expanded in volume and is covered with bubbles.

When the batter is ready to be used, gently stir the baking soda into the mixture. Be careful not to overstir the batter as it must retain its foamy and airy consistency. Let the batter rest for 4 to 5 minutes.

Cut double pieces of cheesecloth into slightly larger rounds or squares than the depressions of the *idli* steamer. Mist the molds lightly with oil. Moisten the cheesecloth with water. Place the cheesecloth in the depressions. Heat water to a depth of 1 inch in an *idli* steamer or a 6- to 8-quart pan in which the *idli* racks will fit. Bring the water to a boil in the steamer. Spoon about 1/4 to 1/3 cup of the batter into each mold. The batter should be thick enough not to fall through the perforations. Assemble the tiered steamer and place it in the steaming vessel. Cover tightly. Steam for 12 to 15 minutes or until a toothpick inserted in the center comes out clean.

Remove the steaming pan from the heat. Lift out the tiered steaming rack. Separate the steaming racks. Pick up each dumpling and peel away the cheesecloth. Transfer the *idlis* to a second steamer or covered dish to keep them warm while steaming the remaining dumplings. Repeat the process until all the dumplings are made. Serve on a plate with a small bowl of *Sambar* (page 261), and Mint-Coriander Chutney (page 285). Spoon the *Sambar* over the dumplings as desired.

YIELD: 28 to 30 dumplings.

ADVANCE PREPARATION: The steamed *idli* may be kept in the refrigerator for 1 to 2 days or in the freezer for 1 month. To reheat, line a steamer with a cloth. Steam for about 10 minutes, covered.

COOK'S TIPS:

1. If you do not have an *idli* steamer, you can improvise by using individual Pyrex cups, muffin tins or any other small mold. Spoon the batter in the containers to a depth of 1/2-inch. Fill a large pan with about 1 inch of water. Place a rack about 1 inch above the bottom of the pan. Put the individual molds on the rack. Cover tightly and steam for 12 to 15 minutes, testing with a toothpick as described in the directions.
2. If you do not want to go through all this preparation, but have the desire for *idlis*, Indian grocery stores carry a prepared packet mix. While it does not compare to the homemade *idlis*, it is quite satisfactory.

36 Calories per serving:

1 G Protein	33 MG Sodium
0 G Fat	0 MG Cholesterol
7 G Carbohydrate	

Inspired by a recipe from K. Natarajan, Executive Chef, The Taj Coromandel, Madras.

Savory Vermicelli

SEVIYA UPPMA

∽∾∾

Here is a simple breakfast or snack food enjoyed by many southerners. Indian whole wheat vermicelli is made flavorful with nutty *urad* and *chana dal*, onions, green chilies and cashew nuts.

The vermicelli is as fine as angel hair pasta and can be found in Indian grocery stores under the name of *sevian* or *sev*.

8 ounces Indian wheat vermicelli, *sevian*
2 teaspoons olive oil
1 teaspoon black mustard seeds
1 tablespoon split *urad dal*
2 tablespoons chopped unroasted cashew nuts
1 tablespoon split *chana dal*
5 fresh curry leaves
3/4 cup chopped onion
3–5 fresh green chilies, slit in half
1/4 teaspoon ground asafetida, *hing*
Salt to taste
Freshly ground black pepper to taste
1 tablespoon fresh lime juice

Bring 8 cups of water to a boil in a large pan. Break the vermicelli into 1-1/2-inch pieces and add to the water. Cook for 1 to 2 minutes until just tender to the bite. Drain and set aside.

Heat the oil in a non-stick wok or stir-fry pan over moderate heat. Add the mustard seeds and stir until they crackle. Add the *urad dal* and cashew nuts. Stir for 30 seconds. Add the *chana dal* and curry leaves and stir until the *dals* and cashew nuts are golden. Add the onion and green chilies and cook, stirring until the onions are translucent. Add the cooked vermicelli. Stir well for 2 minutes. Season to taste with salt and pepper. Sprinkle with the lime juice. Cover and set aside for 4 minutes before serving to allow the flavors to mellow. Serve hot, garnished with lime wedges.

YIELD: 6 servings.

ADVANCE PREPARATION: Prepare ahead. Reheat gently when serving.

194 Calories per serving:
  8 G Protein   28 MG Sodium
  4 G Fat   0 MG Cholesterol
 35 G Carbohydrate

Inspired by Praveen Anand, Executive Chef, Park Sheraton, Madras.

Spiced Vermicelli Chickpeas and Tomatoes

SULTANA SEVIAN

∾⌒∽

This luxuriously seasoned wheat vermicelli, topped with a zesty chickpea, tomato and chili sauce, is a favorite snack or luncheon in northern Rajasthan where it is served with flatbread.

You may wish to serve extra minced green chilies for topping in a separate bowl and let each guest spice the dish to their taste.

1 cup dried chickpeas, *kabuli chana*	1/2 cup chopped onion
2 teaspoons split *urad dal*	1 large ripe tomato, chopped
2 dried red chilies, crushed	1-1/4 cups tomato sauce
1 tablespoon canola oil	Salt to taste
2 teaspoons black mustard seeds	1–2 teaspoons minced fresh green chilies
2 teaspoons *toor dal*	1 tablespoon fresh lemon juice
6 ounces fine wheat vermicelli, preferably Indian, *sevian*	Chopped fresh coriander for garnish

Sort and wash the chickpeas as explained on page 55. Place the chickpeas in a bowl with enough water to cover. Soak for 8 hours or overnight. Drain. Place the chickpeas in a large, heavy saucepan with enough water to cover by 2 inches. Bring to a boil, reduce heat, cover and simmer for about 1-1/2 to 2 hours or until the chickpeas are tender to the bite. (Add more boiling water if the water level falls below that of the chickpeas.) Drain the chickpeas and set aside.

Heat a small non-stick skillet over moderate heat. Add the *urad dal* and stir until it turns golden brown. Transfer to a bowl. Wipe out the pan with paper towels. Add the red chilies to the pan and toast until lightly browned. Add the chilies to the bowl and wipe out the pan. Heat 1 teaspoon of the oil in the pan. Add the mustard seeds and stir-fry until they crackle. Add the *toor dal* and stir until it turns golden brown. Remove from the heat and add to the *urad dal*. Bring 8 cups of water to a boil in a large pan. Break the vermicelli into 1-1/2-inch pieces and add to the water. Cook for 1 to 2 minutes or until firm to the bite. Drain the vermicelli and set aside.

Heat the remaining 2 teaspoons of oil in a large non-stick skillet over medium heat. Add the chopped onion and cook, stirring until translucent. Add the *dal* and chili mixture. Stir for about 5 seconds. Add the chopped tomato and stir for 30 seconds. Reduce the heat and add the cooked vermicelli. Toss the mixture to combine thoroughly. Season to taste with salt. Remove from the heat, cover and set aside.

In a skillet over moderate heat, bring the tomato sauce, cooked chickpeas and half the green chilies to a boil, stirring. Season to taste with salt. Add 3 tablespoons of water and cook, stirring, over moderate heat until the mixture has reduced to a sauce-like consistency. Add the lemon juice and stir. Arrange the vermicelli on a serving plate. Spoon the sauce on top. Garnish with the remaining green chilies and coriander.

YIELD: 6 snack or 4 luncheon or supper servings.

ADVANCE PREPARATION: Prepare the sauce a day ahead. Cool and refrigerate.

VARIATION: Canned chickpeas may be substituted, but you will lose some of the flavor and texture of the cooked dried variety. Be careful not to overcook the canned chickpeas in the sauce as they will become mushy.

443 Calories per serving:
  21 G Protein   675 MG Sodium
   8 G Fat   4 MG Cholesterol
  77 G Carbohydrate

Inspired by G. Sultan Mohideen, Executive Chef, Rajputana Palace, Jaipur, Rajasthan.

Lemon-Flavored Rice Noodles

ELUMBUCHAPAYAM SEVAI

～◌～

Here is a piquant version of rice noodles enhanced with a hint of chili, nutty *dals* and cashew nuts. In south India, it is served as a snack or light meal. You will enjoy this dish as an addition to any meal. Served with Southern Tomato Chutney (page 290).

1/2 pound thin rice noodles (rice sticks)
1 tablespoon canola oil
2 teaspoons black mustard seeds
1 tablespoon split *urad dal*
2 tablespoons chopped raw cashew nuts
2–4 dried red chilies, seeded and broken into small pieces
2 teaspoons split *chana dal*
4 fresh green chilies, slit in half

2 teaspoons chopped fresh ginger
6 fresh curry leaves (optional)
1/2 teaspoon ground turmeric
1/3 teaspoon grated lemon zest
2 to 3 tablespoons fresh lemon juice
2 tablespoons chopped coriander leaves
Salt to taste
Lemon slices for garnish

Bring 4 quarts water to a boil in a saucepan. Turn off the heat. Add the rice noodles and let them soak for 5 minutes. Drain the noodles and rinse immediately with cold water. Set aside.

Heat the oil in a non-stick wok or stir-fry pan over moderate heat. Add the mustard seeds and stir-fry until they crackle. Add the *urad dal* and cashew nuts and stir for 1 minute. Add the red chilies, *chana dal*, green chilies, ginger, curry leaves and turmeric. When the red chilies, *dals* and cashew nuts have darkened, add the cooked noodles. Toss well for 2 minutes to heat the noodles and to coat them evenly with ingredients in the pan. Remove from the heat. Add the lemon zest, lemon juice and coriander. Season to taste with salt. Toss well to combine. Cover and set aside for 4 minutes before serving to allow flavors to mellow. Serve hot. Garnish with lemon slices.

YIELD: 4 to 6 people.

ADVANCE PREPARATION: Prepare ahead. Reheat gently prior to serving. The noodles are also delicious cold.

169 Calories per serving:
  6 G Protein   185 MG Sodium
  10 G Fat   0 MG Cholesterol
  16 G Carbohydrates

Inspired by Praveen Anand, Executive Chef, Park Sheraton, Madras.

Semolina with Mixed Vegetables

SOOJI UPPMA

∼✧∽

One of the most popular—and easy to make—Indian luncheon or snack foods is semolina, as it can be served in a variety of ways. Prem Sharma prepares this fluffy version using quick-cooking Cream of Wheat or Farina, frozen vegetables and spices for a subtly-flavored vegetarian dish. She serves it with yogurt, Spiced Chickpeas in Sauce (page 251) and Lemon Pickles (page 292).

1 tablespoon canola oil
1/2 teaspoon mustard seeds
6 fresh curry leaves
1 tablespoon split *urad dal*
1 tablespoon split *chana dal*
1/2 teaspoon cumin seeds
1/8 teaspoon asafetida, *hing*
1–2 dried red chilies
1 black cardamom
2 cloves
3 black peppercorns
1/2 teaspoon salt, or to taste

1/2–3/4 teaspoon red pepper powder
1 medium ripe tomato, coarsely chopped
1 small onion, coarsely chopped
1 cup frozen mixed vegetables or vegetables of your choice
1 cup fine-grained quick cooking Cream of Wheat or Farina
1–2 tablespoons fresh lime juice
chopped fresh coriander leaves for garnish

Heat the oil in a large non-stick skillet over moderate heat. Add the mustard seeds and stir-fry until they crackle. Add the curry leaves, *urad dal* and *chana dal*. Stir until the *dals* are golden brown. Add the cumin seeds, asafetida, chilies, black cardamom, cloves, peppercorns, salt and red pepper. Stir for 30 seconds. Add the tomato and onion to the skillet. Stir-fry for 1 minute. Add frozen vegetables and 1/4 cup of water. Bring to a boil, stirring. Reduce the heat to moderate. Cover and cook until the vegetables are crisp-tender. Slowly stir in the Cream of Wheat and reduce the heat to moderately low. Cook, stirring for 6–8 minutes or until the water is absorbed and the mixture is light and fluffy. Sprinkle with the lime juice and garnish with coriander.

YIELD: 5 to 6 servings.

ADVANCE PREPARATION: Prepare ahead completely. Cool, cover and refrigerate or freeze. Reheat gently to serve.

209 Calories per serving:
- 7 G Protein   338 MG Sodium
- 4 G Fat   0 MG Cholesterol
- 37 G Carbohydrate

Inspired by a recipe from Prem Sharma, Burr Ridge, IL, formerly from New Delhi.

Spicy Chicken Salad

MURGH CHAT

ೂಀಀ

Serve this dish as an appetizer or as a cool, refreshing salad.

2 pounds boneless, skinless chicken breast cooked, cut into 1/2-inch cubes
1 medium onion, minced
1 fresh green chili, seeded and minced
2 teaspoons chopped fresh coriander leaves
2 teaspoons dry roasted cumin

seeds, ground to a powder
1 tablespoon *garam masala* (page 43)
2 teaspoons tomato purée
1 tablespoon fresh lime juice
1/2 teaspoon salt, or to taste
1 teaspoon freshly ground black pepper
8–10 lettuce leaves

In a bowl, combine cooked chicken, onion, chili, coriander, cumin, *garam masala*, tomato purée and lime juice. Season to taste with salt and black pepper. Cover and chill for a few hours or overnight. Serve each portion on a lettuce leaf.

YIELD: 6 or more as an appetizer or 4 as a main dish.

205 Calories per serving:
- 35 G Protein   381 MG Sodium
- 4 G Fat   91 MG Cholesterol
- 5 G Carbohydrate

Pineapple Sesame

ANANNAS SASME

∽○∾

This easily prepared appetizer or accompaniment, combining sweet pineapple with a touch of spice, comes from Mangalore.

1 medium-size ripe pineapple
2–3 tablespoons sugar
1/2 teaspoon salt, or to taste
2 teaspoons canola oil

TEMPERING:
1/2 teaspoon black mustard seeds
2 dried red chilies
7 fresh curry leaves
1 teaspoon white sesame seeds
2 teaspoons unsweetened ground coconut

Cut the pineapple in half lengthwise. Using a sharp knife, carefully remove the fruit. Remove the core and cut the pineapple into 1/2-inch wedges. Rub the sugar and salt into the pineapple wedges. Set aside to marinate in a cool place for 30 minutes.

Heat 2 teaspoons of the oil in a non-stick wok or large skillet over moderate heat. Add 2 red chilies and stir until darkened. Add the ground coconut and the marinated pineapple. Sauté until the pineapple is heated throughout. Set aside.

TEMPERING: Heat the remaining 2 teaspoons of oil in a small non-stick skillet. Add the mustard seeds and stir-fry until they crackle. Add the remaining red chilies and stir-fry until lightly browned. Add the curry leaves and sesame seeds and stir-fry until the sesame seeds are very lightly browned. Remove from heat and add to the pineapple. Transfer to a bowl and refrigerate until chilled. Serve in the pineapple shells.

YIELD: 6 servings.

ADVANCE PREPARATION: Prepare 1 day in advance. Cover. Refrigerate. Serve chilled.

120 Calories per serving:
   1 G Protein   205 MG Sodium
   5 G Fat   0 MG Cholesterol
   1 G Carbohydrate

Inspired by P.N. Raman, Head Department of Food & Beverage, Welcomgroup School of Hotel Administration, Manipal.

Spiced Fruit Salad

CHAT

ᕬᕲᕲ

Here is a favorite treat sold by the many street-side *chat* vendors. This tasty combination of spiced fruits is delicious as an appetizer, an accompaniment to the main course to refresh the palate and soothe the senses, or as a spiced dessert. You may use any fresh fruits in season.

2 small oranges, peeled, sectioned and tough outer white membrane removed

2 bananas, peeled and sliced

2 apples, peeled, cored and sliced into 1/4-inch pieces

2 pears, peeled, cored and sliced into 1/4-inch pieces

1 large ripe mango, peeled and cut into 1/4-inch pieces

1/2 ripe pineapple, peeled, cored and cut into 1-inch pieces

20 seedless grapes

Juice of 1–2 fresh limes

1 tablespoon peeled, shredded fresh ginger

2–4 fresh green chilies, seeded and finely shredded

1-1/4 teaspoons ground cinnamon

1/2 teaspoon ground cardamom

1/2 teaspoon freshly ground black pepper

Pinch of ground cloves

1 tablespoon sugar

Salt to taste

Fresh mint leaves to garnish

In a bowl combine the fruits and the lime juice and mix well to prevent the fruit from discoloring. In a small bowl, combine the ginger, chilies, cinnamon, cardamom, black pepper, cloves, sugar and salt. Add the mixture to the fruit. Toss until the fruit is coated. Chill covered in refrigerator for 2 hours. Serve garnished with mint leaves.

YIELD: 6 servings.

COOK'S TIP: If oranges are large, cut sections in half. Mandarin oranges may be substituted for the oranges.

208 Calories per serving:
  3 G Protein
  1 G Fat
  51 G Carbohydrate
  30 MG Sodium
  0 MG Cholesterol

Inspired by Executive Chef G. Sultan Mohideen, Rajputana Palace, Jaipur, Rajasthan.

Fruit Chat

CHAT

∽∾

Here is a simple fresh fruit appetizer or snack food.

1 apple, peeled, cored and sliced
1 banana, sliced
1 kiwi, sliced
15 seedless grapes
6 pitted dates, chopped

3 tablespoons raisins
4 walnuts, chopped
1-1/2 teaspoon *chat masala*
(page 44)
2 tablespoons fresh lime juice

In a bowl combine the fruit, walnuts, *chat masala* and lime juice. Mix well. Chill in the refrigerator for 2 hours before serving.

YIELD: 4 servings.

172 Calories per serving:
3 G Protein
5 G Fat
33 G Carbohydrate

3 MG Sodium
0 MG Cholesterol

Inspired by Meena Mohindra, Burr Ridge, IL, formerly from New Delhi.

Lentil Wafers

PAPPADUMS

✿

These delicate, crisp wafers are made from a paste of ground lentils seasoned with black pepper, garlic, fiery chilies or cumin seeds. Since the process of making them and drying the paper-thin wafers in the sun is laborious and time consuming, they are usually purchased ready made in the form of dried round, fragile disks in Indian grocery stores. The number of *Pappadums* in a package varies so you will need to check this when purchasing. As a general rule, allow one *Pappadum* per person.

The traditional method of cooking *Pappadum* is to deep fry them or to roast them over a flame. I prefer to broil them for a few seconds, keeping them free of oil and making them easier to prepare.

They are marvelous when served alone as appetizers or with a dip such as Southern Mixed Vegetable Salad (page 280), Spiced Eggplant, Tomato and Yogurt Salad (page 267) or as an accompaniment to any Indian or Western meal.

1 package of 4 *Pappadums* (1 *Pappadum* per serving)

COOKING METHODS:

1. Broiler or barbecue. Place *Pappadums* on a rack 2 inches from heat source. Watch the *pappadums* carefully, as they cook very quickly. When the *pappadums* have expanded or bubbles have formed, using tongs turn and cook them for 1 to 2 seconds more. Watch carefully to make sure they do not burn.

2. Microwave oven. Arrange in a single layer on a paper towel in the microwave oven. Microwave on HIGH for 30 seconds to 2 minutes or until *Pappadums* bubble and are golden, turning once or twice.

3. Deep fried. Heat 1-1/2-inches of oil in a wok or frying pan over medium heat to 350°F. Gently slide 1 or 2 *pappadums* into the hot oil. They will puff up in seconds and cook quickly. Remove them with a slotted spoon to prevent them from burning. Drain on paper towels. Serve immediately or keep warm in the oven.

YIELD: 6–8 servings or more, depending on size of package.

Sago Wafers

PHUL BADI

∽◡∾

These wafers are a combination of tapioca and rice flours made into a thick paste, spread into thin rounds and then dried in the sun. They are easy to cook and make interesting hors d'oeuvres or snacks. The dried wafers are available in Indian grocery stores.

Corn oil to fill a pan to a depth of 1-1/2 inches

16 sago wafers

Heat 1-1/2 inches of oil in a wok or frying pan to 350°F. Using a pair of tongs, put the wafer into the hot oil, turning as it cooks. The wafer will puff up to twice its original size in about 3 to 5 seconds. If it does not, the oil is not hot enough. Remove the wafer. Drain on paper towels. Continue cooking in the same manner until all the wafers are cooked. Serve at room temperature. The wafers will keep for several days in an airtight container.

YIELD: 8 servings.

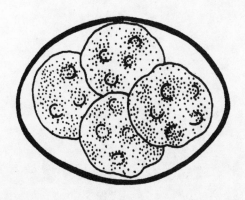

Soups

〜〜〜

In India, soups as we know them are little known and a thin curry that is part of a meal might be construed as a soup.

Today, there are some soups, particularly Mulligatawny (page 89), which might be served as a first course. For those who enjoy soups, I have also included some of the non-traditional recipes from famous chefs, which I am sure you will enjoy.

Carrot Soup   GAAJAR SHORBA
Mulligatawny Soup   MURGH MULLIGATANNI
Vegetarian Mulligatawny Soup   SABZI MULLIGATANNI
Settu Soup   SETTU SHORBA
Spiced Chicken Soup   JEHANGIRI SHORBA
Spicy Tomato-Flavored Lentil Soup, Madras Style
TAMATAR RASAM
Yogurt, Radish and Spinach Soup   PUDINA DAHI SHORBA
Chilled Mint-Flavored Yogurt Soup   DAHI KA SHORBA
Rice and Coriander Soup   CHAWAL DHANIA SHORBA

Carrot Soup

GAAJAR SHORBA

This vividly spiced clear soup will perk up your dinner.

8 cups vegetable or chicken stock
1-1/2 cups peeled, chopped carrots
1/4 teaspoon crushed black peppercorns
1/4 teaspoon crushed cardamom seeds
4 cloves

1 2-inch stick cinnamon
2 bay leaves
1/4 teaspoon red pepper powder
Salt to taste
2 tablespoons chopped fresh coriander leaves to garnish

Heat the stock in a saucepan. Add the carrots, peppercorns, cardamom seeds, cloves, cinnamon, bay leaves and red pepper. Add salt to taste. Bring to a boil. Reduce the heat and let simmer until the liquid is reduced by half. Remove from the heat, discard the peppercorns, cardamom, cloves, cinnamon and bay leaves.

Process the soup in a food processor or blender until smooth. Force the soup through a strainer into a clean pan. Bring the soup to a boil, skim if necessary. Pour the soup into bowls and garnish with chopped coriander. Serve with an Indian bread of your choice.

YIELD: 4 servings.

ADVANCE PREPARATION: Prepare 1 day ahead. Reheat and garnish when serving.

64 Calories per serving:
5 G Protein
2 G Fat
7 G Carbohydrates
180 MG Sodium
0 MG Cholesterol

Inspired by Chef Manu Mehta, Maurya Sheraton, New Delhi.

Mulligatawny Soup

MURGH MULLIGATANNI

∽∾∾

There are as many variations of this soup as there are tales of its origin. In Madras, where the soup is said to have originated, the name is derived from a local Tamil word *mullaga* meaning "pepper" and *tanni* meaning "broth" or "water." Executive Chef Mohideen, who is from Madras, said that it is believed this was originally a "pepper water" drink served centuries ago by the brahmin yogis of the south, who were strict vegetarians. The local cooks for the British Raj adopted the soup and even added chicken to this strictly vegetarian "drink"—which would have horrified the brahmins. Since then, Indian cooks have exercised their creativity and now there are a multitude of appealing variations of this soup around the world. The following is Executive Chef Mohideen's full-bodied version.

1/2 cup peeled, chopped potatoes
1 tablespoon canola oil
2–3 dried red chilies
1 tablespoon coriander seeds
2 teaspoons chopped garlic
1/4 cup chopped onion
2 teaspoons minced fresh ginger
1/2 teaspoon ground turmeric
2 teaspoons Madras curry powder
2 tablespoons ground coconut
2 tablespoons chickpea flour, *besan*
1 cup chopped cooking apple
3 bay leaves

3 tablespoons fresh coriander stems, chopped
3 cups homemade chicken stock or low-sodium canned chicken broth
1 whole boneless, skinless chicken breast
Salt to taste
Freshly ground black pepper to taste
1–2 tablespoons fresh lemon juice
2 tablespoons chopped fresh coriander leaves

Soak potato cubes in water just to cover for 10 minutes.

In a 6-quart non-stick saucepan, heat the oil over moderate heat. Add the chilies, coriander seeds and garlic. Stir for 10 seconds. Add the onion and stir for 2 minutes. Add the ginger, turmeric and curry powder. Stir for 10 seconds. Add the coconut and stir for 10 seconds, being careful the mixture does not burn. Add the chickpea flour. Stir constantly for about 2 minutes, being careful not to burn, until golden brown in color. Add the potato cubes and soaking water, apples and bay leaves. Stir for 30 seconds. Add the coriander stems and chicken stock. Bring almost to a boil.

Reduce heat to a simmer and allow to cook, covered, for 25 minutes. Add the chicken and cook for 8 to 10 minutes or until no longer pink. Remove the soup from the heat. Using a slotted spoon remove the chicken and cut into 1/4-inch cubes. Purée the stock, spices and potato in batches in a food processor or blender. Pass the mixture through a fine-mesh sieve, pressing to extract as much liquid as possible. Season to taste with salt and pepper. Add the lemon juice and cooked chicken. Stir. Reheat the soup gently. Serve sprinkled with chopped coriander.

YIELD: 6 to 8 servings.

ADVANCE PREPARATION: Prepare 1 to 2 days in advance. Add the lemon juice, cooked chicken and freshly ground black pepper when reheating.

COOK'S TIP: To make a heartier soup, add 1 to 2 cups cooked rice to the soup and cook for 5 minutes to blend flavors before serving.

206 Calories per serving:
- 14 G Protein
- 11 G Fat
- 15 G Carbohydrate
- 272 MG Sodium
- 23 MG Cholesterol

Inspired by G. Sultan Mohideen, Executive Chef, Rajputana Palace, Jaipur.

Vegetarian Mulligatawny Soup

SABZI MULLIGATANNI

~~~

Here is a a vegetable-laden version of Mulligatawny Soup that I enjoyed in Madras. It is an extraordinary light and tasty soup.

1 tablespoon olive oil
2–3 dried red chilies
1 teaspoon coriander seeds
2 teaspoons chopped garlic
1/4 cup finely chopped onion
2 teaspoons minced fresh ginger
2 teaspoons Madras curry powder
2 tablespoons chickpea flour
2 tablespoons ground coconut
1 cup chopped cooking apple
3 bay leaves

2 tablespoons chopped fresh
 coriander stems
3 cups chopped mixed vegetables
 (carrots, onions, cauliflower,
 potatoes, celery, zucchini, bell
 pepper) in any proportion
3 cups homemade vegetable stock
Salt to taste
Freshly ground black pepper
1 tablespoon coriander leaves

In a 6-quart non-stick saucepan, heat the oil over moderate heat. Add the chilies, coriander seeds, and garlic. Stir for 10 seconds. Add the onion and stir for 2 minutes or until translucent. Add the ginger and curry powder. Stir for 10 seconds. Add the chickpea flour. Stir constantly for 2 minutes, being careful not to burn. The mixture should be golden brown. Add the coconut and stir for 10–20 seconds. Add apple and bay leaves. Stir for 30 seconds. Add coriander stems, and vegetables and the stock. Bring to a boil, reduce the heat to a simmer and cook, covered, for 30 minutes. Purée the stock, spices and vegetables in batches in a food processor or blender. Pass the mixture through a fine-mesh sieve, pressing to extract as much liquid as possible. Reheat the soup gently. Season to taste with salt and freshly ground black pepper. Serve in soup bowls sprinkled with coriander leaves.

YIELD: 4 servings.

ADVANCE PREPARATION: Prepare 1 to 2 days in advance. If the soup is too thick when reheating, add water. Season with salt and ground black pepper prior to serving.

COOK'S TIPS: To make a heartier soup, add 1 to 2 cups cooked rice to the soup and cook for 5 minutes before serving.

193 Calories per serving:
  6 G Protein   386 MG Sodium
  8 G Fat   0 MG Cholesterol
 28 G Carbohydrate

Inspired by Mrs. A. Mullens, Principal, Institute of Hotel Management Catering Technology & Applied Nutrition, Madras.

Settu Soup

SETTU SHORBA

⚬⚬⚬

This enticing vegetarian soup is laced with the subtle flavor interplay of fennel, cinnamon and *chana dal*. It is traditionally served at elaborate south Indian Chettinad wedding feasts. Teams of male chefs, who have passed down their craft for generations, travel in a *set* or *settu* to the wedding to prepare a feast, which may last as long as five days. When served with a flatbread, this soup makes a splendid starter for both Western and Indian dinners. As it can be easily doubled or tripled, and as it tastes even better the next day, it is perfect for entertaining. The soup tastes delicious served hot or chilled.

6–8 green chilies, slit in half lengthwise

4 teaspoons whole black peppercorns, crushed

1 tablespoon roasted fennel seeds, crushed

4 2-inch cinnamon sticks, broken in half

2 bay leaves

1 cauliflower, about 2 pounds, trimmed and cut into florets

2 medium ripe tomatoes, cut into eighths, about 2 cups

3/4 cup sliced onion

1 cup split *chana dal*

Salt to taste

GARNISH:

2 tablespoons chopped coriander leaves

12 small cauliflower florets, parboiled or steamed until crunchy

In a 6-quart saucepan combine the chilies, peppercorns, fennel seeds, cinnamon, bay leaves, cauliflower, tomatoes, onion and *dal.* Add water to cover the vegetables by 2 inches. Bring to a boil. Reduce the heat to a simmer. Skim off any residue that rises to the surface, being very careful not to remove any of the spices in the soup. Cook, stirring occasionally, for 40 to 45 minutes or until the soup is reduced by one-third. Strain the soup. Add salt if desired. Serve garnished with chopped coriander leaves and cauliflower florets.

YIELD: 4 servings.

ADVANCE PREPARATION: The soup tastes even better when cooked 1 to 2 days ahead.

277 Calories per serving:
18 G Protein   246 MG Sodium
 2 G Fat   0 MG Cholesterol
52 G Carbohydrate

Inspired by Praveen Anand, Executive Chef, Dakshin Restaurant, Park Sheraton, Madras.

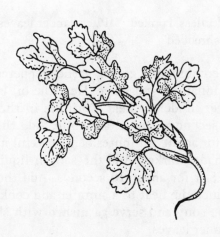

Spiced Chicken Soup

JEHANGIRI SHORBA

⁓⌒⁓

Emperor Jehangir, the father of Emperor Shah Jahan (who constructed the famous Taj Mahal in memory of his wife Mumtaz Mahal), chose this as his favorite soup. Chicken stock heightened with the flavors of fresh herbs, saffron and apple will be the perfect starter for your meal. Executive Chef Misri said the soup can be made vegetarian by using a vegetable stock, and for an extra richness, he often adds a touch of cream to each serving. Serve hot or chilled.

2 teaspoons minced fresh ginger
1-1/2 teaspoons minced garlic
1/4 teaspoon black peppercorns
3 bay leaves
4 green cardamom pods
1 2-inch cinnamon stick, crushed
1/2 teaspoon ground mace
2 teaspoons canola oil
1 tablespoon chickpea flour,
    besan

8 saffron threads, soaked in
    2 tablespoons warm water for
    10 minutes
1 teaspoon ground turmeric
1/2 teaspoon red pepper powder
1 large cooking apple, peeled,
    cored and chopped
4 cups low-sodium homemade
    chicken stock or low-sodium
    canned chicken broth

GARNISH:

1/3 cup boneless, skinless, cooked
    chicken breasts, shredded

12 coriander leaves, chopped

In a small bowl combine the ginger, garlic, peppercorns, bay leaves, cardamom pods, cinnamon and mace. Heat the oil in a 2-quart non-stick saucepan over moderate heat. Sprinkle in the spices. Stir for approximately 15 seconds or until aromatic. Add the chickpea flour and cook, stirring for about 2 minutes being careful not to burn, until the flour is 2–3 shades darker. Add the saffron liquid, turmeric, red pepper and apple. Stir for about 10 seconds. Add the chicken stock. Bring to a boil, reduce the heat to a simmer and cook, covered, for 30 minutes. Strain the soup and serve garnished with shredded chicken and chopped coriander leaves.

YIELD: 4 servings.

ADVANCE PREPARATION: Prepare ahead. Reheat and garnish with chicken and chopped coriander prior to serving.

96 Calories per serving:
  6 G Protein   76 MG Sodium
  4 G Fat   8 MG Cholesterol
10 G Carbohydrate

Inspired by Anil Misri, Executive Chef, Mughal Sheraton, Agra.

Spicy Tomato-Flavored Lentil Broth, Madras Style

TAMATAR RASAM

∼୬ఁ∽

Rasam, a highly seasoned tomato-lentil broth, abundant with the flavors of turmeric, garlic and pepper, and *Sambar*, a thicker spicy lentil soup, are both made daily in south Indian households. The *toor dal* is boiled with lots of water then strained, and the liquid is used for the *Rasam*. The reserved thick *dal* is used for *Sambar* (page 261). They are both either mixed with rice or served in separate small bowls as a soup accompanying other dishes such as Mixed Vegetables in Yogurt Sauce (page 207), a yogurt salad and rice. During my travels throughout South India, I sampled many variations. This is one of my favorites.

1 cup *toor dal*
1 teaspoon ground turmeric
1 1-inch piece tamarind pulp
2-1/2 cups chopped ripe tomatoes
2-1/2 teaspoons chopped garlic
1 teaspoon ground cumin

1/2 teaspoon ground black pepper
1-2 teaspoons red pepper powder
1 tablespoon ground coriander
1/8 teaspoon asafetida
4 fresh green chilies, slit in half
    lengthwise

2 teaspoons olive oil

2 teaspoons black mustard seeds

3 dried red chilies

7 fresh curry leaves

1/2 teaspoon salt, or to taste

2 tablespoons chopped fresh
coriander leaves to garnish

Clean and wash *toor dal* following the directions on page 55. In a 3-quart saucepan combine *dal*, turmeric and 6 cups of water. Bring to a boil over medium-high heat. Reduce heat and simmer, partially covered, for 35 minutes, or until the *dal* is tender. Stir mixture occasionally to prevent sticking. Remove from the heat and set aside.

Strain the cooked *dal* liquid into a bowl. There should be about 4 cups of liquid. If there is not, add more water. Reserve the thick *dal* and use it for making *Sambar* (page 261).

Place tamarind pulp in a bowl. Pour 1/2 cup of hot water over the tamarind pulp and soak for 15 minutes. Mash the pulp with a spoon or with your fingers. Pour the tamarind and the liquid into a sieve and strain into a small bowl, squeezing out as much of the tamarind liquid as possible. Discard the fiber.

In a food processor or blender, process 2 cups of the tomatoes, the garlic and 1/2 cup water until smooth.

Return the strained *dal* liquid to the saucepan. Add the tamarind liquid, tomato mixture, cumin, black pepper, red pepper, coriander, asafetida and green chilies. Bring the liquid almost to a boil over medium heat, being careful not to let it actually boil. Reduce the heat to low and simmer, partially covered, for 15 minutes. Add the remaining 1/2 cup of chopped tomatoes and cook for 30 seconds. Remove pan from heat.

TEMPERING: Heat the oil in a small non-stick skillet. Add mustard seeds and cook until they crackle. Add the red chilies and curry leaves. Cook until the chilies are lightly browned. Add spice mixture to the soup and stir. Season to taste with salt and serve the soup garnished with chopped coriander leaves.

YIELD: 6 to 8 servings.

ADVANCE PREPARATION: Prepare 1 to 2 days ahead to the tempering. Refrigerate. Reheat gently, temper the *Rasam* and garnish with coriander when serving.

186 Calories per serving:
 11 G Protein   368 MG Sodium
  3 G Fat   0 MG Cholesterol
 31 G Carbohydrate

Inspired by K. Natarajan, Executive Chef, Taj Coromandel Hotel, Madras.

Yogurt, Radish and Spinach Soup

PUDINA DAHI SHORBA

ᔐᐧᓂ

This delicate soup is a specialty of Executive Chef Helmant Oberoi of
the famous Taj Mahal Hotel in Bombay.

1-1/2 cups water
1 teaspoon chickpea flour, *besan*
3/4 teaspoon sugar
3/4 teaspoon salt

1 ounce white radish, *daikon*
  (Japanese turnip), peeled
1-1/2 cups nonfat plain yogurt

TEMPERING:
2 teaspoons canola oil
1/4 teaspoon black mustard seeds
8 fresh curry leaves

Pinch of asafetida
1 tablespoon steamed spinach
  leaves, shredded

   In a wok, whisk the water, chickpea flour, sugar and salt thoroughly. Add the peeled radish. Bring to a boil. Reduce the heat and
simmer for 20 minutes. Remove the radish and grate finely. Return
the grated radish to the soup. Whisk the yogurt and add to the soup a
little at a time. Simmer for 2 to 3 minutes to allow flavors to mellow.
Be careful not to let the soup come to a boil or it will curdle. Remove
from the heat.

TEMPERING: Heat oil in a small non-stick skillet. Add the mustard seeds and stir until they crackle. Add the curry leaves and asafetida and stir for about 10 to 20 seconds. Pour over the soup. Serve garnished with spinach leaves.

YIELD: 4 servings.

79 Calories per serving:
6 G Protein   494 MG Sodium
3 G Fat   2 MG Cholesterol
9 G Carbohydrate

Inspired by Helmant Oberoi, Executive Chef, The Taj Mahal Hotel, Bombay.

Chilled Mint-Flavored Yogurt Soup

DAHI KA SHORBA

❧

This cool, tasty soup is especially refreshing during the hot summer months. Throughout India, yogurt soup is used in one form or another almost every day. While mild homemade yogurt offers the best flavor, you may purchase nonfat yogurt.

1 large cucumber, peeled, seeded   1 teaspoon dry roasted cumin
and finely shredded   seeds, coarsely ground
2-1/2 cups nonfat plain yogurt   Ground white pepper to taste
2 tablespoons finely chopped fresh   Fresh mint springs to garnish
mint leaves

In a food processor or blender, process the cucumber and yogurt until just smooth. Transfer the mixture to a bowl. Add the mint and ground cumin and stir to combine. Add white pepper to taste. Cover and chill. Serve in chilled bowls, garnished with sprigs of fresh mint.

YIELD: 4 servings.

ADVANCE PREPARATION: Prepare ahead completely. Chill. When serving, garnish with mint leaves.

COOK'S TIP: If soup is too thick for your taste, add a little nonfat milk.

91 Calories per serving:

9 G Protein   104 MG Sodium
0 G Fat   3 MG Cholesterol
14 G Carbohydrate

Inspired by Mrs. A. Mullens, Principal, Institute of Hotel Management Catering Technology & Applied Nutrition, Madras.

Rice and Coriander Soup

CHAWAL DHANIA SHORBA

෴

Here is a soup from the Jai Mahal Palace Hotel, Jaipur, Rajasthan. From its name it might sound rather mundane, but once you have tried it, you will find this tomato-based soup, overlaced with coriander and fiery Indian spices, to be spectacular! It tastes even better when made a day ahead.

2 teaspoons peeled, chopped fresh
  ginger
2 teaspoons chopped garlic
2 teaspoons canola oil
1 2-inch stick cinnamon
4 cloves
6 green cardamom pods
8 black peppercorns
2 teaspoons cumin seeds
2 bay leaves
2/3 cup chopped fresh coriander
  stems

1–2 fresh green chilies, seeded and
  minced
2/3 cup peeled, sliced carrots
2/3 cup sliced red onion
2 pounds ripe tomatoes
2 tablespoons long-grain rice
3 tablespoons fresh lemon juice
Salt to taste
2 tablespoons chopped coriander
  leaves

In a mini food processor or blender, process the ginger, garlic and 2 tablespoons of water to a paste.

Heat the oil in a large non-stick saucepan over moderate heat. Add the cinnamon stick, cloves, cardamom, peppercorns, cumin seeds and bay leaves. Cook, stirring, until the spices crackle. Add the ginger and garlic paste. Cook, stirring, until lightly browned. Add the coriander stems and green chilies and stir for 1 minute. Add the carrots and onion. Stir until onion is transparent. Add the whole tomatoes and cook until the skins split and the tomatoes are beginning to soften. Add 6 cups water and bring to a boil. Add the rice. Reduce the heat to low and simmer, covered, for 40 minutes. Strain the soup and add the lemon juice and salt to taste. Serve garnished with chopped coriander.

YIELD: 6 portions.

ADVANCE PREPARATION: Prepare 1 day ahead. Refrigerate. Garnish with coriander when serving.

60 Calories per serving:
 1 G Protein   34 MG Sodium
 2 G Fat   0 MG Cholesterol
10 G Carbohydrate

Inspired by Arvind Saraswat, Director, Food Production, Taj Mahal Group of Hotels.

MEAT

Meat is known as mutton in India, and it is usually lamb or very fresh goat. It is part of the daily fare in the north, where the lush lands are particularly good for grazing. Hindus do not eat beef because the cow is sacred and Muslims do not eat pork because the pig is considered unclean. In the mostly vegetarian south, meat is rarely eaten because of religious beliefs.

Common to all Indians is a strong dislike for the raw taste of meat. They prefer well-done meat that has been marinated in a mixture of spices and often yogurt. The marinade allows the spices to permeate the meat while tenderizing it. It is then cooked in a slow oven or in a *tandoor*, or grilled.

Many of the slow-cooked dishes in this chapter, such as Lamb Braised in Spiced Yogurt, *Gosht Pasanda* (page 104), taste better the next day when the flavors have a chance to mellow. Others, like Grilled Spiced Lamb Kebabs, *Boti Kababs* (page 113), can be marinated ahead and barbecued or broiled prior to serving. Most dishes are suitable for both Indian and Western meals and are excellent for entertaining, as most of the preparation can be done well in advance of serving. If you desire, beef may be substituted for lamb in the dishes in this chapter.

Lamb Braised in Spiced Yogurt   GOSHT PASANDA
Lamb, Rajasthani Style   LAL MAAS
Ground Lamb Cutlets, Parsi Style   PARSI CUTLACE
Baby Lamb Stew, Parsi Style   KID NU GOSHT
Minced Lamb with Peas   KEEMA MATAR
Minced Lamb Kebabs   SEEKH KABABS
Grilled Spiced Lamb Kebabs   BOTI KABABS
Grilled Lamb Kebabs   GOSHT KABABS
Goan Hot and Sour Pork   VINDALOO

Lamb Braised in Spiced Yogurt

GOSHT PASANDA

∽≈∾

This superb example of Mughlai cooking is usually served for wedding feasts or other special occasions, according to Ghulam Naqshband. Lamb fillets, *pasanda,* are gently braised in a black cumin, *shahi jeera,* and green cardamom-laced yogurt sauce. The dried plums *(aloobukhara)* add a tangy and fruity flavor. *Gosht Pasanda* is a favorite in my house as it is extremely tasty, can be made ahead and can be easily doubled or tripled. Serve with Lamb Biryani, Dum Pukht Style (page 216), Eggplant Topped with Tomato Sauce and Coriander-Flavored Yogurt (page 186) and a yogurt salad of your choice.

In India, lamb fillets are used because they are more tender and juicy when cooked. However, lamb in America is naturally tender and juicy, making it unnecessary to use such an expensive cut of lamb.

1 tablespoon chopped garlic
1 tablespoon chopped fresh ginger
2 pounds boneless lamb, preferably from the leg, trimmed and cut into strips 1/4-inch thick by 2-1/2-inches long and 1-inch wide
4 teaspoons canola oil
2 cups finely chopped onions
1-1/4 cup nonfat plain yogurt
1 tablespoon white poppy seeds

1 teaspoon ground turmeric
1 teaspoon red pepper powder
1/2 teaspoon salt
7 dried plums
3/4 teaspoon ground cinnamon
1 teaspoon ground cardamom
1 teaspoon ground black cumin seeds
1–2 seeded, minced green chilies
1 teaspoon mace

GARNISH:
2 tablespoons chopped fresh coriander leaves

16 blanched toasted almonds (optional)

In a mini food processor or blender, process the garlic, ginger and 1 tablespoon of water to a paste. In a shallow dish combine the lamb with the garlic and ginger paste. Cover and marinate in the refrigerator for 30 minutes.

In a large non-stick saucepan heat 2 teaspoons of the oil over moderate heat. Add the onions and cook, stirring for one minute. Lower the heat and add 2 tablespoons of water. Cook, stirring until the onions are golden brown, about 20 minutes. Remove from the heat and cool slightly. In a mini food processor or blender, process to a paste.

Heat the remaining 2 teaspoons of oil in a non-stick pan over moderate heat. Add the meat in batches, searing evenly on all sides. Remove meat from the pan and set aside.

Add the cooked onion paste, yogurt, poppy seeds, turmeric, red pepper, salt and dried plums to the pan. Add the seared lamb and stir. Add the cinnamon, cardamom, black cumin, chilies and mace. Add 1/3 cup of water and bring to a boil. Reduce the heat to low, cover and cook for 1 to 1-1/2 hours or until the meat is very tender and the sauce is thick. Stir occasionally to prevent the mixture from sticking to the bottom of the pan and burning.

Yield: 6 servings.

Advance Preparation: The flavor of this dish improves when made ahead. Make it several hours prior to serving or a day before and refrigerate. It also can be frozen successfully. Defrost thoroughly prior to reheating. Reheat gently over low heat. If the sauce looks thick, add a little water.

Variation:
1. Substitute boneless lean beef round, cut into strips 1/4-inch thick, 2-1/2 inches long, and 1 inch wide.
2. For a very rich *Gosht Pasanda*, add 1/4 cup heavy cream prior to serving.

271 Calories per serving:
28 G Protein   286 MG Sodium
11 G Fat   77 MG Cholesterol
13 G Carbohydrate

Inspired by Ghulam Naqshband, Managing Director, SITA World Travel, New Delhi.

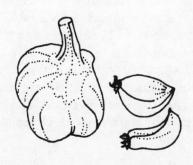

Lamb, Rajasthani Style

LAL MAAS

∽⌖∼

Rajasthan's extraordinary lamb dish is only for those with steel-lined stomachs, according to Executive Chef Sultan Mohideen. If cooked as in Rajasthan, where at least 30 dried red chilies plus a heap of red pepper powder is used, it could easily be the hottest dish in this book. When showing me this recipe, the chef used fewer chilies and less red pepper powder but managed to retain some of the fire. If you wish to dine as the Rajasthanis, add more dried red chilies and red pepper powder! Serve with rice, a yogurt salad and *Chapatis* (page 298). It can easily be doubled or tripled, and tastes even better next day.

1 cup nonfat plain yogurt
15 dried red chilies, seeded
1 teaspoon dry roasted cumin
    seeds, ground
3 teaspoons ground coriander
1/2 teaspoon ground turmeric
2 teaspoons canola oil
1 tablespoon minced garlic
4 green cardamom pods
3 bay leaves

2 2-inch cinnamon sticks
2 black peppercorns
1-1/4 cups finely sliced onions
2 pounds boneless lamb, prefer-
    ably from the leg, trimmed and
    cut into 1-1/2-inch pieces
1/4 teaspoon salt
2 tablespoons chopped fresh
    coriander leaves

Place the yogurt in a sieve. Let stand for 20 minutes to remove excess moisture. Whisk the yogurt in a bowl. Add the chilies, cumin, coriander and turmeric. Mix well. Set aside for at least 10 minutes.

Heat the oil in a large non-stick saucepan over moderate heat. Add the garlic and sauté until golden brown. Add the cardamoms, bay leaves, cinnamon and black peppercorns and cook for 30 seconds. Add the onions and cook for 2 minutes. Add 2 tablespoons water, reduce the heat to low and cook 10 to 15 minutes or until golden brown. Add the lamb to the pan in batches, searing evenly on all sides. Add the yogurt mixture and stir until the liquid has evaporated. Add 3/4 cup water. Bring to a boil, reduce the heat to low and cook, covered, stirring occasionally until the lamb is tender and the sauce thickened. Season to taste with salt. Garnish with chopped coriander and serve with rice or a flatbread.

YIELD: 6 servings.

ADVANCE PREPARATION: The flavors improve when prepared one to two days ahead. To reheat, simmer gently over very low heat until warmed through. If necessary, add a little water.

COOK's TIP: Lean beef may be substituted for the lamb.

261 Calories per serving:
   31 G Protein   197 MG Sodium
    9 G Fat   77 MG Cholesterol
   12 G Carbohydrate

Inspired by G. Sultan Mohideen, Executive Chef, Rajputana Palace, Jaipur.

Ground Lamb Cutlets, Parsi Style

PARSI CUTLACE

❧

These juicy, subtly spiced patties are marvelous when accompanied by Savory Rice and Green Pea Pilaf (page 234) and Tamarind Chutney (page 286).

3 slices fresh white bread, crusts removed and cut into cubes
1 tablespoon chopped fresh ginger
1 tablespoon chopped garlic
1 medium onion, minced
1/4 cup loosely packed mint leaves, minced
1/2 cup loosely packed coriander leaves, minced

1/2 teaspoon ground turmeric
1/2–1 teaspoon red pepper powder
1 teaspoon ground coriander
Salt to taste
1 pound lean ground lamb
1-1/2 cups dry breadcrumbs
3 egg whites, lightly beaten
1 tablespoon canola oil

Soak the bread cubes in water to cover for 5 minutes or until pulpy. Squeeze dry.

In a mini food processor or blender, process the ginger, garlic and 1 teaspoon of water to a paste.

In a bowl combine the onion, mint, coriander leaves, turmeric, red pepper, coriander powder, ginger and garlic paste and salt to taste. Mix thoroughly. Add the ground lamb and soaked bread. Mix well. Divide the mixture into 8 to 10 portions and form into 1/2-inch thick patties.

Spread breadcrumbs on a tray. With a wet hand, pat each patty lightly in the breadcrumbs. Dip each breaded cutlet into the egg whites. Heat the oil in a non-stick skillet over moderate heat. Add the cutlets to the pan and cook for about 3 to 4 minutes per side or until cooked through. Serve hot.

YIELD: 8 to 10 portions.

ADVANCE PREPARATION: Cook the patties one day ahead. Refrigerate or freeze. Defrost. Reheat in a moderate oven for about 10 to 15 minutes.

COOK'S TIP: Ground beef or turkey can be used instead of lamb.

196 Calories per serving:
14 G Protein   265 MG Sodium
6 G Fat   29 MG Cholesterol
22 G Carbohydrate

Inspired by Gev Desai, Executive Chef, Maurya Sheraton, New Delhi.

Baby Lamb Stew, Parsi Style

KID NU GOSHT

∞⌇∞

This hearty stew is a must for every Parsi wedding. Its subtle flavors are ideal for American tastes and would make a heart-warming winter meal when served with an American salad and crusty bread or with an Indian salad such as Onion Salad, Parsi Style (page 279), and an Indian flatbread. It is perfect for entertaining, as it can be easily doubled or tripled and tastes better the next day when the flavors have mellowed. Beef can be substituted for lamb.

1 cup skim milk
2 tablespoons nonfat dry milk
2 tablespoons coconut
1/2 teaspoon cumin seeds,
   crushed
1/2 cup white poppy seeds
1 tablespoon chopped fresh ginger
5 cloves garlic, chopped
2–4 green chilies, seeded and
   chopped
6 raw cashew nuts

1 pound lamb, trimmed of fat,
   preferably from the leg and cut
   into 1-inch pieces
1 tablespoon canola oil
1 large onion, finely chopped
1 2-inch cinnamon stick
4 cloves
1 bay leaf
1/2 teaspoon black peppercorns
2 large potatoes, peeled and cut
   into 2-inch pieces

In a food processor or blender, combine the skim milk, dry milk and ground coconut. Set aside.

In a mini food processor or blender, grind the cumin seeds and poppy seeds to a powder. Add the ginger, garlic, chilies, cashew nuts and 1 tablespoon water and process to a paste.

In a shallow dish combine the lamb with the paste mixture. Cover and marinate for 3 hours, or overnight in the refrigerator.

Heat the oil in a large non-stick saucepan over moderate heat. Add the onion and cook, stirring for 2 minutes. Reduce the heat to low. Add 2 tablespoons water and continue cooking for 10 to 15 minutes or until the onions are golden brown. Add the cinnamon, cloves, bay leaf and peppercorns. Cook over moderate heat for 1 minute. Add the marinated meat in batches and cook, stirring until the meat has been seared on all sides. If the meat sticks to the pan, add a little water to prevent burning. Add 2 cups of water to the meat. Bring to a boil, reduce the heat to low and cook, covered, for 40 minutes, stirring occasionally. Add the potatoes and cook for 20 minutes more or until the meat is tender and the potatoes are cooked. Add the coconut and milk mixture and simmer for 1 minute. Remove from the heat. Serve hot with *basmati* rice.

YIELD: 6 servings with other dishes.

ADVANCE PREPARATION: Prepare 1 to 2 days ahead. Refrigerate or freeze. Reheat gently. For best flavor, add the coconut milk mixture and cook for 1 minute prior to serving.

284 Calories per serving:
   18 G Protein   78 MG Sodium
   13 G Fat   39 MG Cholesterol
   23 G Carbohydrate

Inspired by Gev Desai, Executive Chef, Maurya Sheraton, New Delhi.

Minced Lamb with Peas

KEEMA MATAR

⌒⌒⌒

This traditional dish from north India has tremendous versatility. It can be served as an entrée or used as a stuffing for baked eggplant, green peppers, tomatoes and zucchini. When *Keema Matar* is gently stirred into cooked rice, it makes tasty ground lamb pilaf.

2 teaspoons canola oil
1 teaspoon cumin seeds
1 1-inch stick cinnamon
1 bay leaf, crumbled
1 tablespoon minced fresh ginger
1 tablepoon minced garlic
2 medium onions, minced
1/2 teaspoon salt (optional)
2 medium tomatoes, coarsely chopped
3 tablespoons nonfat plain yogurt

1/2 teaspoon ground nutmeg
1 teaspoon ground coriander
1/4 teaspoon ground turmeric
1/2 teaspoon red pepper powder (optional)
1 pound lean ground lamb
1 cup frozen peas
1 teaspoon *garam masala* (page 43)
2 teaspoons fresh lemon juice
2 tablespoons chopped fresh coriander leaves

Heat the oil in a large non-stick saucepan over moderate heat. Add the cumin, cinnamon and bay leaf. Stir until the cumin has darkened, about 10 seconds. Add the ginger and garlic and stir for 30 seconds. Add the onions and salt if desired. Stir for 2 minutes. Add 2 tablespoons water. Reduce the heat to low and cook, stirring occasionally for 20 minutes or until the onions are golden brown. Add the tomatoes and cook until soft. Lightly beat the yogurt until smooth. Add the yogurt to the pan gradually, stirring constantly. Cook for about 5 minutes. Add the nutmeg, coriander, turmeric and red pepper powder and stir for about 10 seconds. Add the lamb and cook, stirring to break up the lumps, until it is no longer pink and starts to brown. Add 1/4 cup of hot water. Reduce the heat. Cover and simmer, stirring occasionally, for 30 minutes or until the lamb is tender. Add the peas, cover and cook for 3 minutes more or until the peas are tender. If the liquid is not totally absorbed, uncover the pan and cook until evaporated. Remove from the heat. Stir in the *garam masala* and lemon juice. Serve garnished with chopped coriander leaves.

YIELD: 6 servings with other dishes.

VARIATION: Substitute minced turkey or beef for the lamb.

145 Calories per serving:
- 14 G Protein
- 6 G Fat
- 10 G Carbohydrate
- 48 MG Sodium
- 38 MG Cholesterol

Minced Lamb Kebabs

SEEKH KABABS

~~~

Tender baked or grilled rolls of spiced minced lamb shaped like sausages and wrapped around skewers are extremely popular in north India. But, because it is sometimes tricky to keep the meat from falling off the skewer and into the fire, you may want to make small lamb patties for grilling or broiling. As a patty, they are really the Indian equivalent to our hamburger, but more tasty! This dish is excellent with drinks, as an appetizer or to take on picnics. If you wish, you may substitute beef or minced turkey for the lamb.

4 whole cloves
8 black peppercorns
1 tablespoon chopped fresh ginger
4 garlic cloves, chopped
1 fresh green chili, seeded and chopped
1 teaspoon ground nutmeg
1 teaspoon ground cinnamon

1 teaspoon red pepper powder
1 tablespoon minced fresh coriander leaves
1 pound lean lamb, ground three times
1 egg, beaten
Chat masala to taste (page 44)

GARNISH:

1 lemon, cut into wedges
1 onion, thinly sliced
1 medium tomato, sliced

In a mini-food processor or blender combine the cloves and peppercorns. Grind to a powder. Add the ginger, garlic, and chili. Process into a smooth paste. Add the nutmeg, cinnamon, red pepper powder and coriander leaves and process just enough to combine thoroughly. Add the egg and mix well.

Heat the charcoal grill until the coals are gray and very hot. Meanwhile, in a large bowl combine the lamb and the spice paste. Mix well with your hands. (Do not use a food processor.) Divide the mixture into 4 portions. Using a wet hand, press each portion of meat along the length of a skewer and making each kebab 5 inches long. Be very careful to distribute the meat evenly around the skewer. If the meat is not evenly balanced, it might fall off the skewer. Grill over hot coals or under a preheated broiler for approximately 6 to 8 minutes, turning the skewers. Brush with oil once or twice during cooking. Sprinkle *chat masala* on kebabs. Serve hot, garnished with lemon wedges, onion and tomato slices.

YIELD: 6 portions.

ADVANCE PREPARATION: Prepare the meat mixture 1 day ahead. Cover and refrigerate overnight. Return to room temperature. Cook. The patties may be cooked ahead and reheated in a moderate oven or in the microwave. The cooked patties also may be frozen and reheated prior to serving.

COOK'S TIPS:
1. It is important that the meat have a coarse grainy texture yet be smooth enough to be shaped into a kebab. Do not let it turn into paste. I usually have my butcher grind the meat three times for me.
2. To make patties, roll each portion into a round ball and then flatten. Spray a large non-stick skillet with olive oil spray and cook the patties for 3–4 minutes on each side or until cooked through.

VARIATION: Substitute beef or turkey that has been ground three times.

178 Calories per serving:
21 G Protein   71 MG Sodium
 7 G Fat   111 MG Cholesterol
 8 G Carbohydrates

Inspired by Madan Lal Jaiswal, Master Chef, Bukhara Restaurant, Maurya Sheraton, New Delhi.

Grilled Spiced Lamb Kebabs

BOTI KABABS

∽∾∽

Exotically spiced grilled lamb kebabs that have been marinated in aromatic yogurt and a multitude of Indian spices are unsurpassed when served hot or cold. To obtain the full flavor of the spices it is important that the lamb be cooked slowly and thoroughly, otherwise the spices will taste raw.

The kebabs are delightful for a Western buffet, a barbecue, picnic or as part of an Indian meal. Serve with Green Pepper and Yogurt Salad (page 268); a rice pilaf, such as Tomato Rice (page 229); and if you desire, Potatoes, Green Peas and Tomatoes and a flatbread such as *Chapati* (page 298).

3/4 cup nonfat plain yogurt
1 tablespoon cumin seeds
1 tablespoon coriander seeds
1 tablespoon white poppy seeds
1 small onion, coarsely chopped
5 cloves garlic, coarsely chopped
2 tablespoons fresh ginger, coarsely chopped
1/4 cup fresh lemon juice

1 tablespoon *garam masala* (page 43)
3/4 teaspoon red pepper powder
1/2 teaspoon salt
1 teaspoon canola oil
2-1/2 pounds lamb, preferably from the leg, trimmed and cut into 1-inch pieces

GARNISH:

1 lemon, cut into wedges
1 small onion, thinly sliced

1 medium tomato, cut into wedges

Place the yogurt in a strainer over a bowl. Let the yogurt hang and drain for 30 minutes to remove excess liquid. Discard the liquid. Whisk the drained yogurt until smooth and creamy.

In a small skillet dry roast the cumin, coriander and poppy seeds over moderate heat, stirring for 15 seconds or until the spices are fragrant. In a spice grinder, grind the spices to a powder. In a mini food processor or blender, process the onion, garlic, ginger and the lemon juice to a paste. Add the *garam masala*, red pepper powder, salt and the oil. Add the roasted ground spices and blend to combine. Add the yogurt and mix until combined. Do not overprocess.

Place the yogurt mixture in a bowl. Prick the lamb cubes and add them to the yogurt mixture. Toss them until they are thoroughly coated. Cover the bowl and marinate for at least 4 hours or overnight in the refrigerator.

Heat the charcoal grill until the coals are gray and very hot. Bring the lamb to room temperature. Thread the lamb pieces on skewers leaving 1-inch between each piece of meat. Grill the kebabs about 5 inches above the coals for about 5 to 7 minutes on each side or until cooked. Using a brush, baste the kebabs occasionally with the remaining marinade. Serve garnished with lemon wedges, onion and tomato.

YIELD: 10 servings with other dishes.

ADVANCE PREPARATION: The lamb may also be cooked ahead and served at room temperature.

COOK'S TIP: The kebabs may be broiled in the oven. Place the meat about 4 inches from the heat and broil for about 7 minutes on each side.

VARIATION: Substitute lean, trimmed beef for the lamb.

251 Calories per serving:
  33 G Protein   291 MG Sodium
  9 G Fat   96 MG Cholesterol
  8 G Carbohydrate

Inspired by Master Chef Madan Lal Jaiswal, Bukhara Restaurant, Maurya Sheraton, New Delhi.

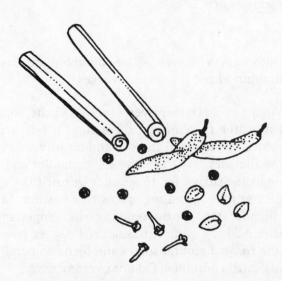

Grilled Lamb Kebabs

GOSHT KABABS

∽⌒∾

Low in calories and easily prepared, this favorite north Indian kebab bursts with exciting flavors.

1 pound boned lamb, preferably from the leg, trimmed and cut into 1-inch pieces	1/2 teaspoon red pepper powder
	1/2 teaspoon ground turmeric
	1 tablespoon malt vinegar
Juice of 1 lemon	1/2 teaspoon salt
1 small onion, peeled and quartered	1 teaspoon ground black pepper
	1/2 cup nonfat plain yogurt
2 cloves garlic, chopped	Lemon wedges for garnish

Place the lamb in a bowl. Add the lemon juice and mix. In a mini food processor or blender, put the onion, garlic, red pepper powder, turmeric, vinegar, salt and pepper. Blend to a coarse paste. Add the yogurt to the paste and mix. Pour the mixture over the lamb and mix well. Cover and marinate for 4 hours or overnight in the refrigerator.

Heat the charcoal grill until the coals are gray and very hot. Thread the lamb on skewers leaving 1 inch between each piece of meat. Grill the kebabs about 5 inches above the coals for about 5 to 7 minutes on each side, or until cooked. Using a brush baste kebabs occasionally with the remaining marinade. Serve hot with lemon wedges.

YIELD: 4 servings.

COOK'S TIP: Beef may be substituted for the lamb.

157 Calories per serving:
- 20 G Protein
- 5 G Fat
- 7 G Carbohydrate
- 355 MG Sodium
- 58 MG Cholesterol

Inspired by Sous Chef Kalam Kumar Channa, Tandoor Restaurant.

Goan Hot and Sour Pork

VINDALOO

❧

Here is a favorite dish from the Kokani-speaking Christians of Goa on India's west coast. Generally the Muslims and Hindus do not eat pork but the Indian Christians do.

Auntie Pauline de Sousa, a grandmotherly cook, taught me her mother's recipe for this Portuguese-influenced dish. She used the local coconut vinegar made from coconut toddy—the fermented liquid found in the center of the coconut. I have substituted white wine vinegar with good results.

Although a *vindaloo* is usually very, very hot, Auntie said you can control the heat by putting in as many dried red chilies as you wish. Marvelous for entertaining, this dish can be doubled or tripled. It tastes even better next day! Serve with plenty of fluffy rice.

4–8 dried red chilies
2 teaspoons black peppercorns
2 teaspoons cumin seeds
4 green cardamom pods, crushed
6 cloves
3 medium onions
6 large cloves garlic, chopped
1 tablespoon chopped fresh
　ginger
3 tablespoons white wine
　vinegar

2 pounds boneless pork tenderloin,
　trimmed and cut into 1-inch
　cubes
2 teaspoons canola oil
1 3-inch stick cinnamon, crushed
1–2 teaspoons red pepper powder
1 teaspoon ground turmeric
　powder
3 tablespoons tamarind liquid
　(page 54)
1/2 teaspoon salt (optional)

In a small skillet, dry roast the red chilies, peppercorns, cumin, cardamom and cloves until the cumin seeds begin to change color. Let cool slightly. Grind to a powder in a spice grinder.

Chop one of the onions coarsely. Finely slice the remaining onions. In a mini food processor or blender, process the garlic, ginger and 1 tablespoon of water to a smooth paste. Add the chopped onion and 1 to 2 tablespoons water, if necessary, and process again until smooth. Add the ground spices and vinegar and process until thoroughly combined.

Put the pork in a shallow bowl. Rub the paste mixture into the pork pieces. Cover and marinate for at least 1 hour in the refrigerator, stirring occasionally.

Heat the oil in a large non-stick pan over moderate heat. Add the crushed cinnamon. Allow to cook for a few seconds. Add the reserved onion rings. Cook, stirring for 2 minutes. Reduce the heat to low. Add 2 to 3 tablespoons water. Cook, stirring occasionally, until the onions are golden brown, about 20 minutes. If necessary, add a little water to prevent the onions from burning and sticking to the pan. Add the red pepper powder and turmeric and stir for 20 seconds. Add the meat to the pan in batches and stir until it is seared on all sides, taking care the mixture does not stick to the bottom of the pan. Add 1 cup warm water to the pork and bring to the boil. Reduce the heat to low, cover and simmer until the liquid has reduced by half. Add the tamarind liquid and salt to taste. Continue cooking, covered, until the pork is tender, stirring occasionally. The approximate cooking time should be about 40 minutes to 1-1/4 hours. Remove from heat. Serve with lots of rice and a yogurt salad.

YIELD: 4 servings.

ADVANCE PREPARATION: Prepare one to two days ahead. Refrigerate. Reheat when serving.

VARIATION: Skinless chicken, lamb or shrimp may be substituted.

359 Calories per serving:
  52 G Protein   129 MG Sodium
  11 G Fat   161 MG Cholesterol
  11 G Carbohydrate

Inspired by Auntie Pauline de Sousa, Goan Chef, Cicade de Goa.

POULTRY

Until recently, poultry was expensive in India and considered a delicacy. The rich Mughuls served lavish chicken dishes that took hours to prepare. Now, chicken is mass produced and fairly inexpensive. Its status has been greatly reduced and eating it has become an everyday occurrence, just as it is in the United States.

Chicken is often extravagantly spiced in the south, while in the north chicken dishes are often rather subtle. Andrah Chili Chicken (page 127), with exciting nuances of chili, is typical of an easily prepared south Indian chicken dish. Magnificently Spiced Chicken Breasts (page 125) are prepared in the *dum* method of the north, where chicken is cooked first and then finally sealed to ensure the seasonings are incorporated into the chicken for a final baking in the oven.

∾◡∾◡∾◡∾◡∾◡∾◡∾◡∾◡∾◡∾◡∾

Chicken with Saffron-Flavored Yogurt   CHOOZA-E-NIMBU
Chicken in Fragrant Yogurt Sauce   DAHI MURGH
Spiced Chicken Breast   KHUROOS-E-TURSH
Fragrant Simmered Chicken   MURGH HANDI LAZEEZ
Andhra Chili Chicken   MIRPUKAI KODI
Pepper Chicken, Chettinad Style
KODI MELLAGU CHETTINAD
Black Pepper Chicken, Bengali Style
MURGH KALI MIRCHI-BENGALI
Fenugreek Chicken, Bengali Style   METHI MURGH BENGALI
Fenugreek Chicken, New Delhi Style
METHI MURGH NEW DELHI
Chicken Masala   DUM MURGH MASSALAM
Chicken Tandoori   MURGH TANDOORI
Easy Chicken Tandoori   MURGH TANDOORI
Chicken in Tomato Sauce   KADHAI MURGH
Mustard Chicken   RAI SARSON MURGH
Grilled Chicken Kebabs   MURGH MALAI KABABS
Chicken Kebabs   MURGH TIKKA
Chicken Curry, Bangalore Style   MURGH KORMA
Piquant Turkey Dumplings in Tomato Sauce
CUCCHA KOFTA

∾◡∾◡∾◡∾◡∾◡∾◡∾◡∾◡∾◡∾◡∾

Chicken with Saffron-Flavored Yogurt

CHOOZA-E-NIMBU

∽⌒∾

This flavorful chicken delicacy, spiced with cumin and chilies and highlighted with a touch of saffron and mint, was served by Ghulam Naqshband in his lovely art-laden New Delhi home. Easy to prepare and very tasty, it is elegant as an appetizer or entrée.

The method of partially cooking the chicken first and finishing the process in a tightly sealed pan originated with the Avadh Nawabs of Lucknow in the eighteenth century and is known as *dum pukht* or *dum* cooking.

3/4 cup nonfat plain yogurt
1 tablespoon blanched slivered almonds
2 teaspoons minced fresh ginger
2 teaspoons minced garlic
1/2 cup finely sliced red onions
2–3 fresh green chilies, seeded and minced
1/2 teaspoon black cumin seeds, *shahi jeera*
1/2 teaspoon ground white pepper powder

1 tablespoon plus 2 teaspoons fresh lime juice
4 whole chicken breasts, skinned, boned and divided
Extra-virgin olive oil spray
1/4 teaspoon saffron threads, soaked in 2 tablespoons warm skim milk
10 mint leaves, chopped
8 romaine or Boston lettuce leaves (optional)

Place the yogurt in a fine sieve over a bowl. Cover and refrigerate for 4 hours or overnight in the refrigerator to remove the excess liquid. Discard the liquid.

In a mini food processor or blender, process the almonds with 1 tablespoon water to a smooth paste. Remove from the processor and set aside. Combine the ginger, garlic and 1 tablespoon water and process to a smooth paste. Do not process the ginger and garlic paste and almond paste together.

Whisk the yogurt in a large bowl until smooth and creamy. Add the almond paste, ginger and garlic paste, onions, chilies, cumin, white pepper and lime juice. Marinate the chicken in the yogurt mixture for at least 30 minutes, turning once.

Preheat the oven to 300°F. Arrange the chicken breasts in a single layer in a shallow ovenproof pan without overlapping. Spread the marinade over the breasts evenly. Mist lightly with olive oil. Bake the chicken for 15 minutes. Remove from the oven, drizzle with the saffron mixture and place mint leaves on top. Cover the chicken with foil. Place a tight cover over the foil. Cook in the oven for 5 to 10 minutes, or until cooked through. To serve, place chicken on a lettuce leaf, if desired.

YIELD: 8 servings with other dishes.

147 Calories per serving:
 25 G Protein   18 MG Sodium
  3 G Fat   1 MG Cholesterol
  5 G Carbohydrate

Inspired by Ghulam Naqshband, Managing Director, SITA World Travel, New Delhi.

Chicken in
Fragrant Yogurt Sauce
DAHI MURGH

෬ᏻᏺ

Chicken cooked in yogurt, Indian seasonings and onions is a mainstay in Indian households. It is easily prepared and uses few of the spices associated with Indian cuisine. Serve this dish to your friends who are timid about trying Indian food.

1 teaspoon white poppy seeds
1 tablespoon olive oil
3 cups thinly sliced onions
1 tablespoon peeled, chopped fresh
  ginger
2 teaspoons chopped garlic
1/2–1 teaspoon red pepper powder

2 tablespoons chopped fresh
  coriander leaves
1 cup nonfat plain yogurt
3 whole chicken breasts, skinned,
  boned and divided
1/2 teaspoon salt, or to taste

In a small skillet, dry roast the poppy seeds over moderate heat until aromatic. Let cool. Grind to a powder in a spice grinder or blender.

Heat 2 teaspoons oil in a non-stick pan. Add the onions and stir for 2 minutes. Add 2 tablespoons water. Turn the heat to low. Cook, stirring, until the onions are light brown, about 8 minutes. Add the ginger and garlic and cook another 2 minutes. Add the red pepper powder, ground poppy seeds and 1 tablespoon of the coriander leaves. Stir for 30 seconds. Let cool slightly. Put the mixture and 1/4 cup water in a food processor or blender and process to a smooth paste. Add the yogurt and process long enough to blend. Do not overprocess. Set aside

Heat the remaining teaspoon of oil in a large non-stick skillet over moderate heat. Add the chicken breasts and sauté on each side until they are very lightly browned. Add the yogurt mixture and bring almost to a boil. (Do not boil or the yogurt will separate.) Reduce the heat and simmer, covered, until the chicken is tender and no longer pink inside, about 8 to 10 minutes. Stir occasionally during cooking to make sure the sauce is not sticking to the pan and burning.

The yogurt sauce should have thickened to a velvety, smooth consistency that just forms a glaze on the chicken. If the sauce is too thin, remove the cover and boil until the sauce reduces. If it is too thick, add skim milk tablespoon by tablespoon until the sauce is the correct consistency. Sprinkle remaining coriander leaves over the top and serve.

YIELD: 6 servings with other dishes.

ADVANCE PREPARATION: The chicken flavors reach their full peak when prepared 1 to 2 days ahead. Refrigerate covered. Reheat gently, adding skim milk if necessary to adjust the sauce.

186 Calories per serving:
 26 G Protein   223 MG Sodium
  4 G Fat   1 MG Cholesterol
 11 G Carbohydrate

Spiced Chicken Breast

KHUROOS-E-TURSH

⌒◡⌒

Subtle spices and herbs impart delicate flavors and aromas to chicken cooked in the *dum* manner, where the chicken is first baked and then finally sealed to ensure that the seasonings are completely incorporated into the meat. This process originated in Avadh, which is now known as the Lucknow District of Utter Pradesh.

1/2 cup nonfat plain yogurt
8 blanched almonds, slivered
1 tablespoon plus 2 teaspoons
  chopped fresh ginger
1 tablespoon plus 2 teaspoons
  chopped garlic
1 medium onion, halved and
  thinly sliced
1 green bell pepper, finely sliced
1–2 fresh green chilies, seeded and
  minced

3/4 teaspoon black cumin
1/2 teaspoon ground white pepper
1 tablespoon fresh lime juice
Salt to taste
3 whole chicken breasts, skinned,
  boned and divided
Olive oil spray
1/2 teaspoon saffron, dissolved in
  2 tablespoons warm skim milk
6 mint leaves, chopped

Place the yogurt in a fine sieve over a small bowl. Let the yogurt drain for 4 hours or overnight in the refrigerator.

In a mini food processor or blender, grind the almonds with 4 teaspoons water to a smooth paste. Remove from the processor and set aside. Grind the ginger, garlic and 1 tablespoon water. Process to a smooth paste.

Whisk the yogurt in a large bowl. Add the almond paste, ginger and garlic paste, onion, green bell pepper, chilies, black cumin, white pepper, lime juice and salt to taste. Combine well. Add the chicken breasts and marinate for 30 minutes, turning once.

Preheat oven to 300°F. Lightly mist a shallow, ovenproof pan with oil. Arrange the chicken breasts in the pan without overlapping. Spread remaining marinade evenly on the chicken. Bake for 20 minutes. Remove from oven. Drizzle saffron and sprinkle mint over the chicken breasts. Cover the pan tightly with foil. Return to the oven for 10 minutes. Remove the foil and serve.

142 Calories per serving:
  25 G Protein   41 MG Sodium
   2 G Fat   1 MG Cholesterol
   6 G Carbohydrate

Inspired by Master Chef Mohammed Imtiaz Qureshi, Dum Pukht Restaurant, Maurya Sheraton, New Delhi.

Fragrant Simmered Chicken

MURGH HANDI LAZEEZ

Boneless pieces of chicken sautéed and simmered in chicken stock are made heady with mace, cardamom and saffron.

1 teaspoon chopped, fresh ginger
1 clove garlic, chopped
1 tablespoon canola oil
6 cloves
1 cinnamon stick
1 teaspoon cardamom seeds
1 medium onion, finely sliced
3 whole chicken breasts, skinned,

boned and cut into 1-1/2-inch pieces
1/2 teaspoon red pepper powder
3 cups chicken stock
1/2 teaspoon saffron threads, dissolved in 2 tablespoons warm water

Combine the ginger and garlic in a mini food processor or blender. Add 2 teaspoons water. Process to a smooth paste.

Heat the oil in a non-stick saucepan over moderate heat. Add the cloves, cinnamon and cardamom. Stir until they crackle. Add the ginger and garlic paste and sauté for 20 seconds. Add the onion and stir for 2 minutes. Add 2 tablespoons of water and stir. Reduce the heat to low and cook, stirring, for 10 to 15 minutes or until the onions are golden brown. Add the chicken and red pepper powder. Cook, stirring, for 3 to 4 minutes. Add the chicken stock, bring to a boil. Remove the chicken pieces and set aside. Force the cooking liquid through a sieve into a clean pan. Return to the heat and bring to a boil and cook until the liquid is reduced to a saucelike consistency. Add the cooked chicken and cook for 2 to 3 minutes more or until the chicken is cooked. Stir in the saffron liquid. Serve.

YIELD: 4 to 6 servings.

ADVANCE PREPARATION: Prepare 1 to 2 days ahead. Reheat prior to serving.

312 Calories per serving:
  54 G Protein   53 MG Sodium
  7 G Fat   0 MG Cholesterol
  5 G Carbohydrate

Inspired by Chef Manu Mehta, Maurya Sheraton, New Delhi.

Andhra Chili Chicken

MIRPUKAI KODI

೧ುಲ

Chili punctuates this chicken entrée from Andhra Pradesh where they like their food with a lot of zing! Serve with fried Sago Wafers (page 84), Lemon Pickle (page 292) and Yogurt Rice (page 228).

1 teaspoon chopped, fresh ginger	1/2 teaspoon ground turmeric
2 teaspoons chopped garlic	1 teaspoon red pepper powder
6 fresh green chilies	2 whole chicken breasts, skinned,
2 teaspoons canola oil	boned and divided
1/3 cup chopped onion	12 curry leaves
Pinch of salt	

In a mini food processor or blender, combine the ginger, garlic and 2 tablespoons of water. Process to a smooth paste. Remove from the blender and set aside. Chop 1 green chili and process to a paste in the processor, adding 1 to 2 teaspoons of water as needed. Slit 3 chilies in half lengthwise.

Heat the oil in a non-stick saucepan over moderate heat. Add the onion, and cook until translucent, about 1 minute. Lower the heat. Add 2 tablespoons water. Cook, stirring occasionally, until the onion turns golden brown, about 15 to 20 minutes. Add the ginger and garlic paste mixture. Cook, stirring to combine, until the mixture is no longer raw, about 20 to 30 seconds. Add the turmeric, red pepper powder, slit green chilies, green chili paste and 2 tablespoons water. Stir for 30 to 40 seconds. Add 1/4 cup of water and stir. Add the chicken and 7 of the curry leaves. Stir to coat chicken with pan mixture. Cook, turning the chicken occasionally and basting it with the sauces in the pan, until the chicken is tender and cooked. To prevent burning, it may be necessary to add water occasionally. The finished chicken dish should be dry in consistency. When serving, garnish with the remaining green chilies, slit lengthwise, and curry leaves.

YIELD: 4 servings with other dishes.

168 Calories per serving:
25 G Protein   44 MG Sodium
 4 G Fat   0 MG Cholesterol
 7 G Carbohydrate

Inspired by Chef C. S. Ramnath, Windsor Manor, Bangalore.

Pepper Chicken, Chettinad Style

KODI MELLAGU CHETTINAD

~~~

As I dined with Executive Chef Natarajan in the enchanting garden of the Raintree Restaurant in Madras, he said his authentic Pepper Chicken was typical of the enticing nuance of spices of the south's Chettinad cuisine. This is a must for lovers of spicy food!

The easily prepared dish tastes even better the next day, making it a perfect selection for entertaining. Serve with Tomato Rice (page 229) and Spinach and *Dal* Purée, Chettinad Style (page 259).

3 teaspoons minced fresh ginger
3 teaspoons minced garlic
1–2 teaspoons red pepper powder
1/2 teaspoon ground turmeric
2–3 tablespoons black peppercorns, coarsely crushed
1/2 teaspoon salt (optional)
3 whole chicken breasts, skinned,
   boned and cut into 1-1/2 inch
   pieces

2 teaspoons canola oil
1 3-inch stick of cinnamon,
   crushed
4 green cardamom pods, crushed
4 whole cloves, crushed
10 fresh curry leaves (optional)
1 cup chopped onion
3/4 cup chopped tomatoes

GARNISH:
Coriander leaves
8 slices cucumber

8 slices tomato

In a mini food processor or blender, combine the ginger, garlic and 1 tablespoon of water and process to a smooth paste.

Combine the ginger and garlic paste, red pepper powder, turmeric, and 1 tablespoon of the crushed black pepper. Rub the mixture into the chicken, cover and marinate for one hour.

Heat oil over moderate heat in a non-stick saucepan. Add the cinnamon, cardamom and cloves. Stir for 30 seconds or until fragrant.

Add the curry leaves. Stir. Add the chopped onion and sauté for 2 minutes. Reduce the heat to medium-low. Add 2 tablespoons water. Sauté, stirring occasionally, until the onions are golden brown. Add 1 to 2 tablespoons additional water to pan if necessary to prevent the onions from sticking to the pan and burning. Increase the heat to moderate. Add the chicken and cook, stirring, until the chicken is seared on all sides. Add 1/2 cup of water and bring to a boil.

Reduce the heat to a simmer, cover. Simmer for 10 minutes, stirring occasionally. To prevent burning or sticking, add 1 to 2 tablespoons water if necessary. Add the tomatoes and cook, stirring occasionally, for 5 minutes. Stir in the remaining black pepper and cook until the meat is tender. The finished dish should be dry in consistency. To serve, garnish with coriander leaves, sliced cucumbers and tomatoes.

YIELD: 4 servings with other dishes.

ADVANCE PREPARATION: Cook until the chicken is tender and some liquid from the tomatoes is remaining in the pan. At serving time, reheat and cook until mixture is dry in consistency.

388 Calories per serving:
67 G Protein   89 MG Sodium
 6 G Fat   0 MG Cholesterol
13 G Carbohydrate

Inspired by K. Natarajan, Executive Chef, Rain Tree Chettinad Restaurant, Madras.

Black Pepper Chicken, Bengali Style

MURGH KALI MIRCHI, BENGALI

⌘

Simply prepared, this fragrant chicken in tomato gravy is brimming with tasty ground black pepper, green chilies and Indian seasonings. As is true of so much Indian food, this tastes even better the next day!

1-1/2 teaspoons chopped fresh
  ginger
1 teaspoon chopped garlic
4 teaspoons canola oil
3 whole chicken breasts, skinned,
  boned and cut into 1-inch pieces
1/2 cup chopped onion
1/2 cup chopped ripe tomatoes

1 to 2 teaspoons minced fresh
  green chilies
2 teaspoons crushed black
  peppercorns
1 tablespoon chopped fresh
  coriander leaves
1/2 teaspoon salt

In a mini food processor or blender, combine 1 teaspoon of the ginger, garlic and 2 teaspoons of water to a smooth paste. Set aside.

Heat 2 teaspoons of oil in a large non-stick skillet over moderate heat. Add the chicken and stir-fry until lightly browned. You may need to cook the chicken in several batches. Remove. Set aside. Wipe pan with paper towels to remove any browned spots that may have stuck to the pan.

Heat the remaining 2 teaspoons of oil in the skillet over moderate heat. Add the chopped onion and remaining 1/2 teaspoon of chopped ginger. Cook for 2 minutes. Add 2 tablespoons of water, reduce the heat and cook, stirring occasionally, until the onions are golden brown. This will take about 20 minutes. Add the chopped tomatoes and ginger and garlic paste. Cook, mashing the tomatoes with a wooden spoon. Add the green chilies and the chicken with 1/2 cup of water. Bring to a boil, reduce heat and simmer for 5 minutes. Add the crushed peppercorns and coriander leaves. Continue cooking until the chicken is cooked, adding more water if necessary to prevent sticking. Add salt to taste. Let stand for a few minutes to allow flavors to develop. Serve.

YIELD: 6 servings with other dishes.

ADVANCE PREPARATION: Prepare 1 to 2 days in advance or freeze. Reheat gently, adding more water if necessary.

229 Calories per serving:
  36 G Protein   337 MG Sodium
   7 G Fat   0 MG Cholesterol
   5 G Carbohydrate

Inspired by S. Charavorty, Area Executive Chef, The Oberoi Grand Hotels, Bombay.

Fenugreek Chicken, Bengali Style

METHI MURGH BENGALI

৵৩৶

This splendid melange of flavors is certain to delight your guests! In Bengal, fresh fenugreek leaves with their pleasingly bitter taste are cherished as a vegetable. They are sometimes found in Indian grocery stores in the United States, so if you find them, use them and omit the fenugreek seeds. Since dried fenugreek often contains more stems than leaves, I do not advise using it. For those who cannot find fresh fenugreek, I have substituted spinach leaves and used the rusty-brown fenugreek seed, which has a delightful pleasant bitter taste with overtones of maple. Serve with Spinach *Dal*, Bengali Style (page 256), Cumin-Flavored Potatoes (page 192), Tangy Chickpeas (page 252) and a yogurt salad.

2 teaspoons canola oil
1-1/2 cups chopped onions
1 tablespoon chopped fresh ginger
2 teaspoon chopped garlic
1 teaspoon dry roasted coriander seeds, ground
1 teaspoon dry roasted cumin seeds, ground
1/2 teaspoon dry roasted cardamom seeds, ground
1 teaspoon ground turmeric

1/2–1 teaspoon red pepper powder
1/8 teaspoon dry roasted fenugreek seeds, ground
2 teaspoons mustard oil
1 teaspoon black mustard seeds
4 whole chicken breasts, skinned, boned and cut in half
3 tablespoons washed, trimmed fresh fenugreek leaves or 1/2 cup fresh spinach leaves
2 teaspoons fresh lime juice

Heat the canola oil in a non-stick skillet. Add the onions, ginger and garlic and stir for 2 minutes. Reduce heat to low. Add about 2 tablespoons water. Continue cooking until onions are golden brown.

In a mini food processor or blender, process the cooked onion mixture and 1/4 cup water to a paste. Add the coriander, cumin, cardamom, turmeric, red pepper powder and fenugreek to the paste mixture. Process just to combine.

Heat the mustard oil to smoking point in a large non-stick saucepan. Add the mustard seeds and cook until they crackle. Add the chicken breasts and lightly brown on both sides. Add the ground paste mixture and stir for 1 minute. Add about 1 cup water, bring to a boil. Reduce the heat and simmer, covered, for 10 to 15 minutes or until chicken is tender and cooked. Add more water if necessary during cooking to prevent burning and sticking to the pan. Stir occasionally. Add the fenugreek leaves and cook until tender. Sprinkle with lime juice before serving.

YIELD: 6 to 8 servings with other dishes.

ADVANCE PREPARATION: Prepare dish 1 to 2 days ahead. Refrigerate. Reheat on moderate flame. Add lime juice just before serving.

COOK'S TIP: When dry roasting fenugreek seeds, be careful not to burn them as they will become bitter. If mustard oil is unavailable, substitute canola oil.

200 Calories per serving:
- 32 G Protein
- 5 G Fat
- 5 G Carbohydrate
- 8 MG Sodium
- 0 MG Cholesterol

Inspired by Sudha Mehrotra, Calcutta.

Fenugreek Chicken, New Delhi Style

METHI MURGH NEW DELHI

જ∞≈

A titillating bouquet of subtle spices including warm aromatic green cardamom provides an excellent counterpoint to this savory chicken. Serve hot with flatbread.

3 whole chicken breasts, skinned
and boned
1 cup nonfat plain yogurt
1/2 teaspoon salt
2 teaspoons canola oil
5 green cardamom pods
5 cloves
1 1-inch stick cinnamon
1 bay leaf
Pinch of ground mace
1-1/2 cups chopped onion
2 tablespoons plus 2 teaspoons
chopped fresh ginger

5 teaspoons chopped garlic
2–4 teaspoons minced, seeded
fresh green chilies
1/2 teaspoon ground turmeric
1 teaspoon ground coriander
1/2–1 teaspoon red pepper
powder
1 cup chopped tomatoes
1/2 teaspoon roasted fenugreek
seeds
2 tablespoons chopped fresh
coriander leaves

Cut chicken into 12 pieces. Combine the yogurt and salt in a bowl. Marinate the chicken pieces in the yogurt for 30 minutes.

Preheat the oven to 300°F. Heat the oil in a non-stick ovenproof pan over moderate heat. Add the cardamom pods, cloves, cinnamon, bay leaf and mace. Stir for 30 seconds or until aromatic. Add the onion and cook, stirring, for 2 minutes. Add 2 tablespoons of water. Reduce the heat to low. Cook onion for about 10 to 15 minutes, stirring occasionally, until golden brown. Add 2 tablespoons of the ginger, the garlic and green chilies. Stir for 1 minute. Add the turmeric, coriander and red pepper powder. Stir for 30 seconds. Add the chopped tomatoes and cook for 2 to 3 minutes. Add the chicken and 1/4 cup water. Bring almost to a boil. Cover. Reduce heat and let the chicken simmer, covered, for 10 minutes until almost cooked. Sprinkle the chicken with the remaining 2 teaspoons of ginger, fenugreek seeds and coriander leaves. Cover the pan with foil. Place a tight cover over the foil and put the pan in the oven and cook for 10 minutes.

YIELD: 6 servings with other dishes.

ADVANCE PREPARATION: Prepare dish 1 to 2 days ahead. Refrigerate. Reheat gently in the oven.

239 Calories per serving:
39 G Protein   228 MG Sodium
4 G Fat   1 MG Cholesterol
11 G Carbohydrate

Inspired by Inder Sharma, Chairman, SITA World Travel, New Delhi.

Chicken Masala

DUM MURGH MASSALAM

～⌒〜

The subtle juxtaposition of almonds, ginger, turmeric, cardamom, mace and saffron makes this famous Mughlai dish, created by the chefs of the Royal House of Avadh, a winner. In Dum Pukht Restaurant in New Delhi, Master Chef Qureshi garnishes the chicken with saffron soaked hard boiled eggs and carrots. The dish is then covered with dough to seal in the juices and cooked in the *dum* style in the oven.

1 cup plus 1 tablespoon nonfat
   plain yogurt
3 tablespoons chopped fresh ginger
2 tablespoons chopped garlic
3 whole chicken breasts, skinned,
   boned and divided
1/2 teaspoon ground turmeric
1/2–1 teaspoon red pepper
   powder
1 tablespoon paprika

1 tablespoon canola oil
2 tablespoons slivered blanched
   almonds
1/2 teaspoon ground cardamom
1/3 teaspoon ground mace
1/2 teaspoon salt
1/2 teaspoon saffron threads,
   soaked in 2 tablespoons warm
   skim milk for 20 minutes

GARNISH:
2 tablespoons coriander leaves

12 dry roasted pistachio halves
(optional)

Place 1 cup of the yogurt in a sieve over a bowl. Let drain for 30 minutes. Discard liquid in bowl. Whisk yogurt until smooth and creamy. Set aside.

In a mini food processor or blender, combine the ginger, garlic and 1 tablespoon of water. Process to a smooth paste.

Place the chicken breasts in a shallow pan. Combine 3 tablespoons of the ginger and garlic paste mixture, turmeric, red pepper powder, paprika and remaining 1 tablespoon of yogurt. Rub the spice paste into the chicken breasts. Marinate the chicken, covered, for 30 minutes in the refrigerator.

Scrape off any excess marinade. Heat 2 teaspoons of the oil in a non-stick skillet over moderate heat. Add the chicken and cook on both sides until light brown. Remove the chicken from the skillet and set aside.

Preheat oven to 300°F.

In a mini food processor or blender, combine the almonds and 2 tablespoons of water to a smooth paste. Add the yogurt, cardamom, mace, almond paste, salt and saffron liquid and combine just enough to mix. Heat the remaining 1 teaspoon of oil over moderate heat in the skillet. Add the remaining ginger and garlic paste. Cook, stirring, for 30 seconds. Add the yogurt mixture and cook, stirring until a moderately thick sauce has formed.

Arrange the cooked chicken in a single layer in a shallow ovenproof dish. Pour the yogurt mixture over the chicken. Wrap the dish tightly with foil. Place a tight cover over the foil. The seal on the cover must be very tight. If necessary, place an ovenproof weight on top of the cover. Bake the chicken in the oven for 10 to 15 minutes or until cooked through. Remove the chicken from the oven. Garnish with coriander leaves and pistachio nuts. Serve immediately with Indian bread, *Dal* Qureshi (page 243) and a yogurt salad.

YIELD: 6 servings with other dishes.

ADVANCE PREPARATION: Prepare the chicken one day ahead. Refrigerate, covered. Bring to room temperature. Bake in oven as directed. Serve.

VARIATION: Precook 2 small carrots. Hard cook 2 eggs. Soak eggs in saffron water (4 teaspoons saffron threads to 1/2 cup water) until they are a brilliant yellow color. Slice eggs. Place carrots and eggs over the chicken prior to sealing it with foil.

175 Calories per serving:
  26 G Protein   226 MG Sodium
   5 G Fat   1 MG Cholesterol
   6 G Carbohydrate

Inspired by Master Chef Mohammed Imtiaz Qureshi, Dum Pukht Restaurant, Maurya Sheraton, New Delhi.

Chicken Tandoori

Murgh Tandoori

∽◡◠∾

The famous north Indian dish Chicken Tandoori has a distinctive bright reddish-orange color and unforgettable flavor. It is cooked with fragrant Indian spices in a *tandoor* oven, a large clay pit heated by very hot, glowing coals. The juices from the chicken—cooked on a long skewer in the center of the oven—drip down onto the coals, causing a unique sweet aroma.

Sous Chef Channa says that one of the secrets of Chicken Tandoori is the long marinating in fragrant spices, which flavor and tenderize the bird. I have designed this recipe for cooking in a conventional oven or on a charcoal grill.

4 whole boneless chicken breasts,
  skinned, boned and divided
3 tablespoons fresh lemon juice
1/2 teaspoon salt
1 tablespoon chopped fresh ginger
3 cloves garlic, chopped
1-1/2 teaspoons ground cumin

1 teaspoon red pepper powder
2 tablespoons paprika
1 teaspoon ground coriander
1/2 teaspoon ground cardamom
3/4 cup nonfat plain yogurt
Canola oil spray
Lemon slices to garnish

With a sharp knife, make short slashes in the chicken about 1/2 inch deep and 1 inch apart. Rub the chicken with lemon juice and salt. Place chicken in a shallow dish.

In a mini-food processor or blender, combine the ginger and garlic adding 1 tablespoon of water to make a smooth paste. Add the cumin, red pepper powder, paprika, coriander and cardamom. Add the yogurt and blend to a smooth paste. Do not overprocess. Place the chicken in a shallow dish. Rub the marinade thoroughly into the chicken. Cover and marinate for 4 hours or overnight in the refrigerator.

Remove the chicken from the refrigerator. Preheat the oven to 500°F. Lightly spray the chicken with oil and place on a wire rack in a large, shallow roasting pan. Cook the chicken for 15 to 20 minutes or until cooked throughout. Garnish with lemon slices.

OUTDOOR BARBECUING METHOD: Prepare coals for the barbecue 1 hour in advance. Coals are ready when a white ash forms. Rub the grill generously with oil and place 5 inches from the coals. Place the chicken slashed side up on the grill and brush with oil. Cook for 10 minutes. Turn the chicken, brush with oil and cook about 10 minutes longer or until the chicken is cooked.

YIELD: 8 servings with other dishes.

ADVANCE PREPARATION: Marinate the chicken one day ahead. Cook at time of serving or cook ahead and serve at room temperature.

COOK'S TIP: Marinating of the chicken is a tenderizing process. The cooking time will take less than that of the usual roasted or barbecued chicken.

153 Calories per serving:
- 31 G Protein
- 2 G Fat
- 1 G Carbohydrate
- 191 MG Sodium
- 0 MG Cholesterol

Inspired by Chef Kalum Kumar Channa, Tandoor Restaurant.

Easy Chicken Tandoori

MURGH TANDOORI

∽⌇∾

Here is a version of Chicken Tandoori in the form of kebabs. It uses ready-made *tandoori* paste, which can be purchased from Indian grocers and specialty food stores. It is ideal to have on hand when preparing a quick dinner, barbecue or picnic.

2 whole chicken breasts, skinned, boned and divided
3 tablespoons *tandoori* paste
6 tablespoons nonfat plain yogurt
1-1/2 teaspoons minced garlic

1-1/2 teaspoons ground ginger
1/2 teaspoon red pepper powder
Salt to taste
Olive oil spray (optional)

Make slashes in the chicken as for Chicken Tandoori (page 137). Place the chicken in a shallow dish. In a bowl combine the *tandoori* paste, yogurt, garlic, ginger, red pepper powder and salt. The mixture should be a thick paste. If it is not, add more yogurt. Mix well. Pour over the chicken and marinate, covered, in the refrigerator for 2 to 4 hours.

Remove the chicken from the refrigerator. Preheat oven to 400°F.

Bake the chicken for 8 minutes. Turn the chicken over and bake for 8 to 10 minutes or until the chicken is no longer pink. Mist with olive oil spray if desired. Serve hot or at room temperature.

YIELD: 4 servings.

ADVANCE PREPARATION: Marinate and cook chicken ahead. Serve at room temperature.

VARIATION: Barbecue the chicken over hot coals for 8 to 10 minutes on each side, misting occasionally with olive oil spray.

137 Calories per serving:
  24 G Protein   54 MG Sodium
   1 G Fat   0 MG Cholesterol
   3 G Carbohydrate

Chicken in Tomato Sauce

KADHAI MURGH

∽৩৫∾

This spectacular dish is so popular at the Taj Mahal's New Delhi Haveli Restaurant that it has remained on the menu for fifteen years! If you are a lover of spicy food, try this magnificent dish cooked with an abundance of tomatoes and flavored with fenugreek and chilies. It can be easily doubled or tripled and tastes even better when prepared ahead. Serve with Piquant Lemon Rice (page 226), a flat bread and a yogurt salad, such as Spiced Yogurt Salad (page 266).

2 teaspoons chopped garlic
2 teaspoons canola oil
6–8 dried red chilies, crushed
2 teaspoons coriander seeds, crushed
1-1/2 pounds ripe tomatoes, chopped
1/2 teaspoon salt, or to taste
1–3 hot fresh green chilies

2 tablespoons chopped fresh ginger
1/4 cup chopped fresh coriander
3 whole chicken breasts, skinned, boned and divided
1-1/2 teaspoons *garam masala* (page 64)
3/4 teaspoon toasted fenugreek seeds, ground

In a mini food processor or blender, process the garlic and 1 tablespoon water to a paste.

Heat the oil in a non-stick wok or large non-stick saucepan over moderate heat. Add the garlic paste and stir for 20 seconds. Add the crushed chili and coriander seeds. Stir for 30 seconds. Add the tomatoes and salt to taste. Bring the mixture just to a boil. Add the green chilies and 1 tablespoon each of the ginger and coriander. Reduce the heat and simmer tomato mixture for about 4 to 5 minutes. Add the chicken and bring just to a boil. Reduce the heat and simmer, covered, until the chicken is tender and no longer pink. Remove from the heat. Add the *garam masala* and fenugreek and stir. Garnish with remaining ginger and coriander.

YIELD: 6 servings with other dishes.

ADVANCE PREPARATION: Prepare chicken 1 to 2 days ahead. Refrigerate. Reheat before serving. Add the *garam masala* and fenugreek and garnish just prior to serving.

231 Calories per serving:
   38 G Protein   208 MG Sodium
    4 G Fat   0 MG Cholesterol
    9 G Carbohydrate

Inspired by Arvind Saraswat, Director, Food Production, Northern Region, Taj Mahal Group of Hotels, Bombay.

Mustard Chicken

RAI SARSON MURGH

༄◦༅

Inviting nuances of mustard combined with the spark of chilies lend titillating flavors to savory chicken. Serve with Vegetable Pilaf (page 230) and Mint-Coriander Chutney (page 285).

1 tablespoon plus 2 teaspoons
    black mustard seeds
1/2 teaspoon ground turmeric
1/4 teaspoon freshly ground black
    pepper
3 whole chicken breasts, skinned,
    boned and divided
1 tablespoon plus 2 teaspoons
    minced fresh ginger

1 tablespoon canola oil
1 tablespoon plus 2 teaspoons
    minced garlic
1/2–1 fresh green chili, seeded and
    thinly sliced
3 medium potatoes, peeled and cut
    into 1-1/2-inch cubes
Salt to taste

In a spice grinder or blender, combine the mustard seeds and 2 tablespoons water to a fine paste. Add the turmeric and black pepper. Process just enough to mix thoroughly.

Rub the spice paste mixture into the chicken breasts and marinate, covered, for 2 to 3 hours in the refrigerator.

In a large non-stick skillet, heat the oil over moderate heat. Add the ginger, garlic and green chili and stir-fry for 45 seconds. Add the chicken and sear on both sides. Add the potatoes and 1/4 cup water. Bring to a boil. Reduce the heat to simmer. Cook, covered, stirring occasionally, for about 20 minutes or until the chicken and potatoes are tender. If the mixture sticks to the pan, add about 1 tablespoon of water during cooking. Add salt to taste. Remove from heat. Let stand, covered, for a few minutes before serving.

YIELD: 6 servings.

ADVANCE PREPARATION: Prepare 1 day ahead. Reheat prior to serving.

213 Calories per serving:
  26 G Protein   29 MG Sodium
   4 G Fat   0 MG Cholesterol
  17 G Carbohydrate

Inspired by Sudha Mehrotra, Calcutta.

Grilled Chicken Kebabs

MURGH MALAI KABABS

～∽

Master Chef Madan Lal Jaiswal prepares this tasty combination of
tandoori herbs and spices with an Indian processed cheese called
amul, which is unavailable in the United States. I have substituted
nonfat cream cheese combined with skim milk with great success.
The dish is excellent served at room temperature with drinks prior to
dinner, or hot as part of a meal.

4 tablespoons chopped fresh ginger
3 tablespoons plus 2 teaspoons
 chopped garlic
1/2 teaspoon salt
1 tablespoon malt or red wine
 vinegar
4 whole chicken breasts, boned,
 skinned and cut in 16 pieces
3/4 cup nonfat cream cheese

1 tablespoon skim milk
3/4 teaspoon ground mace
3/4 teaspoon ground cardamom
3/4 teaspoon black cumin
2 tablespoons minced fresh
 coriander stems
3 teaspoons seeded, minced fresh
 green chilies

1 lemon, cut into wedges
1 small onion, thinly sliced
1 ripe tomato, sliced

1 cucumber, seeded and sliced
Chat masala (page 44)

In a mini food processor or blender, combine the ginger, garlic, salt
and vinegar to a paste. Rub the mixture into the chicken pieces, cover
and marinate for 15 minutes. In a large bowl, whisk the cream cheese
with skim milk until smooth and creamy. Add the mace, cardamom,
black cumin, coriander and chilies to the cheese and mix well. Add
the chicken pieces and coat with the cheese mixture. Cover and
allow to marinate for a least 3 hours in the refrigerator.

Heat the charcoal grill until the coals become gray and are very hot.
Thread the chicken pieces lengthwise on the skewers leaving 1 inch
between pieces. Barbecue the chicken about 5 inches above the coals
for approximately 3 to 5 minutes on each side or until the chicken is
no longer pink. Brush with marinade during the cooking. Serve gar-

nished with lemon wedges, sliced onions, tomato slices and cucumber slices. Sprinkle the *chat masala* over the chicken.

YIELD: 8 servings with other dishes.

ADVANCE PREPARATION: Cover the chicken and marinate overnight in the refrigerator. If serving at room temperature, cook one day ahead. Refrigerate. Bring to room temperature prior to serving.

VARIATION: Broil in the oven.

187 Calories per serving:
  26 G Protein   297 MG Sodium
   5 G Fat   13 MG Cholesterol
   7 G Carbohydrate

Inspired by Executive Chef Madan Lal Jaiswal, Bukhara Restaurant, Maurya Sheraton, New Delhi.

Chicken Kebabs

MURGH TIKKA

⤳⤳⤳

This succulent kebab is one of India's most popular dishes. It makes a superb cocktail snack as well as a main course. Traditionally Chicken Kebabs are cooked in the *tandoor* oven; however, I find it very tasty when cooked in the oven, under the broiler or on a charcoal grill.

2 tablespoons chopped fresh ginger
2 tablespoons chopped garlic
1/4 cup nonfat yogurt
1/2 teaspoon ground white pepper
1/2 teaspoon ground cumin
1/4 teaspoon ground mace
1/4 teaspoon ground nutmeg
1/4 teaspoon ground cardamom
1/2 teaspoon red pepper powder

1/2 teaspoon ground turmeric
1/4 cup fresh lemon juice
2 tablespoons chickpea flour
2 teaspoons canola oil
Salt to taste
3 whole chicken breasts, boned,
   skinned and cut into 18 pieces
Olive oil spray

GARNISH:

6–8 lemon wedges   Lettuce leaves
6–8 tomato slices

In a mini food processor or blender, combine the ginger, garlic and 1 tablespoon water to a smooth paste.

Place the yogurt in a large bowl and whisk until smooth. Add the ginger and garlic paste, pepper, cumin, mace, nutmeg, cardamom, red pepper, turmeric, lemon juice, chickpea flour and oil. Season to taste with salt. Whisk to combine thoroughly. Add the chicken pieces to the marinade. Mix thoroughly to coat. Cover and marinate for approximately 3–4 hours in the refrigerator.

Remove chicken from the refrigerator.

Preheat the oven to 350°F. or prepare the charcoal grill.

Place the chicken pieces on skewers at least 1 inch apart. Place the skewers on a rack over a pan and bake in the oven for about 8 minutes, or until cooked, turning occasionally. Remove from the oven. Immediately mist lightly with olive oil spray.

Cook the chicken over charcoal for 6 to 7 minutes, or until cooked, turning once. Remove from grill. Immediately mist lightly with olive oil spray. Garnish with lemon wedges, tomato slices and lettuce.

YIELD: 10 to 12 appetizer servings or 6 dinner servings with other dishes.

113 Calories per serving:
 21 G Protein   1 MG Sodium
  2 G Fat   0 MG Cholesterol
  1 G Carbohydrate

Inspired by Madan Lal Jaiswal, Master Chef, Bukhara Restaurant, New Delhi.

Chicken Curry, Bangalore Style

MURGH KORMA

ᘓᕟᘒ

In southern Bangalore, this aromatic chicken curry is enriched with freshly made coconut milk. Kitty Basith marinates the chicken in yogurt before cooking, producing a light, subtly spiced dish.

3/4 teaspoon minced fresh ginger
3/4 teaspoon minced garlic
5 green cardamom pods
10 cloves
2 tablespoons coriander seeds
2/3 cup nonfat plain yogurt
1/2 teaspoon ground turmeric
2 whole chicken breasts, boned, skinned and cut into 1-inch pieces

2–4 fresh green chilies, chopped
1/3 cup tightly packed fresh mint leaves
2 teaspoons canola oil
2/3 cup chopped onions
1/2 teaspoon salt (optional)

In a mini food processor or blender, combine the ginger, garlic and 2 tablespoons water to a smooth paste. In a spice grinder or blender, grind the cardamom pods, cloves, and coriander to a fine powder. In a large bowl whisk the yogurt, ginger and garlic paste, turmeric and ground spices. Add the chicken and stir to coat. Cover and marinate for 30 minutes or overnight in the refrigerator.

In a mini food processor or blender, process the green chilies, mint leaves and 1 teaspoon water to a paste.

Heat the oil in a non-stick pan. Add the onions and cook, stirring, until translucent. Add the chicken with the marinade and the chili mixture. Stir to combine. Add the salt if desired. Bring the mixture almost to a boil. Do not let the yogurt boil or it will curdle. Reduce the heat to a simmer. Cover and cook, stirrring occasionally, for 10 to 20 minutes, or until chicken is cooked through. Remove from heat. Let stand for about 10 minutes to allow flavors to mellow. Serve with rice.

YIELD: 4 servings with other dishes.

ADVANCE PREPARATION: Prepare 1 day in advance. Reheat gently on low heat.

COOK'S TIP: If sauce is too thin, add 1/4 teaspoon cornstarch combined with a little cold water and cook, stirring until thickened.

181 Calories per serving:
27 G Protein	30 MG Sodium
4 G Fat	1 MG Cholesterol
9 G Carbohydrate	

Inspired by Kitty Basith, Willowbrook, IL, formerly from Bangalore.

Piquant Turkey Dumplings in Tomato Sauce

CUCCHA KOFTA

∽✄∾

This classic dish from Bengal combines tasty turkey dumplings with a fragrant tomato sauce. Traditionally the dumplings are fried before being added to the tomato sauce, and sour cream is added at the end of cooking to produce a rich *kofta*. Anna Sanyal eliminates the frying and cooks the meatballs directly in the tomato sauce for a lighter, lower calorie *kofta*. For a richer dish, she often adds lightly beaten yogurt a teaspoon at a time to the finished dish until the desired consistency is reached.

TURKEY DUMPLINGS:

1 pound lean ground turkey	1/2 teaspoon *garam masala* (page 43)
2 teaspoons minced fresh ginger	
1 teaspoon finely minced garlic	1/2 teaspoon salt
1/2 teaspoon ground turmeric	1 teaspoon minced onion
1/2 teaspoon ground cumin	1/3 cup fresh bread crumbs
	1 large egg white

TOMATO SAUCE:

1-1/2 teaspoons peeled, chopped fresh ginger

1/2 cup chopped onion

2 teaspoons canola oil

1/2 teaspoon ground turmeric

1/2 teaspoon ground cumin

1/4 teaspoon red pepper powder

1 teaspoon paprika

1 cup finely chopped ripe tomatoes

1/2 teaspoon salt

1/4 teaspoon sugar

1/2 teaspoon *garam masala* (page 43)

1/4 cup chopped fresh coriander leaves

DUMPLINGS: Combine all the ingredients for the turkey dumplings in a bowl and mix, kneading the mixture until well blended. Shape into walnut-sized balls. Cover and chill for 30 minutes.

TOMATO SAUCE: In a mini food processor or blender, combine the ginger, onion and 2 tablespoons water to a smooth paste. In a non-stick pan, heat the oil over moderate heat. Add the ginger and onion paste and cook, stirring, for about 1 to 2 minutes. Add the turmeric, cumin, red pepper and paprika. Stir for 2 minutes, adding 1 tablespoon water if necessary to prevent burning. Add the tomatoes and cook for 4 to 5 minutes to blend the flavors.

Add 2 cups of water and bring mixture to a boil. Season with salt and sugar. Add the dumplings a few at a time, allowing the tomato sauce to come to a boil before adding additional dumplings. When all the dumplings are in the pan, reduce the heat. Cook for 5 minutes or until all the dumplings are cooked through. Place in a serving bowl. Sprinkle with *garam masala* and coriander leaves.

YIELD: 6 servings with other dishes.

ADVANCE PREPARATION: Prepare the dumplings 1 to 2 days ahead and refrigerate or freeze. Reheat gently when serving.

VARIATION: Extra lean ground lamb, beef or chicken may be substituted for the turkey.

COOK'S TIP: If the *kofta* sauce is too thin, remove the turkey dumplings and reduce the sauce to desired consistency.

164 Calories per serving:

17 G Protein

7 G Fat

6 G Carbohydrate

894 MG Sodium

61 MG Cholesterol

Inspired by Anna Sanyal, Darien, IL, formerly of Calcutta.

Seafood

Seafood is popular in the coastal towns, particularly in Bengal and along the southern coasts of Bombay, Goa, Kerala and Madras.

Many of the seafood dishes are marinated and cooked on top of the stove, such as the exotically Spiced Shrimp (page 164) from Goa, or broiled or barbecued, such as the enticing Mustard Tuna (page 153), and can easily be incorporated into both Western and Indian dining.

~~~~~~

Fragrant Mackerel, Goan Style   MACCHI RECHAD
Mustard Tuna   RAI SARSON MACCHI
Grilled Salmon Steaks with Carom   MACCHI AJWAINI
Grilled Swordfish, Chettinad Style   MEEN VARUVAL
Broiled Spiced Swordfish, Mangalore Style
MACCHI MASALA MANGALORE
Fish Parcels, Parsi Style   PATRA NI MACCHI
Fish in Tomato Sauce, Parsi Style   SAAS NI MACCHI PARSI
Hot and Sour Fish, Parsi Style   MACCHI NI VINDALOO
Barbecued Ginger Shrimp   JHINGA ADRAKI
Shrimp in Spiced Sauce   JHINGA SAMURKUNDH
Spiced Shrimp   JHINGA BALCHAO
Spicy Stir-Fried Shrimp, Mangalore Style
MEEN VARUVAL MANGALORE

~~~~~~

Stuffed Mackerel, Goan Style

MACCHI RECHAD

~~~

The vivaciousness of Goa is deeply imbued in this vibrantly spiced yet simply prepared fish. In Goa, this local favorite is prepared with freshly caught mackerel from the local waters. You may use any lean firm white fillet with great success.

6 dried red chilies
1/2 teaspoon cumin seeds
3 black peppercorns
1-1/4 inch piece of fresh ginger, chopped
1 teaspoon chopped garlic
1/2 cup chopped onion
2 teaspoons sugar
1-1/2 teaspoons tamarind concentrate

2 tablespoons white wine vinegar
1 teaspoon *garam masala* (page 43)
1 teaspoon ground turmeric
1/2 teaspoon salt, or to taste
4 8-ounce mackerel fillets, cleaned
2 teaspoons canola oil
1 lime, cut into wedges

In a mini food processor or blender, grind the red chilies, cumin seeds, peppercorns, ginger, garlic, onion, sugar, tamarind concentrate and vinegar to a paste. Add the *garam masala*, turmeric and salt and process until combined.

Rinse the mackerel and pat dry with paper towels. Rub the paste mixture on both sides of the each fillet.

Heat the oil in a non-stick skillet. Add the fish and fry until both sides are brown and the fish almost flakes. This should take about 3 to 5 minutes. Serve with lime wedges.

YIELD: 4 servings.

ADVANCE PREPARATION: Prepare the paste mixture a day ahead. Rub the paste mixture into the fish several hours ahead. Cook prior to serving.

427 Calories per serving:
48 G Protein
21 G Fat
9 G Carbohydrate
491 MG Sodium
107 MG Cholesterol

Inspired by Peter Goes, Goan Chef, The Oberoi Bagmalo Beach, Goa.

Mustard Tuna

RAI SARSON MACCHI

∽∾

Enticing nuances of mustard lend intriguing flavors to succulent tuna. Instead of pan frying, you may want to try grilling the tuna for your next barbecue.

2 teaspoons black mustard seeds
4 5-ounce tuna steaks, washed and dried with paper towels
1/2 teaspoon chopped garlic
1/2 teaspoon peeled, chopped fresh ginger

1/2 teaspoon red pepper powder
1 tablespoon fresh lemon juice
1 teaspoon mustard oil
2 tablespoons drained nonfat plain yogurt
Lemon wedges to garnish

Grind 1 teaspoon of the mustard seeds in a spice grinder or processor to a powder. Add 1 tablespoon of warm water and mix to a thin paste. Let stand for 30 minutes to allow the flavors to develop.

Rinse the tuna and pat dry with paper towels. Place tuna in a shallow dish. In a mini food processor or blender, process the garlic, ginger and 1 tablespoon of water to a smooth paste. Add the mustard paste, red pepper powder and lemon juice. Process to combine. Crush the remaining teaspoon mustard seeds and combine with the mixture. Add the mustard oil and yogurt and process just to combine. Rub the mixture into the fish. Cover and marinate in the refrigerator for 1 hour.

Heat a non-stick skillet over moderate heat. Add the tuna steaks and cook until the tuna is browned on the outside and still rare on the inside, about 2 to 3 minutes on each side. Baste the tuna with marinade while cooking. Serve with lemon wedges.

YIELD: 4 servings with other dishes.

ADVANCE PREPARATION: Marinate the fish several hours ahead.

COOK'S TIP: For medium-rare fish, press the fish with your finger during cooking. If it yields gently it is ready.

VARIATIONS:
1. Grill the fish on the barbecue.
2. Substitute red snapper fillets, skewered shrimp or chicken.
3. Substitute canola oil for mustard oil.

178 Calories per serving:
  35 G Protein   66 MG Sodium
  2 G Fat   73 MG Cholesterol
  3 G Carbohydrate

Inspired by a recipe from S. Charavorty, Area Executive Chef, The Oberoi Grand Hotels.

Grilled Salmon Steaks with Carom

MACCHI AJWAINI

~~~

Bengalis are passionate about fish and without it no meal is considered complete. Executive Chef Alphonso Gomes, of The Oberoi Grand, Calcutta, showed me the preparation of this dish using the prized *bekti*, a local fresh-water fish. He said that salmon, swordfish or mackerel could be substituted for the *Bekti*. Carom seeds, *garam masala* and lemon juice lend a delicate fragrance, which is highlighted by a hint of red pepper powder.

4 6-ounce boneless salmon steaks, 1-1/4 inches thick
1 teaspoon cumin seeds, crushed
1 teaspoon carom seeds, *ajwain,* crushed
1 teaspoon ground ginger
1 teaspoon *garam masala* (page 43)
1/2 teaspoon ground turmeric

3/4 –1 teaspoon red pepper powder
1/2 teaspoon *chat masala* (page 44)
1 tablespoon fresh lemon juice
5 tablespoons nonfat plain yogurt
1/2 teaspoon salt (optional)
1 teaspoon canola oil
1 lemon, cut into wedges

Rinse the salmon and pat dry with paper towels.

In a shallow dish combine the cumin, carom, ginger, *garam masala*, turmeric, red pepper powder, *chat masala*, lemon juice, yogurt and salt if desired. Whisk together until the mixture is smooth. Add the salmon to the yogurt mixture and turn to coat. Cover and marinate in the refrigerator for at least 1 hour.

Preheat the charcoal grill. When the coals are gray and very hot, brush the grill lightly with the oil. Grill the salmon until lightly browned on both sides, about 6 to 7 minutes on each side, or until the fish almost flakes. Brush occasionally with the marinade while grilling. Serve with lemon wedges.

YIELD: 4 servings.

ADVANCE PREPARATION: Marinate the salmon several hours ahead.

VARIATIONS:
1. The fish may be broiled. Preheat the broiler. Place the fish on the lightly oiled rack of the broiler pan. Cook the salmon 4 inches from the heat source, turning once.
2. Substitute chicken for the fish.

256 Calories per serving:
27 G Protein   84 MG Sodium
15 G Fat   78 MG Cholesterol
1 G Carbohydrate

Inspired by Alphonso Gomes, Executive Chef, The Oberoi Grand, Calcutta.

Grilled Swordfish, Chettinad Style

MEEN VARUVAL

ᔕᕓᕈ

Grilling is one of the best ways to cook full-flavored swordfish. In this simply prepared southern Chettiar dish, swordfish is enlivened with chilies and fragrant with turmeric. Chef Anand usually deep fries the fish until it is crisp, but varies his cooking method by grilling. He uses local *seer* Fish, but suggests using swordfish as an alternative.

4 4-ounce swordfish steaks,
  1/2–1 inch thick
1/2 teaspoon ground turmeric
2–3 teaspoons red pepper powder

1/2 teaspoon salt
2 tablespoons plus 2 teaspoons
  fresh lime juice
Olive oil spray

GARNISH:

2 tablespoons chopped fresh
  coriander leaves

Lime wedges

Rinse the swordfish and pat dry with paper towels. In a shallow dish combine the turmeric, red pepper powder, salt and lime juice. Add the swordfish and rub the mixture on each side. Cover and refrigerate for at least 3 hours, or overnight.

Preheat the charcoal grill. When the coals are gray and very hot, brush the grill lightly with olive oil. Grill until the swordfish almost flakes, approximately 3 to 4 minutes on each side.

To serve, transfer the fish to a serving platter. Mist the fish very lightly with olive oil spray. Garnish with chopped coriander. Serve with lime wedges.

YIELD: 4 servings

COOK'S TIPS:
1. The fish may be broiled on a non-stick baking sheet that has been sprayed lightly with olive oil.
2. Swordfish may be pan fried in a non-stick skillet. Spray fish lightly on each side with olive oil spray.
3. Any firm-fleshed fish such as salmon, tuna, halibut or mackerel may be substituted.

148 Calories per serving:
23 G Protein   402 MG Sodium
 5 G Fat   44 MG Cholesterol
 3 G Carbohydrate

Inspired by Executive Chef Praveen Anand, Dakshin Restaurant, Park Sheraton, Madras.

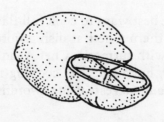

Broiled Spiced Swordfish, Mangalore Style

MACCHI MASALA MANGALORE

∽∾∽

Chili paste lends intensity and complexity to simple grilled fish. In Mangalore on the west coast, the locals love fiery food and would prepare this with three times as much red pepper powder. Here, the dish is made with a local lady fish, so named because of its long, lean and delicate shape. As an alternative, Chef Shankaran suggested using swordfish and broiling it instead of the traditional frying.

4 4-ounce boneless swordfish
   steaks, 1/2–1 inch thick
2 teaspoons chopped fresh ginger
2 teaspoons chopped garlic
2–3 tablespoons red pepper powder

1/2 teaspoon salt
5 tablespoons fresh lemon juice
Olive oil spray

GARNISH:
Fresh coriander leaves
Lemon wedges

Wash the swordfish and pat dry with paper towels. Place the swordfish in a shallow dish.

In a mini food processor or blender, process the ginger, garlic, red pepper powder, salt, lemon juice and 1 tablespoon of water to a smooth paste.

Rub the paste mixture on each side of the swordfish. Cover and marinate in the refrigerator for at least 1 hour or overnight.

Preheat the broiler. Mist the broiling pan with olive oil spray. Arrange the fish on the pan and broil 4 inches from the heat source until the fish almost flakes, about 2 to 3 minutes on each side. Mist the fish with olive oil spray. Garnish with coriander leaves. Serve with lemon wedges.

Yield: 4 servings.

Cook's Tip:
1. If you prefer to use less red pepper powder, substitute paprika.
2. If desired, the fish may be fried. Mist the fish on each side with olive oil. Fry in a nonstick skillet for 2 to 3 minutes on each side.

160 Calories per serving:
23 G Protein   428 MG Sodium
5 G Fat   44 MG Cholesterol
5 G Carbohydrates

Inspired by Chef C. B. Shankaran, Manjuram Hotel, Mangalore.

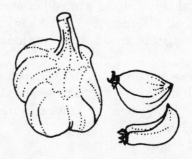

ƒish Parcels, Parsi Style

PATRA NI MACCHI

Roshani Kerawalla, a Parsi friend, joined me for lunch at the Landmark Restaurant, Bombay, where we delighted in this light, steamed fish, combining delicate coconut, coriander and mint chutney with fragrant banana leaves. She said that *Patra ni Macchi* is the leitmotif for every auspicious Parsi occasion, especially a wedding. It is traditionally prepared with pomfret, a local fish, but as this is rarely available in the United States, I have substituted sole, with excellent results.

This dish is delicious when served hot as an entrée or chilled as a first course.

6 6-ounce skinned fillets of sole, flounder or other firm white fish.
1/3 cup plus 1 teaspoon fresh lime juice
1/2 teaspoon salt
Ground white pepper, to taste
4 cloves garlic, chopped
2 teaspoons chopped fresh ginger
3–5 fresh green chilies, seeded and chopped
1/2 cup plus 2 tablespoons loosely packed fresh coriander leaves
1/3 cup loosely packed fresh mint leaves
1/4 cup coconut
1-1/2 teaspoons ground cumin
6 banana leaves, cut into 10-inch squares
6 thin lemon slices

Rinse the sole and pat dry with paper towels. Rub both sides of the sole with 2 tablespoons of the lime juice. Season on both sides with salt and pepper. Cover and allow the sole to marinate for 10 minutes.

In a mini food processor or blender, combine the garlic, ginger, chilies, coriander, mint, coconut, cumin and remaining lime juice. Process to a smooth paste.

Pour boiling water over each square of banana leaf to soften and prevent splitting. Spread the garlic and ginger paste thickly on each side of the fish. Place the fish in the upper third of a square of banana leaf. Top with a slice of lemon. Wrap the fish with the banana leaf, envelope-style, into a neat parcel, keeping seam side on top. Secure with a metal skewer, toothpick or staples. (See diagram on page 159.)

Place parcels in a single layer, without overlapping, on a wire steaming rack in a steamer or a large roasting pan. Fill the steamer with boiling water to within 1 inch of the rack. Cover the pan with a tight-fitting lid and steam the parcels over medium-high heat for about 7 to 8 minutes or until the fish almost flakes. Serve banana leaf–wrapped parcels intact.

YIELD: 6 servings.

ADVANCE PREPARATION: Wrap the parcels several hours ahead. Refrigerate. Steam just before serving.

VARIATIONS:
1. Substitute 12 large spinach or Boston lettuce leaves for the banana leaves. Bring 4 quarts of water to a boil. Plunge the leaves into the boiling water and cook until just pliable, about 1 minute. Drain. Refresh under cold running water. Drain again. Pat dry carefully. Set aside. To wrap, place 2 leaves on a work surface, overlapping them slightly. Place the prepared fish in the center of the leaves. Fold over the leaves and wrap into a neat parcel. Secure with a skewer.

2. Substitute 10-inch squares of aluminum foil for the banana leaves.
3. Substitute haddock, flounder, salmon or cod fillets for the sole.

COOK'S TIP: If the banana or vegetable leaves split, wrap the leaves with aluminum foil. The fragrance of the banana leaves will be imparted, but none of juices will be lost.

190 Calories per serving:

32 G Protein	287 MG Sodium
4 G Fat	74 MG Cholesterol
5 G Carbohydrate	

Inspired by the chefs of the Parsi Ratan Tata Institute, Bombay.

1
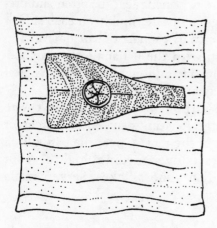

2
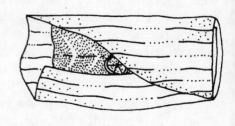

3
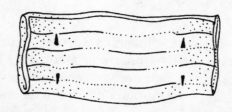

Fish in Tomato Sauce, Parsi Style

SAAS NI MACCHI PARSI

∽✺∾

Here is a Parsi favorite that has the delicate combination of sweet, sour and spice so distinctive of their cuisine. It is often served at weddings and other festive gatherings, as fish is highly regarded. It is almost always served with a steaming hot dish of Steamed Rice and Lentils, Parsi Style (page 233) and Onion Salad, Parsi Style (page 279).

1 tablespoon canola oil
7 cloves garlic
1/2 teaspoon ground cumin
1/2 cup fresh coriander leaves
2–4 fresh green chilies, seeded and chopped
3 tablespoons chickpea flour
2 ripe tomatoes, quartered
1/2 teaspoon red pepper powder (optional)

2 tablespoons sugar
1 pound cod, halibut or other firm white fish, skinned and cut into 2-inch pieces
2 eggs
1/2 cup distilled white vinegar
Salt to taste

Heat the oil in a non-stick saucepan over medium heat. Add the garlic and stir-fry until lightly browned. Add the cumin, coriander leaves, chilies and chickpea flour and stirfry until light brown in color. Add the tomatoes, 2 cups of water and cook, stirring, for 4 minutes. Add the red pepper powder, if desired, and the sugar. Stir until dissolved. Add the cod and bring the mixture to a boil. Reduce the heat and simmer for 2 to 3 minutes. Remove the pan from the heat. In a bowl whisk the eggs with vinegar and stir them into the pan. Return the pan to a low heat and cook until the fish almost flakes. Season to taste with salt. Serve hot.

YIELD: 4 servings with other dishes.

259 Calories per serving:
27 G Protein   137 MG Sodium
 8 G Fat   155 MG Cholesterol
21 G Carbohydrates

ADVANCE PREPARATION: Prepare ahead to the point of adding the eggs. Add the eggs and continue cooking as in recipe.

VARIATION: Substitute shrimp for the fish.

Inspired by Gev Desai, Executive Chef, Maurya Sheraton, New Delhi.

ꤟoτ and Sour ꤟish, ꤡarsi Sτyle

MACCHI NI VINDALOO

∽ᗡᏅᏜᎦᏄ

The Parsis of Bombay have borrowed from southern Goa, where Vindaloo originated, to create their own version of this tangy dish with a spark of fire. Serve with Savory Rice and Green Pea Pilaf (page 234) and Cucumber and Yogurt Salad (page 271).

3–5 dried red chilies, seeded
1/2 cup plus 1 tablespoon white
   wine vinegar
3 cloves garlic, coarsely chopped
1/2 teaspoon cumin seeds

4 8-ounce skinned flounder fillets,
   or other firm white fish
1 tablespoon olive oil
1 medium onion, finely chopped
Salt to taste

Soak the red chilies in 1 tablespoon of the vinegar for 10 minutes. Drain.

In a mini food processor or blender, process the chilies, garlic and cumin seeds to a paste. Add the remaining 1/2 cup vinegar and process to a thin paste.

Rinse the flounder and pat dry on paper towels. Place the flounder in a shallow dish and rub the chili paste on both sides. Cover and marinate for 20 minutes. Meanwhile, heat the oil in a non-stick skillet over moderate heat. Add the onions and cook for 2 minutes.

Reduce the heat to low. Add 2 tablespoons of water. Cook until the onions are golden brown, about 10 to 15 minutes. Add the flounder and cook on both sides until the fish almost flakes, about 2 to 3 minutes on each side. Remove from the pan and serve.

YIELD: 4 servings.

245 Calories per serving:
42 G Protein   163 MG Sodium
 5 G Fat   99 MG Cholesterol
 7 G Carbohydrate

Inspired by Kyrus Vazifidar, Air India, Detroit, MI, formerly from Bombay.

Barbecued Ginger Shrimp

JHINGA ADRAKI

⤳⤳⤳

This recipe represents Indian-style barbecued shrimp and it easily translates to the Western kitchen.

2 tablespoons peeled, chopped
   fresh ginger
2 teaspoons chopped garlic
1/2 teaspoon salt
2 tablespoons fresh lemon juice
3/4 cup nonfat plain yogurt
3/4 teaspoon red pepper powder

1 teaspoon ground carom, *ajwain*
1 teaspoon ground coriander
1 teaspoon olive oil
1-1/2 pounds large shrimp, peeled,
   washed and deveined
1 lemon cut into wedges

In a mini food processor or blender, process the ginger, garlic, salt and lemon juice to a paste.

In a bowl combine the paste mixture, yogurt, red pepper powder, carom, coriander and olive oil. Add the shrimp and toss to cook. Cover and marinate for 30 minutes.

Preheat the charcoal grill. Thread the marinated shrimp onto skewers, leaving about 3/4 inch between each shrimp. When the coals are gray and very hot, grill the shrimp, basting with the marinade, for 1 to 2 minutes per side, or until the shrimp are just pink and opaque. Serve with lemon wedges.

YIELD: 4 to 6 servings.

170 Calories per serving:
29 G Protein
3 G Fat
6 G Carbohydrate
607 MG Sodium
250 MG Cholesterol

Inspired by Inder Dhawan, Executive Chef, The Oberoi, New Delhi.

Shrimp in Spiced Sauce

JHINGA SAMURKUNDH

༺৩৩৩৩৩༻

Here is an easily prepared, spicy north Indian shrimp dish.

1/2 cup low-fat cottage cheese
1/2 cup skim milk
2 teaspoons canola oil
1 small onion, chopped
1 tablespoon peeled, minced fresh
   ginger
1 tablespoon minced garlic
1 teaspoon red pepper powder
1 tablespoon *garam masala*
   (page 43)

1 teaspoon ground coriander
1 teaspoon ground turmeric
1/2 teaspoon salt
1 pound medium shrimp, peeled
   and deveined
2 tablespoons tomato paste
2 tablespoons chopped fresh
   coriander leaves

In a blender or food processor, combine the cottage cheese and skim milk. Process until thoroughly blended and a creamy consistency.

Heat the oil in a non-stick skillet over moderate heat. Add the onion, ginger and garlic. Stir until softened. Add the red pepper, *garam masala*, coriander, turmeric and salt to the pan and stir to mix. Cook over moderate heat for 1 to 2 minutes to blend the spices. Add the shrimp and tomato paste. Cook, stirring, for 2 minutes. Add the chopped coriander leaves and cottage cheese mixture and cook until the shrimp are pink and opaque and the sauce heated through. Serve.

YIELD: 4 servings.

165 Calories per serving:

24 G Protein	649 MG Sodium
4 G Fat	168 MG Cholesterol
8 G Carbohydrate	

Inspired by Sous Chef Kalum Kumar Channa, Tandoor Restaurant.

Spiced Shrimp

JHINGA BALCHAO

Goa's food is full of color and zest and always made hot with the addition of chilies! It was the Portuguese who introduced the chili to India when they first arrived in the 16th century, and it has become a fixture of many of the subcontinent's cuisines. If you prefer a less spicy dish, reduce the dried red chilies. Serve with plenty of rice!

1/2 teaspoon minced fresh green
  chilies
10 dried red chilies
1/2 teaspoon cumin seeds
4 green cardamom pods
1 teaspoon cloves
2 teaspoons chopped garlic
1 tablespoon plus 2 teaspoons
  chopped fresh ginger
2 tablespoons malt vinegar

1 teaspoon ground cinnamon
1 teaspoon ground turmeric
1/2 teaspoon ground black pepper
2 teaspoons olive oil
1/2 cup chopped onions
1/4 cup chopped ripe tomatoes
1 pound medium shrimp, peeled
  and deveined
8 fresh curry leaves
Salt to taste

In a mini food processor or blender, process the green and red chilies, cumin seeds, cardamoms, cloves, garlic, ginger and vinegar to a paste. Add the cinnamon, turmeric and pepper to the paste. Process until combined. Set aside.

Heat the oil in a non-stick saucepan. Add the onions and sauté for 2 minutes. Add 2 tablespoons water. Reduce the heat and cook until golden brown, about 20 minutes. Add the tomatoes. Cook, stirring for 1 minute. Add the paste mixture and cook, stirring, for 2 to 3 minutes. Add the shrimp and cook, stirring, until the shrimp are pink and opaque, about 3 to 5 minutes. Add the curry leaves and salt to taste. Serve.

YIELD: 4 servings with other dishes.

172 Calories per serving:
 22 G Protein   263 MG Sodium
  4 G Fat   166 MG Cholesterol
 11 G Carbohydrate

Inspired by Peter Goes, Goan chef, The Oberoi, Bagmado Beach, Goa.

Spicy Stir-Fried Shrimp, Mangalore Style

MEEN VARUVAL MANGALORE

∿✃✄

1 pound medium shrimp, peeled
  and deveined
1/2 teaspoon ground turmeric
1–2 teaspoons red pepper powder
1/2 teaspoon mustard powder

1 teaspoon fresh lime juice
2 teaspoons canola oil
2 tablespoons chopped green
  onions
Salt to taste

Rinse and pat shrimp dry on paper towels. In a bowl, combine the turmeric, red pepper powder, mustard and lime juice. Add the shrimp and toss to coat. Cover and marinate for 30 minutes.

Heat the oil in a non-stick wok or skillet. Add the shrimp and stir-fry the shrimp for 2 minutes. Add the green onions and stir-fry until the shrimp are pink and opaque. Add salt to taste.

YIELD: 4 servings.

112 Calories per serving:
 18 G Protein   221 MG Sodium
  4 G Fat   166 MG Cholesterol
  1 G Carbohydrate

VEGETABLES

Nowhere in the world has the art of vegetarian cooking developed more fully than in southern India. Religious beliefs and scarce supplies of meat have combined to ensure a rich repertoire of vegetarian dishes. Of course, similar dishes are considered essential parts of the daily diet throughout the rest of the country.

A large array of spices and herbs, yogurt and coconut add to the succulence of the extremely fresh vegetables. Only those vegetables in season are used. In India, frozen vegetables would not be a consideration; however, I have used them quite successfully here in the United States to make quickly prepared dishes.

A vegetarian meal should consist of two or three vegetable dishes from this chapter, the usual yogurt salad (raita), a dal, a rice dish, bread and chutney. Once you have tried some of these splendid vegetable dishes, you may be surprised to find yourself depending less on meat and more on vegetables.

Green Beans, Southern Style,   KARI SEM
Spiced Green Beans   MASALA SEM
Spiced Broccoli and Tomatoes   HARI SABZI TAMATAR
Cabbage Porial   GOBHI PORIAL
Cabbage and Carrot Porial   GOBHI GAAJAR PORIAL
Carrot and Green Pea Porial   GAAJAR MATAR PORIAL
Stir-Fried Cauliflower   GOBHI BHUNA
Cauliflower Porial   GOBHI PORIAL
Roasted Eggplant Purée with Seasoned Yogurt
BAINGAN BHARTA
Roasted Eggplant and Red Peppers with Spiced
Yogurt   BAINGAN BHARTA TAKARI
Eggplant and Spinach   BAINGAN AUR SAAG
Stuffed Eggplant   BHARVAN BAINGAN
Eggplant Topped with Tomato Sauce and
Coriander-Flavored Yogurt   BADAL JAAM
Stuffed Green Peppers with Velvet Yogurt Sauce
BHARVAN SIMLA MIRCH
Stir-Fried Okra   BHUNA BHINDI
Spiced Potatoes Coondapur   BATATE MASALA COONDAPUR
Cumin-Flavored Potatoes   JEERA ALOO
Potato Curry, Bangalore Style   ALOO PALYA
Fiery Potatoes Smothered with Onions   ALOO PYAZ
Potatoes with Green Onions   ALOO PYAZ KA SABZI
Potatoes, Cauliflower and Peas   ALOO GOBHI MATAR
Potatoes, Green Peas and Tomatoes
ALOO MATAR TAMATAR
Curried Potatoes, Carrots and Green Beans,
Bangalore Style   SABZI PORIAL BANGALORE
Potatoes, Spinach and Tomatoes   ALOO PAALAK TAMATAR
Fragrant Spinach   PAALAK KA SAAG
Stir-Fried Spinach   BHUNA SAAG
Plantain Porial   VAZHAKKAI PORIAL
Savory Stuffed Tomatoes   BHARVAN TAMATAR
Mixed Vegetables in Yogurt Sauce   AVIAL
Mixed Vegetables, New Delhi Style   BHUNA SABZI
Vegetable Medley, Parsi Style   PARSI SABZI
Chettinad Vegetable Curry with Crunchy Urad Dal
KAI KARI MANDI

Green Beans, Southern Style

KARI SEM

A simply prepared, tasty green bean dish. You may use fresh green beans from your garden, if you prefer.

1 tablespoon olive oil
1/2 teaspoon black mustard seeds
1 large onion, chopped
1 fresh green chili, seeded and chopped
1 16-ounce bag frozen French-cut green beans, defrosted and drained

1 teaspoon *sambar masala* (page 42)
1 tablespoon ground coconut
1/2 tablespoon fresh lemon juice
Salt to taste

Heat the oil in a non-stick wok or skillet over moderate heat. Add the mustard seeds and stir-fry until they crackle. Add the onion and cook, stirring, for 2 minutes. Add 2 tablespoons water. Reduce the heat to low. Cook, stirring occasionally, until the onions are golden brown, about 10 to 15 minutes. Add the chopped chili, green beans, and *sambar masala*. Stir-fry until the beans are heated through. Add the coconut and cook, stirring, for 30 seconds. Add the lemon juice and salt to taste. Stir to combine. Serve.

YIELD: 6 servings with other dishes.

66 Calories per serving:
2 G Protein
3 G Fat
9 G Carbohydrate
41 MG Sodium
0 MG Cholesterol

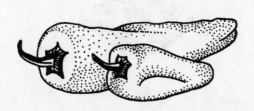

Spiced Green Beans

MASALA SEM

In this recipe I rely on fresh beans rather than frozen. Green beans are easily available fresh all year long.

2 teaspoons olive oil
1 teaspoon cumin seeds
1 dried red chili, crushed
1 tablespoon minced garlic
1-1/2 pounds green beans, trimmed and cut into 3/4-inch lengths

1/2 teaspoon salt
1/2 teaspoon sugar
1 tablespoon plus 2 teaspoons fresh lemon juice
Freshly ground black pepper to taste

Heat the oil in a non-stick wok or skillet. Add the cumin seeds and stir for 5 seconds. Add the red chili and cook until light brown. Add the garlic and cook, stirring, until the garlic turns light brown. Add the green beans, salt and sugar and stir-fry for about 1 to 2 minutes. Reduce the heat to medium-low. Add 1/2 cup of water. Cook the beans, covered, stirring occasionally, for about 5 to 10 minutes until they are tender and have absorbed all the liquid in the pan. Add lemon juice and the black pepper. Stir. Serve.

YIELD: 6 servings.

62 Calories per serving:
3 G Protein
2 G Fat
11 G Carbohydrate
196 MG Sodium
0 MG Cholesterol

Spiced Broccoli and Tomatoes

HARI SABZI TAMATAR

൙ᴄᴂ

The marvelous intermingling of ginger and red pepper powder combined with the vivid colors of broccoli and tomatoes is stunning in this easily prepared dish. I often stir-fry the dish, let it cool and serve it at room temperature. It is perfect for a buffet served at room temperature or chilled.

1 pound fresh broccoli
3 plum tomatoes, peeled and
  seeded
1–2 tablespoons olive oil
1 tablespoon peeled, shredded
  fresh ginger root

1/8 teaspoon red pepper powder, or
  to taste
Salt and freshly ground pepper to
  taste

Separate the broccoli heads into small florets. Peel and slice the stems. Blanch the florets and stems in boiling salted water for 3 to 4 minutes or until crisp-tender. Drain. Refresh in cold water. Drain thoroughly and set aside. Cut the tomatoes lengthwise into eighths. Set aside.

Heat the oil in a non-stick wok or skillet. Add the ginger and stir-fry for a few seconds. Add the broccoli, tomatoes and red pepper powder. Stir-fry for 2 to 3 minutes or until the vegetables are heated through. Add 1 to 2 tablespoons of water and continue to stir-fry for about 30 seconds. Serve hot, at room temperature or chilled.

YIELD: 4 to 6 servings.

83 Calories per serving:
  6 G Protein   57 MG Sodium
  4 G Fat   0 MG Cholesterol
  8 G Carbohydrate

Cabbage Porial

GOBHI PORIAL

❦

After lecturing at the Institute for Hotel Management and Catering Technology in Madras, this dish was one of many vegetarian delights served to me by their chefs. It is easily prepared, light and delicious.

2 teaspoons canola oil
1 teaspoon black mustard seeds
1 teaspoon seeded, chopped fresh green chilies
12 fresh curry leaves (optional)
2 teaspoons split *urad dal*

2 teaspoons split *chana dal*
1 small cabbage, about 1 pound, cored, trimmed and finely shredded
1/4 teaspoon salt, or to taste

Heat the oil in a non-stick wok or skillet over moderate heat. Add the mustard seeds and cook, stirring, until they crackle. Add the chilies, curry leaves, if desired, and *urad dal*. Stir for 1 minute. Add the *chana dal* and stir until both *dals* are a golden brown. Add the cabbage. Mix well. Reduce the heat. Add 2 tablespoons of water. Cover and cook until the cabbage is tender, about 4 to 5 minutes. Add salt to taste. Serve.

YIELD: 4 servings.

70 Calories per serving:
3 G Protein
3 G Fat
10 G Carbohydrate
165 MG Sodium
0 MG Cholesterol

Cabbage and Carrot Porial

GOBHI GAAJAR PORIAL

～◌◌～

Here is an easy, light, "perky" twist to vegetables, contrasting sour cabbage, sweet carrots and spicy chilies. Serve hot or at room temperature with both Indian and Western meals

1/4 teaspoon minced fresh ginger	1/2 head cabbage, finely shredded
1/4 teaspoon minced garlic	4 medium carrots, peeled and
2 teaspoons olive oil	grated
1 tablespoon black mustard seeds	1/2 teaspoon ground turmeric
1/2 medium onion, chopped	1/2 teaspoon salt, or to taste
2 fresh green chilies, cut into	2 tablespoons ground coconut
1-inch pieces	2 tablespoons fresh lime juice

In a mini food processor or blender, process the ginger and garlic to a smooth paste, adding 1 tablespoon water if necessary.

Heat the oil in a non-stick saucepan over moderate heat. Add the mustard seeds and cook, stirring, until they crackle, about 3 to 4 seconds. Add the onion and chilies and cook, stirring, until translucent. Add the ginger and garlic paste. Stir for 10 seconds. Add the cabbage, carrots, turmeric and salt. Stir-fry for 3 to 4 minutes. Cover, reduce the heat and simmer until vegetables are tender, approximately 5 to 10 minutes. Uncover and continue cooking until all the moisture has evaporated. Add the coconut and stir for 1 to 2 minutes. Add the lime juice and stir. Serve with rice and curry.

128 Calories per serving:
3 G Protein	342 MG Sodium
6 G Fat	0 MG Cholesterol
18 G Carbohydrate	

Inspired by Kitty Basith, Willowbrook, IL, formerly from Bangalore.

Carrot and Green Pea Porial

GAAJAR MATAR PORIAL

༄ঌৎৰ

Highlighted by a touch of chili, mustard seeds, nutty *urad* and *chana dals* and coconut, this dish, typical of a Chettinad combination, is a winner! Chef Ramnath says that coconut, traditionally used in home-cooking, is often omitted today. With today's busy lifestyle, there is little time for grating it. However, it is always used on special occasions. Enjoy this with a Western or Indian meal.

2 teaspoons canola oil
2 teaspoons black mustard seeds
2 teaspoons split *urad dal*
2 teaspoons split *chana dal*
   (optional)
1/4 cup chopped onion
2–4 fresh green chilies, slit in half

12 fresh curry leaves (optional)
1/2 cup cooked, cubed carrots
1/2 cup cooked green peas
2 tablespoons coconut (optional)
Salt to taste
1 tablespoon chopped fresh
   coriander leaves

Heat the oil over moderate heat in a large non-stick saucepan. Add the mustard seeds and stir until they crackle, about 5 seconds. Add the *urad dal* and stir until golden brown. Add the *channa dal*, if desired. Stir for 10 seconds or until golden. Add the onion, chilies and curry leaves, if desired. Stir-fry until the onion is translucent. If necessary, add 1 to 2 tablespoons of water to prevent the onions from burning. Add the cooked carrot and green peas. Stir-fry for 30 seconds to blend flavors. Add the coconut, if desired, and stir until combined. Add salt to taste. Garnish with coriander leaves.

YIELD: 4 servings.

ADVANCE PREPARATION: Cook the dish until the addition of the coconut. Add coconut and reheat prior to serving. Garnish with chopped coriander.

COOK'S TIP: Substitute frozen carrots and green peas.

128 Calories per serving:
   3 G Protein   342 MG Sodium
   6 G Fat   0 MG Cholesterol
  18 G Carbohydrate

Inspired by Chef C. S. Ramnath, Windsor Manor, Bangalore.

Stir-Fried Cauliflower

GOBHI BHUNA

A delicious, simply prepared stir-fry.

2 teaspoons vegetable oil	1/2 teaspoon turmeric
2 dried red chilies	2 teaspoons sugar
1 tablespoon white poppy seeds	1/2 teaspoon salt, or to taste
4 cups small cauliflower florets	

Heat the oil in a large non-stick skillet over moderate heat. Add the chilies and poppy seeds.

Cook, stirring, until the chilies are beginning to brown, about 10 seconds. Stir in the cauliflower and sprinkle with the turmeric. Stir-fry for 2 minutes. Add 2 to 4 tablespoons of water. Cover and cook for 10 to 15 minutes, or until the cauliflower is almost cooked. Add the sugar and salt to taste. Remove the cover and cook, stirring, for 2 minutes. Serve.

YIELD: 4 to 6 servings.

75 Calories per serving:
 3 G Protein
 4 G Fat
 9 G Carbohydrate
         319 MG Sodium
           0 MG Cholesterol

Inspired by Anna Sanyal, Darien, Il. formerly of Calcutta.

Cauliflower Porial

GOBHI PORIAL

~~~

This delectable, easily prepared dish contains a lot of chilies. However, it is not as hot as you might think, as the chilies are left whole, so that their heat does not escape. The pleasant subtle combination of chilies combined with cauliflower is remarkably flavorful.

2 teaspoons olive oil
1 teaspoon black mustard seeds
6 fresh curry leaves (optional)
1-1/2 teaspoons split *urad dal*
6 fresh green chilies

2 whole dried red chilies
4 cups small cauliflower florets
1/4 teaspoon salt, or to taste
1 teaspoon coconut (optional)

Heat the oil in a non-stick wok or large skillet over medium heat. Add the mustard seeds and stir until they crackle. Add the curry leaves, if desired, and the *urad dal* and stir until it turns light brown. Add the green and red chilies and cook until the red chilies start to darken.

Stir in the cauliflower. Cook, stirring, for 1 to 2 minutes. Add the salt. Add about 6 tablespoons water gradually. (The amount of water needed will depend upon the age of the cauliflower.) Reduce the heat to low. Add the coconut, if desired. Stir. Cover and cook for 5 minutes or until the cauliflower is tender. Remove the cover. If any liquid remains, continue cooking until evaporated. Serve immediately.

YIELD: 4 to 6 servings

85 Calories per serving:
 4 G Protein   161 MG Sodium
 3 G Fat   0 MG Cholesterol
11 G Carbohydrate

Inspired by Praveen Anand, Executive Chef, Dakshin Restaurant, Park Sheraton, Madras.

Roasted Eggplant Purée with Seasoned Yogurt

BAINGAN BHARTA

❧❧❧

Before gas was a part of the Indian kitchen, the heat for cooking was provided by wood and coal. Never to waste any source of energy, the Indians slowly roasted vegetables, such as eggplant, in the ashes while other food cooked over the flame.

Eggplant *Bharta*, an Indian national favorite, has many variations. Rich in vitamins and minerals, it is colored with many exciting nuances and is a delightful addition to both Indian and Western meals. When served hot, its sparkling combination of spices combined with the smoky flavor of the eggplant is sensational. It is equally tasty when served at room temperature or cold with any flatbread, thin cracker or even as a sandwich spread.

1 medium eggplant, about
   1–1-1/4 pounds
1 tablespoon olive oil
1–2 fresh green chilies, seeded
   and minced
1 teaspoon cumin seeds
2/3 cup chopped onion
1 cup chopped ripe tomato

1 teaspoon ground coriander
1/2 teaspoon salt, or to taste
2 tablespoons chopped fresh mint
   leaves
2 tablespoons chopped fresh
   coriander leaves
1/2 cup nonfat plain yogurt
1 teaspoon *garam masala* (page 43)

Preheat the oven to 450°F.

Prick the surface of the eggplant 7 or 8 times with a fork. Over a moderate gas flame, char the eggplant, turning it frequently, until all the skin has blackened and blistered. Line a baking sheet with foil. Place the eggplant on the baking sheet and bake in the middle of the oven until very soft. Cool slightly. Carefully scrape off most of the charred skin and discard. Coarsely chop the flesh.

Heat the oil in a large non-stick skillet over moderate heat. Add the green chilies and cumin seeds. Stir until the cumin seeds darken, about 20 to 30 seconds. Add the onion and stir-fry until translucent. Add the tomato, eggplant, coriander and salt to taste. Cook, stirring often, until the mixture is a dry, coarse purée, about 10 minutes. Fold in the mint, coriander, yogurt and *garam masala*. Serve hot as part of an Indian meal or cold with any flatbread.

YIELD: 4 to 6 servings.

ADVANCE PREPARATION: Prepare 1 to 2 days ahead. Refrigerate, covered. Reheat gently. Do not let the dish come to a boil.

COOK'S TIP: The eggplant skin may also be charred in the oven. Place the eggplant on a foil-lined tray in a 500°F. oven. Roast the eggplant, turning occasionally, until the skin is charred and blistered all over and the flesh soft. This should take approximately 20 minutes.

101 Calories per serving:
- 4 G Protein   316 MG Sodium
- 4 G Fat   1 MG Cholesterol
- 15 G Carbohydrate

Inspired by Mrs. Bachi Karkaria, Food Editor, Times of India, Bombay.

Roasted Eggplant and Red Peppers with Seasoned Yogurt
BAINGAN BHARTA TAKARI

྾྾྾

Here is a variation of an Indian national favorite, *Baingan Bharta*, which may be served hot as a side dish with a meal, at room temperature or chilled as an appetizer with flatbread or crackers, or as a spread for whole wheat toast. It can even be used as a stuffing for halved pita bread sandwiches. It is best if made a day or two ahead to give the flavors time to heighten.

1 eggplant, about 1–1-1/4 pounds
2 red bell peppers, about 1 pound
1/3 cup nonfat plain yogurt
1 tablespoon chopped fresh mint
  leaves
1 tablespoon chopped coriander
  leaves

1–2 teaspoons seeded, chopped
  fresh green chilies
1 teaspoon dry roasted cumin seeds
1 teaspoon ground coriander
1 teaspoon *garam masala* (page 43)
1/2 teaspoon salt

Preheat the oven to 450°F. Prick the surface of the eggplant 7 or 8 times with a fork. Over a moderate gas flame, char the eggplant, turning it frequently, until all the skin has blackened and blistered. Line a baking sheet with foil. Place the eggplant on the baking sheet and bake in the middle of the oven until very soft. Cool slightly. Carefully scrape off most of the charred skin and discard. Coarsely chop the flesh.

Char the peppers over the flame until blackened and blistered. Place the peppers in a covered pan or in a heavy-duty self-sealing plastic bag. Seal. Let peppers stand 15 minutes. Peel and discard the skins. Halve, seed and cut the peppers into 1-inch pieces. Let cool.

In a bowl, whisk together the yogurt, mint and coriander. In a food processor or blender, combine the chilies, eggplant, peppers, cumin and coriander. Process to a coarse paste. Fold the eggplant mixture and the *garam masala* into the yogurt mixture. Add salt to taste. Serve hot, at room temperature or chilled.

YIELD: 4 to 6 servings.

ADVANCE PREPARATION: Prepare ahead completely. Refrigerate for 1 to 2 days, covered.

VARIATIONS:
  1. Char the eggplant and peppers under the broiler.
  2. Char the eggplant on the barbecue grill.
  3. Cook charred eggplant in a microwave oven until soft.

61 Calories per serving:
  3 G Protein   306 MG Sodium
  1 G Fat   0 MG Cholesterol
13 G Carbohydrates

Inspired by Barchi J. Karkaria, Food Editor, Times of India, Bombay.

Eggplant and Spinach

BAINGAN AUR SAAG

～∽～

Eggplant and spinach complement each other perfectly. Indians tend to cook vegetables longer than we do. If you wish to recreate the dish authentically, cook the eggplant and spinach until almost a purée.

1 medium eggplant, about 1–1/4 pounds, cut into 3/4-inch cubes
2 teaspoons minced fresh ginger
2 teaspoons minced garlic
1/4 cup chopped onion
4 fresh green chilies, slit in half
1/2–1 teaspoon red pepper powder

3/4 pound spinach, washed and trimmed
1/8 teaspoon ground asafetida
2 tablespoons chopped fresh coriander leaves
1/4 teaspoon salt, or to taste
1 teaspoon fresh lemon juice

In a large saucepan, combine the eggplant, ginger, garlic, onion, chilies, red pepper powder and 1 cup of water and cook over moderate heat until the eggplant is tender. Add the spinach, asafetida and coriander leaves. Cook, stirring, for 1 minute or until the spinach is wilted. Add salt to taste and lemon juice. Serve.

YIELD: 4 to 6 servings.

ADVANCE PREPARATION: Prepare 1 day ahead. Reheat gently prior to serving.

78 Calories per serving:
 5 G Protein   220 MG Sodium
 1 G Fat   0 MG Cholesterol
16 G Carbohydrate

Inspired by Mrs. A. Mullens, Principal, Institute of Hotel Management Catering Technology & Applied Nutrition, Madras.

Stuffed Eggplant

BHARVAN BAINGAN

∽◡∾

Two choice Indian favorites, eggplant and Minced Lamb with Peas (page 110), are combined in an elegant and beautifully seasoned preparation.

2 cups Minced Lamb with Peas
(page 110)
3 small eggplants, cut in half
lengthwise

1 egg white, lightly beaten
1 cup fresh bread crumbs
Olive oil spray

Preheat the oven to 325°F.

Prepare the Minced Lamb with Peas. If there is excess liquid in the pan, uncover and cook until it has been absorbed.

Using a grapefruit spoon or sharp knife, carefully scoop out the eggplant pulp leaving only the shell. Finely chop the pulp and add it to the precooked Minced Lamb with Peas, if desired. Otherwise, save it for another dish. Fill each eggplant half with the mixture, mounding it above the side of the shells. Brush the top with the beaten egg white. Sprinkle the bread crumbs over the top of the filling.

Place the eggplants, stuffing side up, on a baking sheet. Mist with olive oil spray. Bake for 15 minutes. Turn off the heat and let the eggplant remain in the oven for 10 minutes. Serve hot.

YIELD: 6 servings.

163 Calories per serving:
  10 G Protein   186 MG Sodium
   4 G Fat   15 MG Cholesterol
  24 G Carbohydrate

Eggplant Topped with Tomato Sauce and Coriander-Flavored Yogurt

BADAL JAAM

৵৽৹

Here is a sumptuous and colorful eggplant delicacy, topped with a garlicky tomato sauce and crowned with creamy, coriander-flavored yogurt. Serve it with both Western and Indian meals. It makes a superb appetizer as well as a vegetable course during dinner.

2-1/4 cups nonfat plain yogurt
3 small eggplants, about 1-1/2 pounds
Olive oil spray
2 teaspoons olive oil
1/3 cup minced onion
1/4 cup minced garlic
1 tablespoon minced fresh ginger

2-1/4 pounds ripe tomatoes, peeled, seeded and chopped
1/2–1 teaspoon red pepper powder
Salt to taste
3 tablespoons chopped fresh coriander leaves
1 tablespoon fresh lime juice

Place the yogurt in a sieve over a bowl. Let the yogurt drain in the refrigerator for 3 hours or until reduced by half.

Preheat the oven to 425°F. Trim eggplants and cut into 1/4-inch thick slices. Lightly brush or mist a non-stick baking sheet with oil. Arrange the eggplant slices in a single layer. Lightly brush the eggplant with oil. Bake in the oven for 25 minutes, turning the slices once, until lightly browned.

Meanwhile heat the 2 teaspoons of oil in a non-stick saucepan over moderate heat. Add the onion and sauté until lightly browned. Add the ginger, all but 1 tablespoon of the garlic, and stir for 1 minute. Add 2 tablespoons of water and sauté until the onions are golden brown. Add the tomatoes, red pepper powder and salt, to taste. Cook, mashing the tomato until the mixture has reduced to a thick sauce. Remove the eggplant from the oven. Reduce the temperature to 350°F.

Mound a spoonful of the tomato mixture on each baked eggplant slice. Tightly cover the baking sheet with foil and bake for 5 minutes more. Meanwhile, whisk the yogurt in a bowl until smooth and creamy. Stir in the coriander, remaining 1 tablespoon of garlic and lime juice.

To serve, transfer the eggplant slices to a serving platter. Place a dollop of yogurt topping on each slice. Serve remaining yogurt as a side dish.

YIELD: 6 to 8 servings.

ADVANCE PREPARATION: Prepare the tomato sauce 1 day ahead. Roast the eggplant several hours ahead. Finish cooking prior to serving.

211 Calories per serving:
12 G Protein   158 MG Sodium
4 G Fat   3 MG Cholesterol
38 G Carbohydrate

Inspired by K. Karmarkar, Executive Chef, Quality Inn Green Park, Hyderabad.

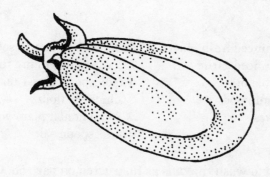

Stuffed Green Peppers with Velvet Yogurt Sauce

BHARVAN SIMLA MIRCH

~~~

Stuffed peppers reach a new height when laced with a velvety sauce of Indian spices and yogurt. In this Rajasthani vegetarian delicacy, the peppers are usually pan-fried until blistered and brown. However, Executive Chef Mohideen bakes them. He likes to use *khoya*, milk that is boiled down to the thickness of heavy cream, but said that nonfat yogurt is a good substitute. The amount of stuffing will vary according to the size of the pepper therefore, the stuffing yields are approximate.

2 tablespoons split *chana dal*
2 tablespoons split *toor dal*
1/2 teaspoon ground turmeric
4 green bell peppers, halved and seeded
1-1/2 cups mashed potatoes
4 teaspoons nonfat plain yogurt
1–2 teaspoons seeded, minced fresh green chilies

3 tablespoons minced fresh coriander leaves
1-1/2 teaspoon minced fresh ginger
1/2 teaspoon salt
1 teaspoon *garam masala* (page 43)
2-1/4 teaspoons olive oil

VELVET SAUCE:
2/3 teaspoon minced fresh ginger
2/3 teaspoon minced garlic
1 teaspoon canola oil
5 green cardamom pods
2 large bay leaves
6 cloves

2/3 teaspoon cumin seeds
2/3 teaspoon ground turmeric
1 tablespoon plus 1 teaspoon chickpea flour
2/3 cup nonfat plain yogurt
1/4 teaspoon salt

Clean, sort and wash the *dals* as instructed on page 55. Combine the *dals* in a bowl and soak for 3 to 5 hours. Drain. In a non-stick saucepan put both the *dals*, turmeric and enough water to cover by 1 inch. Bring the water to a boil. Reduce the heat and simmer, covered, for about 20 to 30 minutes, stirring occasionally. The *dals* should be tender and plump. If necessary, add 2 to 3 tablespoons water to prevent burning. Drain.

Preheat the oven to 350°F. Blanch the pepper halves in the boiling water for 2 minutes. Remove and drain.

In a bowl, combine the *dals*, mashed potatoes, yogurt, chilies, 2 teaspoons of the coriander leaves, ginger, *garam masala* and 1 teaspoon of the olive oil. Mix well. (The mixture should be on the dry side.) Divide the filling between the pepper halves.

Lightly brush a baking dish with a little olive oil. Place the peppers in the dish, barely touching. Lightly brush the stuffing with olive oil. Bake the peppers for 20 to 30 minutes, or until fork-tender. Do not overcook.

SAUCE: In a mini food processor or blender, process the ginger and garlic with 4 tablespoons of water to make a smooth paste. Heat 1 teaspoon of canola oil in a small, non-stick skillet over moderate heat. Add the cardamom pods, bay leaves, cloves and cumin. Stir for about 20 seconds. Add the ginger and garlic paste and stir for 20 seconds. Add the turmeric and chickpea flour and stir for 1 minute. Add the yogurt, 2 tablespoons at a time, stirring constantly. Simmer for 3 minutes. Add salt to taste and additional water if necessary. Remove from the heat. Pour the sauce over each cooked pepper half. Garnish with the remaining coriander leaves.

YIELD: 4 to 8 servings.

ADVANCE PREPARATION: Prepare stuffing and peppers 1 day in advance. Stuff peppers several hours prior to baking. Cover with plastic wrap and chill in the refrigerator.

103 Calories per serving:
  5 G Protein   352 MG Sodium
  2 G Fat   1 MG Cholesterol
 17 G Carbohydrate

Inspired by G. Sultan Mohideen, Executive Chef, Rajputana Palace, Jaipur.

Stir-Fried Okra

BHUNA BHINDI

෴

Okra is gently stir-fried with onions and enhanced with turmeric and red pepper powder in this enticing, easily prepared dish.

1 tablespoon olive oil
1 onion, thinly sliced
1/2 teaspoon ground turmeric
1/2 teaspoon red pepper powder

1 pound fresh okra, trimmed and
    cut into 1/2-inch slices
Salt to taste
2 teaspoons tomato paste

Heat the oil in a non-stick skillet. Add the onion and stir-fry until translucent. Add the turmeric and red pepper powder. Stir for about 15 seconds. Add the okra slices and salt. Stir. Cover and reduce the heat to a simmer. Cook for about 8 to 10 minutes, or until the okra is tender. Add the tomato paste, stir to combine. Cook for 1 minute more. Serve.

YIELD: 6 servings with other dishes.

59 Calories per serving:
  2 G Protein   28 MG Sodium
  2 G Fat   0 MG Cholesterol
  8 G Carbohydrate

Inspired by Suman Sood, Registered Dietitian; President, Club of Indian Woman, Chicago, formerly of New Delhi.

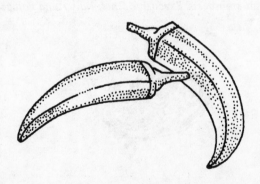

Spiced Potatoes Coondapur

BATATE MASALA COONDAPUR

～∽⌒∽

Here is an excellent potato dish from Coondapur in the southern state of Karnataka. The delightful south Indian combination of chili, coriander, fenugreek and mustard seeds is a perfect foil for the lightly browned potatoes. Chef Namrath says it is important that the potatoes be allowed to cool for 3 to 4 hours after boiling so that they keep their firm texture during shallow-frying. This dish will be a winner at both Western and Indian meals alike!

4 medium potatoes, boiled in the skin and cooled
2/3 teaspoon chopped garlic
1 dried red chili
1 teaspoon coriander seeds
1/4 teaspoon black peppercorns
1/4 teaspoon fenugreek seeds
1/4 teaspoon ground turmeric
1 tablespoon canola oil
1 teaspoon black mustard seeds
1/2 cup chopped onion
10 fresh curry leaves
Salt to taste

Peel the cooked potatoes and cut them into 3/4-inch cubes.

In a mini food processor or blender, process the garlic and 1 tablespoon water to a paste.

Roast the chili, coriander seeds, peppercorns and fenugreek seeds in a dry pan over moderate heat, stirring, for about 30 seconds or until fragrant. Process the mixture to a powder in a spice grinder or blender. Stir in the turmeric. Set aside.

Heat 2 teaspoons of the oil in a non-stick skillet over medium heat. Add the mustard seeds and cook until they crackle, about 5 seconds. Add the onion and stir-fry until very lightly browned. Add the garlic paste and cook, stirring, for about 30 seconds. Add the remaining 1 teaspoon of oil. Add the potatoes and curry leaves. Stir for 2 minutes or until the potatoes have a few light brown spots on them. If the potatoes stick to the pan, add 1 tablespoon water to prevent burning. Add the roasted ground spice mixture. Stir for 30 seconds or until fragrant. Add salt to taste.

YIELD: 4 servings.

ADVANCE PREPARATION: Cook the potatoes 1 day ahead. Peel and cube prior to cooking.

168 Calories per serving:
  3 G Protein   42 MG Sodium
  4 G Fat   0 MG Cholesterol
 31 G Carbohydrate

Inspired by Chef C. S. Ramnath, Windsor Manor, Bangalore.

Cumin-Flavored Potatoes

JEERA ALOO

Here is a delightfully easy potato dish your family will savor with both Western and Indian foods. My family enjoys it prepared with small red potatoes. The delicate skins add a little texture to the dish, but if you prefer, remove them. If you use larger new potatoes, cook them whole and remove the skins when cool.

This is an ideal dish for entertaining as it can easily be doubled or tripled and is flavorful when served hot or at room temperature.

4 medium potatoes, boiled in the skins and cooled
2 teaspoons vegetable oil, preferably mustard oil
1/2 teaspoon black mustard seeds
1-1/2 teaspoons cumin seeds

1/4 teaspoon ground turmeric
2 teaspoons ground coriander
1/4–1/2 teaspoon red pepper powder
2 teaspoons minced fresh ginger
1–2 dried red chilies

TEMPERING:
2 teaspoons olive oil
2 teaspoons peeled, minced fresh ginger
2 dried red chilies
1/2–1 teaspoon seeded, minced fresh green chili

2 teaspoons ground coriander
1/4–1/2 teaspoon red pepper powder
2 teaspoons minced fresh ginger
1–2 dried red chilies

Peel the potatoes and cut into 1-1/2-inch cubes. Heat the oil to smoking point in a non-stick saucepan. Allow to cool slightly. Add the mustard seeds and cook, stirring, until they crackle. Add the cumin seeds, turmeric, coriander, red pepper powder, ginger and red and green chilies. Cook, stirring, for about 30 to 45 seconds. Add the cooked potatoes. Stir, tossing, for about 1 to 2 minutes.

TEMPERING: Heat the oil in a small non-stick skillet. Add the ginger, red and green chilies. Stir for 20 seconds or until the chilies have darkened. Add the coriander leaves and mix well. Sprinkle with the lime juice. Spoon the potatoes into a serving dish and sprinkle the ginger and chili mixture on top. Serve hot or room temperature.

YIELD: 4 servings.

ADVANCE PREPARATION: Prepare the dish 1 day ahead. Refrigerate, covered. Bring to room temperature and reheat gently. Add the coriander leaves, lime juice and tempered mixture when serving.

VARIATION: Substitute small red potatoes, cooked until fork-tender. Cut potatoes in half or quarters depending upon size of potato.

186 Calories per serving:
    4 G Protein   16 MG Sodium
    3 G Fat   0 MG Cholesterol
  37 G Carbohydrate

Inspired by Sudha Mehrotra, Calcutta.

Potato Curry, Bangalore Style

ALOO PALYA

~~~

Here is a subtly spiced potato dish with a hint of spirit.

2 teaspoons olive oil
1 teaspoon black mustard seeds
1 medium onion, coarsely chopped
3 medium potatoes, peeled, cut
   into 1/2-inch cubes and soaked
   in water for 10 minutes

2–3 fresh green chilies, cut in
   3 pieces
2 teaspoons minced fresh
   coriander leaves
1/2 teaspoon salt
2 tablespoons fresh lime juice

Heat the oil in a large non-stick skillet over medium heat. Add the mustard seeds and cook, stirring, until they begin to crackle. Add the onion. Sauté the onion until translucent, stirring, about 2 to 3 minutes. Drain the potatoes and pat dry on paper towels. Add the potatoes, turmeric, chilies, coriander leaves and salt to the skillet. Stir for 2 minutes. Add 1/2 cup of water. Stir. Cover and cook over low heat until the potatoes are tender, about 8 to 10 minutes, stirring occasionally to prevent burning. Sprinkle the lime juice over the potatoes and serve.

YIELD: 4 to 6 servings.

ADVANCE PREPARATION: Prepare 1 day ahead. Reheat when serving. Sprinkle with lime juice when serving.

COOK'S TIP: If you prefer a spicier dish, mince the chilies.

138 Calories per serving:
  3 G Protein   296 MG Sodium
  3 G Fat   0 MG Cholesterol
26 G Carbohydrate

Inspired by Kitty Basith, Willowbrook, IL, formerly of Bangalore.

Fiery Potatoes Smothered with Onions

ALOO PYAZ

∽✑∽

Potatoes laced with red onions, chilies and nutty *urad* and *chana dal* is a favorite vegetarian dish in Madras, according to Saroja Subbaraman. She suggests cutting down on the red pepper powder for a less fiery dish. The potatoes have a wonderful ability to enhance the flavors of the other ingredients. This dish is delightful with any meal, but Saroja serves it with Mixed Vegetables in Yogurt Sauce (page 207), Spicy, Tomato-Flavored Lentil Broth, Madras Style (page 95), Spicy Vegetable and Lentil Stew (page 261) and Green Pepper and Yogurt Salad (page 268) as part of her Sunday vegetarian banana-leaf meal.

For best results, the cooked potatoes should be completely cooled before being added to the dish. I usually cook them a day ahead, refrigerate them and peel them prior to cooking.

4 medium potatoes, boiled in the skin and cooled
1-1/2 tablespoons olive oil
2 teaspoons black mustard seeds
2 cups peeled, sliced red onions
8 fresh curry leaves (optional)
2 teaspoons split *urad dal*
2 teaspoons split *chana dal*

1 teaspoon ground turmeric
1–3 teaspoons red pepper powder
1/2 teaspoon salt
1–2 fresh green chilies, seeded and minced (optional)
2 tablespoons fresh lime juice

Peel and cut the potatoes into 1-inch cubes.

Heat the oil in a non-stick pan over moderate heat. Add the mustard seeds and cook, stirring, until they crackle. Add the onions and curry leaves, if desired, and stir until the onions are soft, about 3 to 4 minutes. Add the *urad dal* and cook 1 minute until lightly browned. Add the *chana dal* and cook until golden. Add the turmeric and red pepper powder. Stir for 30 seconds. Add the cooked potatoes and toss to combine. Continue stirring and tossing for another 2 minutes. Add the salt, green chilies and 1/2 cup of water. Cover and cook for 5 minutes, stirring occasionally. Sprinkle with lime juice.

YIELD: 4 to 6 servings.

ADVANCE PREPARATION: Cook the dish one day ahead. Refrigerate, covered. Reheat gently and add the lime juice prior to serving.

223 Calories per serving:
  5 G Protein   302 MG Sodium
  6 G Fat   0 MG Cholesterol
 39 G Carbohydrate

Inspired by Saroja Subbaraman, Madras.

Potatoes with Green Onions

ALOO PYAZ KA SABZI

❧❧❧

Delicately spiced potatoes are made more interesting with the addition of colorful green onions. Serve with Whole Wheat Bread (page 300) or use as an alternative stuffing for Potato-Stuffed Bread (page 304).

1 tablespoon canola oil
1/2 teaspoon cumin seeds
1/2 teaspoon ground turmeric
3 medium potatoes, peeled and cut into 3/4-inch cubes
12 green onions, sliced into 1/4-inch pieces

Salt to taste
1/4 teaspoon red pepper powder
3/4 teaspoon ground coriander
1 tablespoon fresh lemon juice

Heat the oil in a large non-stick skillet over moderate heat. Add the cumin seeds and stir until darkened, about 2 seconds. Add the turmeric and cook for 2 to 3 seconds. Add the potatoes and toss to coat with the spices and oil. Add 2 tablespoons of water. Cover and reduce the heat to low. Cook for 10 minutes.

Add the green onions, salt to taste, red pepper powder and coriander to the pan. Stir to mix thoroughly. Add more water if necessary to prevent the potatoes from sticking to the pan and burning. Cover, increase the heat to medium. Continue cooking, stirring occasionally, until the potatoes are cooked, about 5 to 6 minutes. If any liquid remains in the pan, uncover and stir until the potatoes are dry. Add the lemon juice and serve.

YIELD: 4 servings.

ADVANCE PREPARATION: Prepare ahead completely. Reheat when serving.

130 Calories per serving:
  3 G Protein   44 MG Sodium
  4 G Fat   0 MG Cholesterol
22 G Carbohydrate

Potatoes, Cauliflower and Peas

ALOO GOBHI MATAR

~~⁓⁓~~

An attractive, colorful north Indian entrée highlighted with a touch of Kashmiri spices, this dish is traditionally served during north Indian banquets and weddings. You may vary the combination of vegetables by substituting green beans, zucchini, green peppers and/or mushrooms.

1 cup cauliflower florets
2 medium potatoes, peeled and cut
   into 1/2-inch cubes
1-1/2 cups fresh green peas or
   10 ounces frozen green peas
1/2 teaspoon ground turmeric
1 teaspoon ground cumin
3/4 teaspoon red pepper powder

1 teaspoon ground coriander
2 teaspoons canola oil
1-1/2 cups finely chopped ripe
   tomatoes
Salt to taste
2 tablespoons chopped fresh
   coriander leaves

Cook the cauliflower, potatoes and fresh peas, separately, in boiling water until almost tender. Drain each vegetable and set aside to dry on paper towels.

In a bowl combine the turmeric, cumin, red pepper powder and coriander. Heat the oil in a large non-stick skillet over moderate heat. Add the spice mixture to the pan. Stir-fry for about 5 seconds to release the flavors. Add the cauliflower, potatoes and peas, if using fresh peas, and stir-fry until they are very lightly browned. Add the tomatoes and continue cooking over low heat for 1 to 2 minutes, crushing the tomatoes with the back of a spoon. Add about 1/4 cup of water. Reduce the heat to low. If using frozen peas, add at this stage. Cover and cook, stirring occasionally, for about 3–4 minutes or until the vegetables are tender. Add salt to taste. Garnish with coriander leaves. Serve.

YIELD: 4 servings

ADVANCE PREPARATION: Prepare ahead and reheat.

158 Calories per serving:
  6 G Protein   197 MG Sodium
  3 G Fat   0 MG Cholesterol
29 G Carbohydrate

Inspired by Sous Chef Kalum Kumar Channa, Tandoor Restaurant.

Potatoes, Green Peas and Tomatoes

ALOO MATAR TAMATAR

⤷∽⤶

The bright colors of turmeric yellow potatoes, red ripe tomatoes and green peas made fragrant by mellow spices make this dish good party fare.

2 medium potatoes, peeled and cut
  into 1/4-inch cubes
2 teaspoons vegetable oil
2 teaspoons minced fresh ginger
1 clove garlic, minced
1 teaspoon cumin seeds
1–2 dried red peppers
1/2 teaspoon ground turmeric

3/4 cup frozen peas, defrosted
1 cup chopped ripe tomatoes
1/2 teaspoon salt, or to taste
Freshly ground black pepper
1–2 tablespoons chopped fresh
  coriander leaves
1 lemon, cut into wedges

Soak the potatoes in water for 15 minutes. Drain the potatoes and pat dry on paper towels. Heat the oil in a non-stick saucepan over medium heat. Add the ginger, garlic, cumin seeds and red peppers. Cook until the garlic and ginger are fragrant and the red pepper has slightly darkened, about 10 seconds. Add the potatoes and turmeric. Stir-fry until the potatoes are lightly browned, about 2 to 3 minutes. Add 1/2 cup of boiling water and bring the mixture to a boil. Reduce the heat, cover and simmer over low heat until potatoes are almost cooked, about 10 minutes. Add the peas and tomatoes and continue cooking for 2 to 4 minutes or until heated throughout, stirring very gently. Season with salt and pepper to taste. Garnish with chopped coriander leaves. Serve with lemon wedges.

YIELD: 4 servings.

117 Calories per serving
  4 G Protein
  3 G Fat
 20 G Carbohydrate
164 MG Sodium
  0 MG Cholesterol

Inspired by Anna Sanyal, Darien, IL, formerly from Calcutta.

Curried Potatoes, Carrots and Green Beans, Bangalore Style

SABZI PORIAL BANGALORE

Carrots, potatoes and green beans are lightly stir-fried in spices to enhance the rich succulent flavors in this tangy, spicy coconut-flavored dish. Kitty Basith serves it with *chapatis* but said it is also delicious with whole-grain toast. Accompany the dish with a *dal* and yogurt salad. It is also a delightful accompaniment to a Western meal.

2 medium potatoes, peeled and cut into 1/4-inch cubes
2 teaspoons olive oil
1 tablespoon black mustard seeds
1/4 teaspoon minced fresh ginger
1/4 teaspoon minced garlic
1/2 medium onion, chopped
2 fresh green chilies, sliced into 1/4-inch pieces

2 carrots, peeled and cut into 1/4-inch pieces
15 green beans, cut into 1/4-inch pieces
1/2 teaspoon ground turmeric
1/2 teaspoon salt, or to taste
2 tablespoons coconut
1–2 tablespoons fresh lime juice

Soak the potatoes in water for 15 minutes. Drain and pat dry on paper towels. In a large non-stick skillet, heat the oil over moderate heat. Add the mustard seeds and cook until they crackle, about 10 seconds. Add ginger, garlic, onion and chilies. Stir until the onion is translucent. Add the carrots, potatoes, green beans, turmeric and salt. Stir-fry for 3 to 4 minutes. Add 1/4 cup water and bring to a boil. Stir, cover and simmer for 5 to 10 minutes, or until the vegetables are tender. Remove the lid. If there is any liquid in pan, cook until evaporated. Add the coconut and stir-fry for 2 minutes. Sprinkle the lime juice over the vegetables and serve.

YIELD: 4 servings.

Cook's Tip: Be sure to cut the vegetables into even size pieces so they cook evenly.

165 Calories per serving:
 4 G Protein   324 MG Sodium
 6 G Fat   0 MG Cholesterol
26 G Carbohydrate

Inspired by Kitty Basith, Willowbrook, IL, formerly of Bangalore.

Potatoes, Spinach and Tomatoes

ALOO PAALAK TAMATAR

∽ఎౡ∾

A colorful medley of potatoes, spinach and tomatoes commingled with Indian spices and a touch of chili provides a winning combination for any meal.

2 medium potatoes, boiled in the skins and cooled
1 12-ounce bag fresh spinach, trimmed and washed
2 teaspoons olive oil
1-1/2 teaspoons cumin seeds
2 medium onions, halved and finely sliced
2 cloves garlic, sliced
1 tablespoon chopped fresh ginger

2 cups chopped ripe tomatoes
1 teaspoon ground turmeric
1/2–1 teaspoon red pepper powder
1 tablespoon ground coriander
Salt to taste
3/4 teaspoon *garam masala* (page 43)
2 tablespoons finely chopped fresh coriander leaves

Peel the potatoes and cut them into 1/2-inch cubes. In a large pan of boiling water, blanch the spinach for 30 seconds or until wilted. Drain and refresh in cold water. Squeeze as much moisture from the leaves as possible. Coarsely chop the spinach and set aside.

Heat the olive oil in a non-stick skillet over medium heat. Add the cumin seeds and stir-fry until they turn medium brown, about 20 seconds. Add the onions, garlic and ginger. Stir for 5 minutes. Add the tomatoes, turmeric, red pepper and coriander. Add salt to taste. Cook for 5 minutes. Add the potatoes and the spinach and mix well, stirring until most of the liquid has evaporated. Stir in the *garam masala*. Sprinkle with coriander leaves and serve.

YIELD: 6 servings.

129 Calories per serving:
  5 G Protein   206 MG Sodium
  3 G Fat   0 MG Cholesterol
  25 G Carbohydrate

Fragrant Spinach

PAALAK KA SAAG

ᢙᢌᠭᠣ

While this appears to be a hot dish, don't let the amount of chilies and garlic deceive you. When chilies and garlic are left whole, they take on a new dimension and impart subtle heat and pungency. This dish is not hot and gives spinach an exciting new twist. Swiss chard is also excellent when prepared this way.

2 12-ounce bags fresh spinach,   1/2 teaspoon cumin seeds
  trimmed and washed   1/2 teaspoon salt, or to taste
2 teaspoons olive oil   3 tablespoons chopped fresh
10 cloves garlic, sliced into   coriander leaves
  1/4-inch slivers   Olive oil spray (optional)
5 dried red chilies

In a large saucepan of boiling water blanch the spinach in batches for 30 seconds or until just wilted. Drain and refresh in cold water. Squeeze the moisture from the leaves, finely chop and set aside.

Heat the oil over medium heat in a non-stick skillet. Add the cumin seeds and stir-fry for 5 seconds. Add the garlic and stir-fry for about 1 minute or until softened but not browned. Add the chilies and stir until lightly browned, about 30 seconds. Add the blanched spinach to the pan, toss well, and sauté until heated through and hardly any liquid remains in the pan, about 1 to 2 minutes. Season with salt. Sprinkle with coriander. Mist the spinach with olive oil spray, if desired. Serve hot.

YIELD: 6 servings

56 Calories per serving:
  4 G Protein   257 MG Sodium
  2 G Fat   0 MG Cholesterol
  7 G Carbohydrate

Inspired by Inder Dhawan, Executive Chef, The Oberoi, New Delhi.

Stir-Fried Spinach

BHUNA SAAG

∽◡∾

This is a splendid way to serve spinach.

1-1/4 pounds fresh spinach,   1 teaspoon black mustard seeds
   trimmed and washed   2–3 dried red chilies (optional)
2 teaspoons mustard or vegetable   3/4 teaspoon minced garlic
   oil   Salt to taste

Heat the oil in a large, non-stick skillet over moderate heat. (If using mustard oil, heat to smoking point. Remove from heat to let cool slightly. Return the pan to the heat. Add the mustard seeds and stir until they crackle, about 5 seconds. Add the chilies and stir until they turn several shades darker. Add the garlic and stir for about 15 seconds. Add the spinach and stir-fry for 3 to 4 minutes or until the spinach has wilted. Pour off any excess liquid. Season to taste and serve warm, at room temperature or cold.

YIELD: 4 servings.

53 Calories per serving:

4 G Protein	101 MG Sodium
3 G Fat	0 MG Cholesterol
5 G Carbohydrates	

Plantain Porial

VAZHAKKAI PORIAL

~✍~

This flavorsome dish from Mangalore has an interesting variety of flavors combining the starch of plantains, tang of tamarind, spice of curry powder, heat of chilies and a touch of coconut. Plantains are large, green-skinned cooking bananas with a higher starch than sugar content. They are available in most supermarkets or Hispanic markets.

1 1/2-inch piece tamarind pulp
3 green plantains, peeled and cut
    into 1/2-inch pieces
1/2 teaspoon ground turmeric
Salt to taste

1–2 fresh green chilies, slit
    lengthwise
1 tablespoon Madras curry powder
1 tablespoon ground coconut

TEMPERING:

2 teaspoons black canola oil
1 teaspoon mustard seeds
2 teaspoons split *urad dal*
2 dried red chilies

1/4 teaspoon ground asafetida
    (optional)
5 fresh curry leaves (optional)

Place the tamarind pulp in a bowl. Pour 3/4 cup of hot water over the pulp and soak for 15 minutes. Mash the pulp with a spoon or with your fingers. Pour the tamarind and the liquid into a sieve and strain into a small bowl, squeezing out as much of the liquid as possible. Discard the fibers.

Place the tamarind juice, plantain, turmeric and salt to taste in a saucepan. Add water to cover by 1 inch. Bring to a boil, reduce the heat to low and cook, covered, until the plantain is tender and the liquid evaporated. Add the green chilies, curry powder and coconut. Cook, stirring, for 1 minute. Remove from the heat.

TEMPERING: Heat the oil in a small non-stick skillet. Add the mustard seeds and cook until they crackle. Add the remaining tempering ingredients and cook, stirring, until the *urad dal* is light brown and the chilies have darkened.

Add the tempered ingredients to the cooked plantain. Return to the heat and cook for 1 to 2 minutes to blend flavors. Serve hot with rice.

YIELD: 4 servings.

ADVANCE PREPARATION: Cook the plantain mixture to the tempering stage. Refrigerate 1 to 2 days. When serving, prepare tempering and add the plantains.

235 Calories per serving:
4 G Protein	53 MG Sodium	
5 G Fat	0 MG Cholesterol	
50 G Carbohydrate		

Savory Stuffed Tomatoes

BHARVAN TAMATAR

⊸⚬⚭⚬⊷

Baked stuffed tomatoes provide an elegant and easy appetizer or vegetable for both Indian and Western meals. Select firm but perfectly ripe tomatoes.

6 medium ripe tomatoes
1 garlic clove, halved
1 tablespoon canola oil
3/4 cup minced onion
1 medium potato, peeled and diced
1–2 fresh green chilies, seeded and
  minced

1 teaspoon tomato purée
1/2 pound medium shrimp,
  peeled, deveined and coarsely
  chopped
1/2 teaspoon salt
18 coriander leaves

Wash and dry tomatoes. Cut off a thin slice from the stem end of each tomato. Using a spoon or small knife, carefully scoop out the pulp. Chop finely and place in a bowl. Invert the tomatoes on a rack to drain for about 15 minutes. Pat dry the inside of the tomatoes with a paper towel. Rub the inside of the tomatoes with the garlic. Preheat the oven to 400°F.

Heat the oil in a non-stick wok or skillet over moderate heat. Add the onion and potato. Stir-fry for about 2 minutes. Add the chilies and tomato purée. Stir-fry for 2 minutes. Add the shrimp and tomato pulp. Cook over low heat for 4 to 6 minutes, stirring occasionally. Add salt to taste.

Spoon the filling into the tomato cups, about 2 tablespoons for each tomato, being careful not to pack the filling.

Lightly brush a large baking pan with oil. Place the tomatoes in the baking pan and bake for 15 to 20 minutes. Garnish the top of each tomato with 3 coriander leaves.

YIELD: 6 servings.

ADVANCE PREPARATION: Prepare filling 1 day in advance. Stuff 3 to 4 hours prior to cooking.

93 Calories per serving:
 7 G Protein   198 MG Sodium
 3 G Fat   43 MG Cholesterol
11 G Carbohydrate

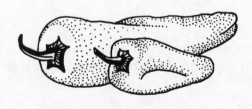

Mixed Vegetables in Yogurt Sauce

AVIAL

∽∾∽

For me, no dish is more typical of Madras than this one. Enticingly simple, colorful fresh vegetables are combined with a vivid masala and tasty yogurt sauce. Saroja Subbaraman, a vegetarian, serves this every Sunday for her family get together over a banana-leaf lunch. She often adds local vegetables in season: green plantains and mangoes, or drumstick, a long, thin Indian vegetable tasting somewhat like asparagus. As side dishes, she serves Fiery Potatoes Smothered with Onions (page 195), Spicy Vegetable and Lentil Stew (page 261), Cucumber and Yogurt Salad (page 271) and Yogurt Rice (page 227).

2 medium carrots, about 6 ounces, peeled and cut into 1/4-inch strips
1 cup green beans, about 6 ounces, cut into 2-inch lengths
1 medium yam, about 6 ounces, peeled and cut into 1/4-inch inch strips
1 medium zucchini, about 6 ounces, cut into 1/4-inch strips

1 small green, red or yellow bell pepper, about 6 ounces, seeded and cut into 1/4-inch strips
1 teaspoon ground turmeric
6–8 fresh curry leaves (optional)
1/3 cup ground coconut
2–3 fresh green chilies, seeded and minced
1/2 cup plain lowfat yogurt
Salt to taste

In a large saucepan combine the carrots, green beans, yam, zucchini, bell pepper, turmeric, curry leaves, if desired, and 1 cup of water. Bring to a boil. Reduce the heat to low and simmer, covered, for 10 minutes or until the vegetables are just tender and have absorbed all the liquid. If the dish becomes too dry, add more water. It is important that the vegetables retain their firm texture.

In a bowl whisk the coconut, chilies and yogurt until smooth. Add this mixture to the cooked vegetables in the pan. Gently stir to mix, adding salt to taste. Cover and simmer over low heat until yogurt mixture is warm, stirring occasionally. Serve.

YIELD: 6 to 8 servings.

ADVANCE PREPARATION: Cook the vegetables and prepare the yogurt mixture several hours ahead. When serving, combine the cooked vegetables and yogurt mixture in the saucepan. Cover. Simmer on low heat until the yogurt is warm and the flavors have blended.

COOK'S TIP: To reduce the fire of the chilies, use whole chilies in place of minced chilies.

102 Calories per serving:
  3 G Protein   51 MG Sodium
  3 G Fat   0 MG Cholesterol
 17 G Carbohydrate

Inspired by Saroja Subbaraman, Madras.

Mixed Vegetables, New Delhi Style

BHUNA SABZI

∽✑

This is an easily prepared, colorful stir-fry. Choose vegetables of your choice, including frozen vegetables.

2 teaspoons chopped fresh ginger
2 teaspoons chopped garlic
2 teaspoons canola oil
1 large onion, chopped
2 green bell peppers, seeded and cut into 1-inch cubes
1/2 pound broccoli, cut into 1-inch florets
1/2 pound cauliflower, cut into 1-inch florets

2 large ripe tomatoes, cut into 1-inch cubes
1/2–1 teaspoon red pepper powder
1/2 teaspoon ground turmeric
2 tablespoons white wine vinegar
2 tablespoons tomato purée
Salt and freshly ground black pepper to taste

In a mini-food processor or blender, process the ginger, garlic and 1 tablespoon water to a paste. Set aside.

Heat oil in a non-stick skillet or wok over moderate heat. Add the onion and ginger and garlic paste. Stir until the onion is translucent. Add the remaining vegetables. Stir-fry for about 5 minutes. Add the red pepper powder, turmeric and vinegar. Stir in the tomato purée and simmer for 4 to 5 minutes or until the vegetables are tender. Season to taste with salt and freshly ground pepper.

YIELD: 4 to 6 servings.

VARIATION: If using frozen vegetables. Heat the oil. Add the defrosted vegetables to the onion mixture and stir for 1 minute. Add the remaining seasonings and simmer until the vegetables are cooked.

100 Calories per serving:
5 G Protein   73 MG Sodium
3 G Fat   0 MG Cholesterol
17 G Carbohydrate

Vegetable Medley, Parsi Style

PARSI SABZI

ᐯᑌᑕᐯ

Here is a magnificent, tangy, hot and sweet vegetable dish from the Parsis of Bombay.

1 tablespoon canola oil
1/2 pound russet potatoes, peeled and cut into 1/2-inch cubes
1/2 pound sweet potatoes, peeled and cut into 1/2-inch cubes
2 medium carrots, peeled and cut into 1/2-inch cubes
1 medium onion, about 4 ounces, chopped

3 tablespoons chopped fresh coriander leaves
2 fresh green chilies, slit in half
1/2 cup white wine vinegar
1 teaspoon sugar
Salt to taste
1 cup frozen peas
8 cherry tomatoes

Heat the oil in a non-stick wok or large saucepan over moderate heat. Add the potatoes, carrots and onion. Stir-fry for 3 to 4 minutes or until the onion is translucent. Add the coriander and green chilies. Stir to combine. Add the vinegar, sugar and salt to taste. Cover and simmer until the vegetables are tender. Add the frozen peas and cherry tomatoes. Cook for about 3 minutes or until the peas and cherry tomatoes are cooked. Serve hot with an Indian bread and Green Pepper and Yogurt Salad (page 268).

YIELD: 8 servings.

ADVANCE PREPARATION: Prepare 1 day ahead. Refrigerate covered. Reheat prior to serving.

103 Calories per serving:
  3 G Protein   47 MG Sodium
  2 G Fat   0 MG Cholesterol
19 G Carbohydrates

Inspired by Kyrus Vazifidar, Air India, Detroit, formerly of Bombay.

Chettinad Vegetable Curry with Crunchy Urad Dal

KAI KARI MANDI

⤜∽⤛

This typical vegetarian dish from the Chettiar community of south India is made even more tasty with the added nutty flavor of *urad dal*, black-eyed peas and tart tamarind. In typical Chettinad cuisine, the vegetables would be cooked for 30 minutes until very soft. I have adapted the recipe to produce tender cooked vegetables. This is delightful with other dishes such as Pepper Chicken, Chettinad Style (page 129) or when served alone as a light meal with Indian breads or toast.

In addition to the shallots, any combination of vegetables may be used so that the total amount is approximately 2 cups. I have chosen cauliflower, carrots, okra and plantain for a colorful presentation. Other vegetables commonly used are pumpkin, beans, peas, eggplant, potato, sweet potatoes, all root vegetables and any others that are not watery. Traditionally, the vegetables are cooked in the water in which *basmati* rice is soaked, known as *mandi*. You may substitute plain water. The black-eyed peas add another dimension to the flavor, but may be omitted if you do not have time for soaking and cooking them.

1/2 cup dried black-eyed peas
1-inch piece of tamarind pulp
2 teaspoons chopped garlic
1 tablespoon canola oil
1 tablespoon split *urad dal*
2 teaspoons fenugreek seeds
8 fresh curry leaves
8 shallots, peeled and cut into
  quarters
1/2 cup cauliflower, cut in 1-inch
  florets

1/2 cup carrots, cut into 2-inch
  shreds
1/2 cup okra, trimmed and cut
  into 1-inch pieces
1/2 cup plantains, cut into 1-inch
  slices
4–6 fresh green chilies, seeded and
  cut into 1/4-inch pieces
Salt to taste

TEMPERING:
2 teaspoons canola oil
10 fresh curry leaves

2–4 dried red chilies

Sort and wash the black-eyed peas as described on page 55. Soak the black-eyed peas in water for 8 hours or overnight. Drain. Add water to cover and bring to a boil. Reduce the heat and simmer, covered, for about 1-1/2 hours or until tender. Drain.

Place the tamarind pulp in a bowl. Pour 1/3 cup hot water over the tamarind pulp and soak for 15 minutes. Mash the pulp with a spoon or with your fingers. Pour the tamarind liquid into a sieve and strain into a small bowl, squeezing out as much of the liquid as possible. Discard the fiber.

In a mini food processor or blender, process the garlic and 1 tablespoon water to a paste.

Heat the oil in a large non-stick saucepan. Add the drained black-eyed peas and sauté for 1 to 2 minutes. Add *urad dal* and cook for 1 minute. Add the fenugreek seeds, curry leaves, if desired, and cook, stirring constantly, until the fenugreek seeds begin to crackle and the *urad dal* turns golden brown, about 2 to 3 minutes. Add the garlic paste and shallots. Stir for 1 to 2 minutes. Add the cauliflower, carrots, okra, plantains and chilies. Add the rice soaking water or plain water to cover the vegetables by about 1 inch. Cook the vegetables until tender to the bite. Add the tamarind liquid. Stir to mix. Simmer for 30 seconds to combine flavors. Season to taste with salt if desired.

TEMPERING: Heat the oil in a non-stick pan. Stir-fry the curry leaves and chilies until the chilies are reddish-brown. Pour over finished dish.

YIELD: 6 servings with other dishes.

ADVANCE PREPARATION: Prepare the dish 1 day ahead. Refrigerate or freeze, covered. Temper the dish prior to serving.

210 Calories per serving:
  10 G Protein   41 MG Sodium
   6 G Fat   0 MG Cholesterol
  30 G Carbohydrate

Inspired by K. Natarajan, Executive Chef, Raintree Chettinad Restaurant, Madras.

RICE

Rice is the staple food in two-third's of India. Each region has created scores of rice dishes, every one varying in taste and texture.

In the south, rice is part of every meal; however, in the north, not every meal will include rice, as bread often takes its place. In this chapter, I have concentrated on rice preparations that illustrate how it may be cooked in a multitude of ways: From plain-steamed as an accompaniment, to the elaborate *biryanis*, where it is combined with exotic spices.

All recipes were tested with the best *dehradun basmati*, which grows in the foothills of the Himalayas. You may substitute any long-grain rice, but it will not be as delicate and naturally perfumed as *basmati* rice. For detailed information on rice, see page 51.

Lamb Biryani, Dum Pukht Style
KACHCHI GOSHT BIRYANI

Lamb Biryani, Hyderabad Style
GOSHT BIRYANI HYDERABADI

Lamb Biryani, Parsi Style   ALOO DAR

Chicken Biryani, Hyderabad Style
MURGH BIRYANI HYDERABADI

Fragrant Lemon Rice   ELUMICHAMPAZHAM SADAM

Piquant Lime Rice   ELUMICHAMPAZHAM SADAM

Yogurt Rice   MASURU ANNA

Tomato Rice   TAMATAR BHAT

Vegetable Pilaf   TEHARI PULLAO

Spiced Rice with Lentils   KICHRI

Spiced Rice with Lentils, Parsi Style   KICHRI PARSI

Savory Rice and Green Pea Pilaf
MASALA HARI MATAR PULLAO

Sweet Saffron Pilaf   ZARDA PULLAO

Lamb Biryani, Dum Pukht Style

KACHCHI GOSHT BIRYANI

∾◡◠∾

Biryani, an elaborate layered meat and *basmati* rice pilaf, is usually made with the best ingredients. It is considered one of the most festive dishes in India with the best *basmati* rice, the most exotic spices and herbs and the finest meat incorporated. The final flourish to this magnificent dish is the garnish of edible silver leaf, *vark*. This type of *biryani*, considered a Mughlai classic art form, originated in Avadh, or what is today the Lucknow District of the state of Utter Pradesh. The following *Kachchi Gosht Biryani* is the creation of Master Chef Mohammed Imtiaz Qureshi, the illustrious scion of a family of master chefs. He now presides over Dum Pukht Restaurant, New Delhi, where he taught me how to make this dish.

In the Avadh version, the *biryani* is prepared by layering partially cooked rice and uncooked meat in a casserole and adding aromatic flavorings, such as saffron, green cardamom and mint. Traditionally, lots of clarified butter, *ghee*, tops the *biryani*, but I have chosen to mist the dish with extra-virgin olive oil, adding a fruity flavor to the *biryani*, with good results.

The entire dish is then steamed by the *dum* method. The cooking vessel is topped by a tight-fitting cover (traditionally sealed with dough around the edges to prevent steam from escaping during the cooking process) and put on very low heat to allow the *biryani* to cook slowly in the perfumed vapor. Master Chef Qureshi covers the entire dish with dough to seal in the juices. I have devised a simpler version, which is to cover the finished dish with foil before putting the cover on the dish. The *dum* process allows the *basmati* rice to relax completely, permitting it to expand to its fullest so that each grain develops exquisite texture and enhances the flavors of the meat and elegant seasonings. Serve with Spiced Yogurt Salad (page 266).

1 cup nonfat plain yogurt
4 teaspoons chopped fresh ginger
2 teaspoons chopped garlic
2 teaspoons red pepper powder
2 teaspoons black cumin
3/4 teaspoon ground turmeric
2 pounds lamb, 1/2-inch loin
 chops, trimmed of all fat
2 cups *basmati* or other long
 grained rice
4 green cardamom pods
6 cloves
Salt to taste
1/2 teaspoon ground cardamom

1/4 teaspoon ground mace
1 onion, halved and thinly sliced
3 fresh green chilies, halved and
 seeded
14 fresh mint leaves
1 teaspoon saffron threads, soaked
 in 4 tablespoons warm water for
 at least 20 minutes
Extra-virgin olive oil spray
2 tablespoons dry roasted slivered
 pistachios
2 3-inch squares silver leaf, *vark*
 (optional)

Place the yogurt in a sieve over a bowl. Cover and allow to drain for 3 hours or overnight in the refrigerator. Discard the liquid. Whisk the yogurt until smooth and creamy.

In a mini food processor or blender, process 2 teaspoons of the chopped ginger, the garlic and 2 tablespoons of water to a paste. Combine the paste mixture with the red pepper powder, black cumin, 1/2 teaspoon of the turmeric and the yogurt. Place the lamb in a shallow dish and pour the yogurt mixture over the lamb. Coat the meat with the mixture. Cover and marinate for 2 hours or overnight in the refrigerator.

Sort, wash and soak the rice as described on page 51. Drain the rice. Bring 8 cups of water to a boil in a non-stick saucepan. Stir in the drained rice. Add the cardamom pods, cloves and salt to taste. Cover with a tight lid. Reduce the heat to low and simmer gently for 5 minutes or until the rice is half cooked. The rice should retain a slim, hard, inner core. Drain the rice.

Preheat the oven to 350°F. Place the marinated lamb chops in a single layer in a non-stick casserole. Sprinkle the ground cardamom and mace, remaining 1/4 teaspoon turmeric, the onion slices, green chilies, remaining 2 teaspoons ginger and half of the mint leaves over the lamb.

Spread half the partially cooked rice over the lamb. Rub the saffron threads between your fingers to extract all of the flavor. Drizzle half the saffron liquid over the rice. If the rice appears dry, sprinkle with 2 to 3 tablespoons of water. Mist very lightly with olive oil spray. Top with the remaining rice. Drizzle the remaining saffron liquid over the rice. Mist very lightly with olive oil spray. Garnish with pistachios, remaining mint leaves and silver leaf, *vark*. Seal the casserole tightly with aluminum foil. Cover tightly with a lid. (If there is not a tight seal, weigh down the cover.) Cook the *biryani* in the middle of the oven for 45 minutes to 1 hour. Test to see if lamb chops are cooked. Quickly cover. Turn off the oven. Let the *biryani* rest in the oven for an additional 10 minutes before serving.

YIELD: 8 servings with other dishes.

ADVANCE PREPARATION: Marinate the meat 1 day ahead. Refrigerate. On day of serving, cook the rice, assemble the *biryani* and bake.

VARIATION: For a richer *biryani*, drizzle clarified butter, *ghee*, over the middle layer of rice and the top of the dish. Omit the olive oil spray.

495 Calories per serving:
  38 G Protein   463 MG Sodium
  17 G Fat   104 MG Cholesterol
  46 G Carbohydrate

Inspired by Master Chef Mohammed Imtiaz Qureshi, Dum Pukht Restaurant, Maurya Sheraton, New Delhi.

Lamb Biryani, Hyderabad Style

GOSHT BIRYANI HYDERABADI

∼✺∼

While the Mughals of the north served their elaborate *biryanis*, the wealthy nizams of Hyderabad in the south served their own ostentatious style of *biryani*. Expert cooks will argue for hours about their particular recipe and each fervently extol the virtues of their local embellishments and style of cooking.

In Hyderabad, the meat is marinated and cooked until it becomes tender. Layers of partially cooked *basmati* rice and the cooked meat are combined with exotic flavorings, such as saffron, black cumin, *shahi jeera*, mint and lots of clarified butter, *ghee*. Again, by using olive oil spray as a substitute, I have found this *biryani* to be quite delightful. The end result, fragrant with saffron, and unexpectedly subtle considering the elaborate *masalas*, is garnished with fried onions, green peas, toasted pistachios and mint. Delicate and delicious, it is an elegant blending of two unsophisticated ingredients. Serve with Tomato and Yogurt Salad (page 269) and Mint-Coriander Chutney (page 285).

When cooking in the *dum* manner, the rice on the bottom cooks first while the rice on top of the layered *biryani* steams. Executive Chef Talwar cooks his *biryani* in the traditional manner over a charcoal fire. His *biryani* is placed in a deep handleless pan, *pateela*. The flat lid *dhakkan* is then sealed to the pan with dough so that no steam escapes. The sealed pan is placed on the coal-fueled fire and hot coals are positioned on top of the lid so that the steam does not condense and the *biryani* cooks and steams at the same time.

1 cup nonfat plain yogurt
1 tablespoon plus 1 teaspoon chopped fresh ginger
1 tablespoon chopped garlic
2 teaspoons ground turmeric
1-1/4 teaspoons red pepper powder
1/4 cup chopped fresh coriander leaves
1 pound lamb, preferably from the leg, trimmed of fat, cut into 1-1/2 inch pieces
2 cups *basmati* or other long-grained rice
1 tablespoon plus 2 teaspoons canola oil
1/2 cup sliced onion
2 teaspoons seeded, minced fresh green chilies

3 tablespoons fresh lemon juice
16 fresh mint leaves
Olive oil spray
6 cloves
4 green cardamom pods
1 3-inch cinnamon stick
1 teaspoon salt, or to taste
2 teaspoons saffron threads, soaked in 4 tablespoons warm water for 20 minutes
1/4 cup frozen peas, defrosted
2 tablespoons pistachio slivers, toasted
2 3-inch squares silver leaf, *vark* (optional)

Place the yogurt in a sieve over a bowl. Allow the yogurt to drain for 3 hours or overnight in the refrigerator. Discard liquid. Whisk the yogurt until smooth and creamy.

In a mini food processor or blender, process the ginger, garlic and 2 tablespoons water to a paste. In a bowl combine half of the ginger and garlic paste, 1 teaspoon of the turmeric, 3/4 teaspoon of the red pepper powder and half of the coriander leaves. Place the lamb in a bowl and rub in the mixture. Allow the lamb to marinate for 2 hours or overnight in the refrigerator.

Sort, wash and soak the rice as described on page 51. Drain.

Preheat the oven to 325°F. Heat 1 teaspoon of the oil in a large non-stick skillet over moderate heat. Add the onions and cook, stirring, for 2 minutes. Reduce the heat to low, add 2 tablespoons water and cook, stirring, until the onions are crisp and brown. Be careful not to burn. Remove the onions and drain on paper towels.

Heat 1 tablespoon of the oil in the pan. Add the lamb mixture, remaining ginger and garlic paste, remaining turmeric and red pepper powder. Cook, stirring, until the meat is lightly brown on all sides. Add half of the browned onions, the green chilies, yogurt and lemon juice. Cook, stirring, for 2 minutes. Add 1/2 cup of water and bring to a boil. Reduce the heat to low and cook the meat, covered, until very tender, about 1-1/2 to 2 hours. Stir the meat occasionally to keep the sauce from sticking and burning. If the sauce evaporates during cooking, add a little more water. When the lamb is cooked, it should have just enough sauce to coat the meat pieces. Stir. Remove from heat.

Meanwhile, bring 8 cups of water to the boil in a non-stick saucepan. Stir in the rice. Add the cloves, cardamom pods, cinnamon stick and salt. Cover with a tight lid and cook on low heat for 5 minutes. Strain the rice. Place a quarter of the rice in the bottom of a non-stick casserole. Spread half of the cooked lamb in a layer. Add a layer of rice. Sprinkle with 2 to 3 tablespoons of water, half of the saffron liquid and half of the mint leaves. Mist with olive oil spray. Add the remaining lamb and the remaining rice. Drizzle the remaining saffron liquid on top. Mist with olive oil spray. Garnish with remaining browned onions and mint leaves, peas, toasted pistachios and silver leaf, *vark*. Cover the pan tightly with aluminum foil. Cover with a tight-fitting lid. Cook the *biryani* in the middle of the oven for 15 minutes. Turn off the oven. Let the *biryani* rest in the oven for an additional 10 minutes. Serve.

YIELD: 6 to 8 servings with other dishes.

ADVANCE PREPARATION: Cook the meat 1 to 2 days ahead. The flavors will improve upon standing. Assemble 1 hour prior to cooking.

VARIATION: Substitute beef for lamb. Check the cooking time for the beef as it may take less cooking time.

403 Calories per serving:
  20 G Protein   455 MG Sodium
  10 G Fat   39 MG Cholesterol
  58 G Carbohydrate

Inspired by G. S. Talwar, Executive Chef, The Krishna Oberoi, Hyderabad.

Lamb Biryani, Parsi Style

ALOO DAR

≈≈≈

The Parsi community of Bombay has its own style of *biryani*, which is always served during weddings and other elaborate occasions. In addition to the layers of rice and meat, Parsis demonstrate their passion for potatoes by adding them to the dish.

In this ornate rice pilaf, partially cooked *basmati* rice is layered with uncooked marinated lamb. Aromatic flavorings imbue the dish with additional exotic flavors.

The dish is cooked by the *dum* method. The cooking vessel is topped with a tight-fitting cover to prevent steam from escaping and cooked on very low heat. This allows the flavors to mellow and permits each grain of rice to expand to its fullest.

1 cup nonfat plain yogurt
2 tablespoons plus 1 teaspoon shredded ginger
2 teaspoons chopped garlic
2 teaspoons red pepper powder
2 teaspoons black cumin, *shahi jeera*
3/4 teaspoon ground turmeric
2 pounds lamb, preferably from the leg, trimmed and cut into 1-1/2-inch pieces
1 tablespoon plus 1/2 teaspoon canola oil
2 medium onions, thinly sliced

1 large potato, peeled and cut into 1-inch cubes
2 cups *basmati* or other long-grained rice
4 green cardamom pods
6 cloves
Salt to taste
1/2 teaspoon ground cardamom
1/4 teaspoon ground mace
1 teaspoon salt, or to taste
3 fresh green chilies, cut in half
2 tablespoons golden raisins
Olive oil spray

Place the yogurt in a sieve over a bowl. Cover and allow the yogurt to drain for 3 hours or overnight in the refrigerator. Discard liquid. Whisk the yogurt until smooth and creamy.

In a mini food processor or blender, process 1 tablespoon plus 1 teaspoon of the shredded ginger, the garlic and 2 tablespoons of water to a paste. Combine the paste mixture with the red pepper powder, black cumin, 1/2 teaspoon of the turmeric, yogurt and the lamb.

Cover and marinate the lamb in the mixture for at least 2 hours or overnight in the refrigerator.

Heat 1 tablespoon of the oil in a non-stick skillet over moderate heat. Add the onions and stir for 2 minutes. Add 2 tablespoons of water and reduce the heat to low. Continue cooking for 10 to 15 minutes, stirring occasionally, until the onions are golden brown. Set aside.

Preheat the oven to 400°F. Soak the potatoes in cold water for 5 minutes. Drain well. Dry thoroughly on paper towels. Place the potatoes in a bowl and toss with the remaining 1/2 teaspoon of oil. Arrange the potatoes in a single layer on a non-stick baking sheet. Bake the potatoes for 15 minutes, tossing occasionally to allow them to brown evenly. Remove and set aside.

Sort, wash and soak the rice as described on page 51. Drain. Bring 8 cups of water to a boil in a non-stick saucepan. Stir in the rice. Add the cardamom pods, cloves and salt. Cover with a tight lid. Reduce heat to low and simmer gently for 5 minutes or until the rice is half cooked. The rice should retain a slim, hard, inner core. Strain the rice.

Preheat oven to 350°F. Place the marinated lamb in a single layer in a non-stick casserole. Sprinkle the ground cardamom and mace, salt, the remaining turmeric and shredded ginger and the green chilies over the lamb.

Spread half the partially cooked rice over the lamb. If the rice appears dry, sprinkle 2 to 3 tablespoons water over the top. Sprinkle half the browned potatoes, fried onions and the raisins over the rice. Mist very lightly with olive oil spray. Top with the remaining rice, potatoes, onions and raisins. Mist very lightly with olive oil spray. Cover the casserole tightly with aluminum foil. Cover with a tight-fitting lid. (If there is not a tight seal, weigh down the cover.) Cook the *biryani* in the middle of the oven for 45 minutes to 1 hour. Test to see if lamb is cooked. Quickly cover. Turn off the oven. Let the *biryani* rest in the oven for an additional 10 minutes. Serve immediately.

YIELD: 8 servings.

ADVANCE PREPARATION: Cook the onions several days ahead, refrigerate or freeze. Defrost completely prior to using.

Marinate the meat 1 day ahead. Refrigerate. On day of serving, cook the rice, assemble the *biryani* 1 hour prior to cooking. Bake.

374 Calories per serving:
  25 G Protein   380 MG Sodium
   8 G Fat   58 MG Cholesterol
  50 G Carbohydrate

Inspired by Gev Desai, Executive Chef, Maurya Sheraton, New Delhi.

Chicken Biryani, Hyderabad Style

MURGH BIRYANI HYDERABADI

∼✺∼

Anna Sanyal has simplified the intricate traditional *biryani* preparation and produced a dish that is a magnificent combination of flavors and colors. In her dish, she uses 4 tablespoons of butter but I have adapted it by using extra-virgin olive oil spray.

1 cup nonfat plain yogurt
1 small onion, chopped
1 tablespoon chopped garlic
2 tablespoons chopped fresh ginger
1 fresh green chili, chopped
1 teaspoon ground turmeric
2 tablespoons fresh lime juice
2–3 whole chicken breasts, skinned, boned and cut into 1-1/2-inch pieces
2 cups *basmati* or other long-grained rice

6 cloves
6 cardamom pods
1 3-inch cinnamon stick, broken into 1-inch pieces
1/2 teaspoon salt
1 teaspoon saffron threads, soaked in warm water for 20 minutes
1/2 cup frozen peas
Extra-virgin olive oil spray

TEMPERING:
2 teaspoons olive oil
2 large onions, sliced (optional)

1 tablespoon toasted blanched almonds
12 fresh mint leaves

Whisk the yogurt with a fork until smooth and creamy. In a mini food processor or blender, process the onion, garlic, ginger, chili and 2 tablespoons water to a smooth paste. In a large bowl combine the yogurt paste mixture, turmeric and lime juice. Add the chicken and mix well to coat. Cover and marinate for 2 hours in the refrigerator.

Meanwhile, sort, wash and soak the rice as described on page 51. Drain. Cover with water and rub the rice between your hands. Drain. Repeat the process until the water runs clear. Let the rice soak in 4 cups water or enough water to cover the rice by about 1 inch for 20 minutes. Drain. Bring 8 cups of water to the boil in a heavy-bottomed pan. Stir in the rice. Add the cloves, cardamom pods, cinnamon stick and salt. Stir gently. Cover with a tight-fitting lid. Reduce the heat and simmer for 5 minutes. Strain the rice in a sieve.

Put the marinated chicken in a heavy-based non-stick saucepan. Place the rice in an even layer on top of the chicken. Drizzle with the saffron water. Cover the pan with aluminum foil. Cover with a tight-fitting lid. Cook on moderate heat for 10 minutes. Sprinkle the green peas over the rice. Mist with olive oil spray. Cover again with the foil and lid. Reduce the heat to very low and cook for 15 minutes. Let the *biryani* rest, covered for 10 minutes.

TEMPERING: Heat the 2 teaspoons oil in a large non-stick skillet. Add the onions and stir over moderate heat for 2 minutes. Reduce heat and add 2 tablespoons water. Let the onions cook, stirring occasionally, until they are crisp and lightly browned. Drain on paper towels. Garnish the cooked *biryani* with the onions, almonds and mint leaves.

YIELD: 8 servings.

ADVANCE PREPARATION: Prepare the marinade 1 day ahead. Cook the rice for 5 minutes several hours ahead. Assemble the dish 1 hour ahead. Cook prior to serving.

VARIATION: Dissolve 1/4 teaspoon turmeric in 2 tablespoons water as a substitute for the saffron.

314 Calories per serving:
29 G Protein   175 MG Sodium
2 G Fat   1 MG Cholesterol
43 G Carbohydrate

Inspired by Anna Sanyal, Darien, IL, formerly from Calcutta.

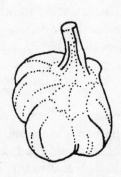

Fragrant Lemon Rice

ELUMICHAMPAZHAM SADAM

∽◦◦∾

A favorite of south Indians, this simply prepared zesty rice is a welcome palate refresher during any meal.

1 tablespoon plus 2 teaspoons split
   chana dal
2 cups basmati or other long-
   grained rice
2 tablespoons olive oil
1 teaspoon black mustard seeds
1 teaspoon cumin seeds
1/2 teaspoon ground turmeric

10 fresh curry leaves (optional)
2–3 green chilies, seeded and
   minced
Salt to taste
2 teaspoons ground coconut
1/3 cup fresh lemon juice
2-1/2 tablespoons chopped
   fresh coriander leaves

Pick over the dal. Rub in a dry towel to get rid of loose powder. If using basmati rice, sort, wash and soak the rice as described on page 51.

Heat the oil in a non-stick saucepan over moderate heat. Add the mustard seeds and stir until they crackle. Add the channa dal, cumin seeds, turmeric, curry leaves, if desired, and the chilies. Add the rice and stir until all the grains are covered with the spice mixture. Continue stirring for another 4 minutes over low heat. Add salt to taste. Add 2 cups of boiling water. Reduce the heat to low. Cover the pan with a tight-fitting lid and cook for 15 to 18 minutes, or until the rice is dry and soft. Gently stir in the coconut, lemon juice and half of the coriander leaves. Replace the lid and let the rice rest for 10 minutes. Transfer to a serving dish and garnish with the remaining coriander.

YIELD: 4 to 6 servings.

441 Calories per serving:
   9 G Protein   45 MG Sodium
   8 G Fat   0 MG Cholesterol
  82 G Carbohydrate

COOK'S TIP: If curry leaves are unavailable, substitute 1 teaspoon minced ginger.

Inspired by Mrs. A. Mullens, Principal, Institute of Hotel, Catering and Technology, Madras.

Piquant Lime Rice

ELUMICHAMPAZHAM SADAM

∾⌇∽

This superb, refreshing, mildly piquant lime-flavored rice dish is enlivened with cashews and the nutty flavor of toasted split *mung dal*. It is a welcome palate refresher for a simple luncheon or a festive banquet.

Whenever I prepare this dish, it brings back memories of lunch with the chefs at the Institute of Hotel Management, Catering and Technology, Bombay. As we dined, we watched the students take their final exam on the proper method of setting a restaurant table. To test them, the instructors had lowered one or two legs of each table, put out slightly varied sizes of dinner plates, flatware, glasses, place-mats and napkins, and placed smudge marks on many of the above. The students were to produce a perfect table in a limited time, and watching them rise to the occasion with spirit and ingenuity was as fascinating as it was educational.

1 cup *basmati* or other long-grained rice
1/2 teaspoon ground turmeric
1 teaspoon fenugreek seeds
1 tablespoon split *urad dal*
1/3 cup fresh lime juice
1 tablespoon canola oil

3 fresh curry leaves (optional)
1/2 teaspoon black mustard seeds
2 dried red chilies
1 tablespoon split *mung dal*
2 tablespoons raw cashew nuts, pan-toasted until golden (optional)

GARNISH:

2 tablespoons chopped fresh coriander leaves

Sort, wash and soak the rice as described on page 51. Drain. Bring 2 cups of water to the boil in a large non-stick saucepan. Stir in the rice and turmeric. Cover with a tight lid. Reduce heat to very low and simmer gently for 20 to 25 minutes or until the water is fully absorbed and the rice is fluffy. Set aside, covered.

In a non-stick skillet, roast the fenugreek seeds and *urad dal* until the *dal* is golden brown. Remove from the heat and let cool. In a spice grinder or mini food processor, grind to a powder. Combine the powdered mixture with the lime juice. Set aside.

Heat the oil in the skillet over moderate heat. Add the curry leaves, if desired, mustard seeds, chilies and *mung dal* to the pan. Cook until the mustard seeds begin to crackle and the *mung dal* is golden brown. Remove from the heat. Gently stir the toasted cashew nuts and the powdered seasoning mixture into the rice. Just before serving, stir in the seasoned oil mixture. Garnish with the chopped coriander leaves. Serve hot.

YIELD: 4 servings.

240 Calories per serving:
  6 G Protein   6 MG Sodium
  4 G Fat   0 MG Cholesterol
 44 G Carbohydrate

Inspired by I. Gomes, Head of Food and Beverage Department, Institute of Hotel, Catering and Technology, Bombay.

Yogurt Rice

MASURU ANNA

∽∾∾

Yogurt Rice or Curd Rice is served at the conclusion of south Indian meals because it has a soothing effect on the palate. It is always served at room temperature.

1 cup *basmati* or other long-grained rice
1 cup nonfat plain yogurt
1/4 teaspoon salt
2 teaspoons canola oil
1/2 teaspoon black mustard seeds
1/4 teaspoon split *urad dal*

8–10 fresh curry leaves (optional)
2 dried red chilies
1–2 fresh green chilies, minced
1-1/2 teaspoons peeled, minced fresh ginger
1 tablespoon finely chopped fresh coriander leaves

Sort, wash and soak the rice as described on page 51. Drain.

Bring 10 cups of water to a boil in a large saucepan. Add the rice and stir. Bring to a boil. Boil vigorously until the rice is cooked and slightly soft, about 20 minutes. Drain and place in a bowl.

In a bowl, combine the yogurt and salt until creamy and smooth. Add the yogurt to the hot rice. Gently stir to mix.

Heat the oil in a small non-stick skillet over moderate flame. Add the mustard seeds. As soon as they crackle, add the *urad dal*. When the *dal* turns light golden brown, add the curry leaves and red chilies. Cook until the chilies start to darken. Remove from heat and pour mixture over the rice. Sprinkle the green chilies, ginger and coriander leaves over the rice. Stir gently to mix. Do not refrigerate. Serve the Yogurt Rice at room temperature.

YIELD: 4 servings with other dishes.

236 Calories per serving:
- 8 G Protein
- 3 G Fat
- 44 G Carbohydrate

189 MG Sodium
1 MG Cholesterol

Inspired by Chef C. Ramnath, Windsor Manor, Bangalore.

Tomato Rice

TAMATAR BHAT

&⤬&

This spirited pilaf combines tomatoes and onions with fragrant mustard seeds and curry leaves. The nutty flavor of the *dals* and the heat of chilies create this specialty of the Chettiars of Tamil Nadu in south India.

1-1/2 cups uncooked rice
2 teaspoons olive oil
1-1/2 teaspoons black mustard
  seeds
2 tablespoons split *urad dal*
2 tablespoons split *chana dal*
10 fresh curry leaves (optional)
1/2 cup minced onion

3 fresh green chilies, slit in half
Pinch of ground turmeric
1 tablespoon red pepper powder
2 cups chopped ripe tomatoes
1/2 teaspoon salt, or to taste
5 cups cold cooked *basmati* or
  other long-grained rice
  (see page 76)

GARNISH:
2 tablespoons chopped fresh
  coriander leaves (optional)

Heat the oil in a large non-stick skillet over medium heat. Add the mustard seeds and cook until they crackle. Add the urad dal and stir until golden brown. Add the chana dal and curry leaves, if desired. Stir for 20 seconds. Add the onions and chilies. Stir-fry until the onion is translucent. Add the turmeric and red pepper powder and cook for about 30 seconds. Add the tomatoes and stir. Cook until the tomatoes are soft. Add 1/2 cup of water and continue to cook, mashing the tomatoes with a wooden spatula until they become a pulpy sauce, about 4 to 5 minutes. Add salt to taste. Gently fold in the cooked rice and toss to mix with the sauce. Cover tightly and steam the rice over low heat for 15 minutes, or until the sauce is absorbed into the rice. Fluff the rice and garnish with coriander.

YIELD: 6 to 8 servings with other dishes.

ADVANCE PREPARATION: Cook the rice one day ahead. Cook the tomato sauce ahead. Combine rice and tomato sauce and complete cooking prior to serving.

191 Calories per serving:
- 6 G Protein
- 3 G Fat
- 37 G Carbohydrate
- 338 MG Sodium
- 0 MG Cholesterol

Inspired by Chef C. S. Ramnath, Windsor Manor, Bangalore.

Vegetable Pilaf

TEHARI PULLAO

⤰⤱

Here is an easily prepared rice dish, combining Indian spices with steamed vegetables.

1 cup *basmati* or other long-grained rice
2 teaspoons olive oil
2-inch cinnamon stick
6 whole cloves
4 green cardamom pods
1 bay leaf

1/4 teaspoon ground tumeric
1/4 teaspoon salt
1-1/2 cups fresh diced mixed vegetables (corn, peas, carrots, green beans, etc.), steamed until tender
1 lemon, cut into 6 wedges

Sort, wash and soak the rice as described on page 51. Drain.

Heat the oil in a large non-stick saucepan over moderate heat. Add the cinnamon, cloves, cardamom and bay leaf. Stir for 10 seconds. Add the rice and stir until the rice is almost opaque, approximately 3 minutes. Add 2 cups of water, turmeric and salt. Bring to a boil. Lower the heat and simmer, covered, until all the water is absorbed, about 18 minutes. Place the steamed vegetables on top of rice, but do not stir. Cover immediately. Remove from the heat. Let stand covered for 10 minutes. Gently fluff the rice, remove the whole spices and stir in the vegetables. Serve with lemon wedges.

YIELD: 4 to 6 servings with other dishes.

ADVANCE PREPARATION: Cook vegetables ahead. Reheat vegetables. Combine with cooked rice when serving.

VARIATION: Substitute cooked mixed frozen vegetables.

316 Calories per serving:
  8 G Protein   183 MG Sodium
  4 G Fat   0 MG Cholesterol
 61 G Carbohydrate

Inspired by G. Sultan Mohideen, Executive Chef, Rajputana Palace, Jaipur.

Spiced Rice with Lentils

KICHRI

≈∾≈

Kichri, meaning hodgepodge, is also known as *Pongal* in the south. It is a nutritious combination of rice and lentils that can be combined with simple spices and ingredients or made quite elaborate by using multiple seasonings and vegetables. This mild version is prepared quickly and goes well with most Indian dishes.

1 cup *basmati* or other long-grained rice
1 cup split *mung dal*
2 teaspoons canola oil
1 medium onion, halved and thinly sliced
1 tablespoon chopped fresh ginger

2 teaspoons chopped garlic
1 dried red chili
3/4 teaspoon ground turmeric
Salt to taste
2 tablespoons fresh lemon juice

GARNISH:
2 tablespoons chopped fresh coriander leaves

8 lemon wedges

Sort, wash and soak the rice as described on page 51. Drain.

Sort, wash and drain the *dal* as described on page 55. In a large non-stick saucepan, heat the oil over moderate heat. Add the onion and stir-fry for 2 minutes or until translucent. Add the ginger, garlic, dried red chili and turmeric. Stir-fry for 1 minute. Add the rice and *dal*. Stir gently to mix. Add boiling water to cover the ingredients by 1/2 inch. Bring to a boil, reduce the heat and simmer, covered, for 20 to 25 minutes or until the liquid is absorbed and the rice and *dal* are tender. Remove the mixture from the heat and let sit, covered, for about 5 minutes. Fluff gently with a fork. Drizzle with lemon juice. Garnish with chopped coriander and serve with lemon wedges.

YIELD: 4 servings with other dishes.

380 Calories per serving:
  16 G Protein   47 MG Sodium
   3 G Fat   0 MG Cholesterol
  72 G Carbohydrate

Inspired by Prem Sharma, Burr Ridge, IL, formerly of New Delhi.

Spiced Rice and Lentils, Parsi Style

KICHRI PARSI

❧

A Parsi would never consider a lunch complete without rice—and a festive meal would never be complete without *Kichri*, a rice and lentil dish. Serve with Fish in Tomato Sauce, Parsi Style (page 161).

1 cup *basmati* or other long-
  grained rice
1/3 cup *masoor dal*
1 tablespoon canola oil
1 medium onion, thinly sliced

1/4 teaspoon ground cumin
1/2 teaspoon fenugreek seeds,
  ground to a powder
1/4 teaspoon ground turmeric
Salt to taste

Sort, wash and soak the rice as described on page 51. Drain.

Sort, wash and drain *masoor dal* as described on page 55. Soak the *dal* in warm water, to cover, for 1 hour. Drain.

Heat the oil in a large, heavy-bottomed non-stick saucepan over moderate heat. Add the onions and cook, stirring for about 2 minutes. Reduce the heat to low. Add 2 tablespoons of water and cook, stirring constantly, for 15 minutes, or until the onions are golden brown. Increase the heat to medium. Add the cumin, fenugreek and turmeric. Cook, stirring, for 30 seconds. Add the drained rice and *dal*. Add salt to taste. Cook, stirring gently, until the rice is almost opaque, about 3 to 4 minutes. Add sufficient boiling water to cover the rice by 1/2 inch. Bring to a boil, stirring gently. Reduce the heat to low and simmer, covered, for 10 to 15 minutes or until most of the water is absorbed and little holes appear on the surface of the rice. Cover the pan with a tight lid. Reduce the heat to low and simmer, covered, for about 10 minutes or until the rice and *dal* are tender. Remove the pan from the heat. Let stand, covered, for 5 minutes. Fluff gently with a fork. Serve immediately.

YIELD: 4 to 6 servings with other dishes.

269 Calories per serving:
8 G Protein
4 G Fat
50 G Carbohydrate
6 MG Sodium
0 MG Cholesterol

Inspired by Gev Desai, Executive Chef, Maurya Sheraton, New Delhi

Savory Rice and Green Pea Pilaf

MASALA HARI MATAR PULLAO

⌒○⌒

A very easily prepared colorful rice dish with a bit of a bite.

1 cup *basmati* or other long-
   grained rice
2 teaspoons canola oil
1 teaspoon cumin seeds
Pinch ground asafetida

1/4 teaspoon ground turmeric
1/2 teaspoon salt
1/2 teaspoon red pepper powder
1 cup frozen peas

Sort, wash and soak the rice as described on page 51. Drain. Let air dry for about 10 to 15 minutes.

Heat the oil in a large non-stick saucepan over moderate heat. Add the cumin seeds and asafetida and stir for 30 seconds. Remove from the heat. Add the turmeric, salt and red pepper powder. Return the pan to the heat. Stir for 30 seconds. Add the rice and peas. Stir for 30 seconds. Add 2 cups of hot water. Cook, partially covered, over medium heat for 5 minutes. Reduce the heat to low, cover tightly and continue cooking for 15 minutes or until all the water is absorbed and the rice is tender and fluffy. Remove from heat and let rice sit for about 10 minutes. Just before serving, fluff up with a fork.

YIELD: 4 to 6 servings with other dishes.

VARIATION: 1/4 cup raw cashews may be added to the rice.

149 Calories per serving:
4 G Protein	218 MG Sodium
2 G Fat	0 MG Cholesterol
29 G Carbohydrate	

Inspired by Prem Sharma, Burr Ridge, IL, formerly of New Delhi.

Sweet Saffron Pilaf

ZARDA PULLAO

Yellow, glistening sweet saffron rice is a favorite of the Muslims. They enjoy this flavorful golden yellow rice with hot, spicy foods or by itself as a snack.

1 cup *basmati* or other long-
   grained rice
1 tablespoon canola oil
2 tablespoons unsalted, shelled
   pistachio nuts
5 cardamom pods
1-1/2 inch stick of cinnamon
5 whole cloves

1/3 teaspoon salt
1/2 teaspoon saffron threads,
   soaked in 2-1/2 tablespoons hot
   water for 15 minutes
5–7 tablespoons sugar, depending
   upon sweetness desired
2 tablespoons golden raisins

GARNISH:
Chopped pistachio nuts

Sort, wash and soak the rice as described on page 51. Drain.

Heat the oil in a large, heavy-bottomed non-stick saucepan. Add the pistachio nuts and stir-fry for 5 seconds or until lightly browned. Remove from the pan and set aside. Add the cardamoms, cinnamon and cloves to the pan and stir-fry until they are lightly browned, about 30 seconds. Add the drained rice and stir-fry for 3 minutes or until the rice is thoroughly coated with the oil and is beginning to brown. Add 1-1/3 cups of water, salt, saffron and its soaking water, sugar and raisins. Stir well to keep the rice from settling. Bring to a boil. Reduce the heat and simmer, partially covered, for 10 minutes or until most of the water is absorbed and the surface of the rice has steamy holes. Cover the pan with a tight-fitting lid and simmer for 10 minutes. Remove from the heat and let the rice rest, covered, for 5 minutes. Do not stir the rice during the final 15 minutes of steaming and resting. Uncover and fluff the rice with a fork. Remove the whole spices. Place the rice in a serving bowl. Sprinkle with chopped pistachio nuts.

YIELD: 4 servings.

COOK'S TIP: The rice will stay warm for 20 minutes after resting.

284 Calories per serving:
  4 G Protein   230 MG Sodium
  6 G Fat   0 MG Cholesterol
53 G Carbohydrates

Inspired by Sous Chef Kalam Kumar Channa, Tandoor Restaurant.

SIDE DISHES AND ACCOMPANIMENTS

Side dishes are served with every Indian meal to balance flavors and provide extra protein and vitamins. They include legumes, *dals;* yogurt salads, *raitas;* vegetable salads; chutneys, *chatneys;* and pickles, *achars.*

Dals are varieties of dried peas and lentils and are consumed in some form, daily, in almost every Indian home. Each state cooks *dal* in a different manner, but a well-prepared *dal* is usually quite thick. When cooked, it might be compared to thin porridge—but not quite as thin as pea soup.

The variety and versatility of *dals* is endless. In the strictly vegetarian south, they are the primary source of protein. Here, they are often intriguingly combined with vegetables and are always consumed with rice or Indian breads. The *dal* can be poured over rice or served in separate bowls called *katori.*

The final spark of the *dal* is the tempering. Oil is heated in a small skillet, whole spices are added and, once lightly browned, poured over the cooked *dal.* This is done immediately prior to serving. More information on *dal* can be found on page 55.

Yogurt Salads, *raitas,* are often served to provide a cool contrast to a spicy meal. A refreshing salad combination of tomato, cucumber and onion or other ingredients can serve the same function.

Chutneys, *chatneys,* and pickles, *achars,* can be spicy, sweet, hot, sour, tart, aromatic or mild. They are best when served with plain dishes such as Dumplings, *Idlis* (page 70) or Potato Patties, *Aloo Tikki* (page 66). Then they do not have to compete with, or overpower, abundantly spiced dishes.

Legumes: Lentils, Dried Peas and Beans *Dals*

Dal Qureshi

Fragrant Roasted   MUNG DAL   BHAJA MUNG DAL

Chickpea Dal   KABULI CHANA DAL

Whole   URAD DAL   SABAT URAD DAL

Hearty Five Dals   DAL PANCHRATAN

Spiced Chickpeas in Sauce   MASALA KABULI CHANA

Tangy Chickpeas   GHUGHNI

Chickpeas with Zucchini   CHANA AUR TORRE

Cabbage Dal   GOBHI DAL

Spinach Dal, Bengali Style   SAAG DAL BENGALI

Spinach Dal, Andhra Pradesh Style
PALAKOORA PAPPU ANDHRA

Spinach and Dal Purée, Chettinad Style
KEERAI MASSIAL

Tomato Dal   TAMATAR PAPPU

Spicy Vegetable and Lentil Stew   SAMBAR

Chickpea Dumplings in Yogurt Sauce, Punjabi Style
PUNJABI KADHI

Yogurt Salads *Raita*

Spiced Yogurt Salad   BHURANNI

Spiced Eggplant, Tomato and Yogurt Salad
BAINGAN BHARTA RAITA

Green Pepper and Yogurt Salad   SIMLA MIRCH RAITA

Tomato and Yogurt Salad   TAMATAR RAITA

Spinach and Yogurt Salad   PAALAK RAITA

Cucumber and Yogurt Salad   KACHUMBAR RAITA

Pineapple and Yogurt Salad   ANANNAS RAITA

Banana and Yogurt Salad   KEELA RAITA

Other Salads

Indian Cottage Cheese Salad   PANEER SALAD

Fresh Mango Salad   AAM SALAD

Shrimp-Stuffed Tomato Salad

JHINGA-TAMATAR

Cucumber and Tomato Salad

KACHUMBAR AUR TAMATAR SALAD

Onion and Tomato Salad, Parsi Style

PYAZ AUR TAMATAR PARSI

Onion Salad, Parsi Style   PYAZ SALAD PARSI

Tomato and Green Pepper Salad, New Delhi Style

TAMATAR AUR SIMLI MIRCH

Southern Mixed Vegetable Salad

THAKKALI-VELLARIKKAI-GAAJAR KOSUMALLI

Mixed Fruit and Vegetable Salad   PHAL KI CHAT

Chutneys, Pickles   *Chatneys, Achars*

Carrot Chutney   GAAJAR CHATNEY

Fresh Coriander Chutney   DHANIA CHATNEY

Mint-Coriander Chutney   PUDINA CHATNEY

Tamarind Chutney   GOR AMLI NI CHATNEY

Tomato Chutney   TAMATAR CHATNEY

Sweet, Hot and Sour Mango Chutney

MAANGAI VELLA PACHCHADI

Southern Tomato Chutney   TAKKALI THOVIYAL

Carrot Pickle   GAAJAR ACHAR

Sour Lemon or Lime Pickle   NIMBU ACHAR

Legumes Dals

⤳⤳

Dal Qureshi

⤳⤳

While in New Delhi, Master Chef Mohammed Imtiaz Qureshi taught me his cherished family recipe from his home in Avadh, presently the Lucknow District of the state of Utter Pradesh. Tender *toor dal* is combined with Indian seasonings and yogurt and exotically tempered with "burned garlic." The result is splendid.

In Chef Qureshi's very rich version, he adds heavy cream after cooking the *dal*, but said that omitting the cream would be delicious. In my version, I have substituted fat-free cream cheese and skim milk, making the *dal* creamy and mellow without the richness of the heavy cream. Serve as a side dish with Lamb Biryani, Dum Pukht Style (page 216), and Spiced Yogurt Salad (page 266).

3/4 cup nonfat plain yogurt
1-1/2 cups split *toor dal*
1 tablespoon mustard oil
2 teaspoons chopped fresh ginger
1-1/2 teaspoons chopped garlic
1/2–3/4 teaspoon red pepper powder

1/2 teaspoon black salt
3/4 teaspoon ground turmeric
1/2 teaspoon salt
1/3 cup fat-free cream cheese
3 tablespoons skim milk

TEMPERING:

1 tablespoon mustard oil
6 dried red peppers, seeded

2 tablespoons chopped garlic

Put the yogurt in a sieve placed over a large bowl. Let the yogurt drain for about 15 minutes. Discard any liquid in the bowl.

Sort the *dal* as described on page 55.

Heat a large non-stick skillet over moderate heat. Add the mustard oil and heat until it reaches the smoking point. Remove the pan and let the oil cool slightly. Return the pan to the heat. Add the *dal* to the skillet and stir-fry over low heat until it turns golden brown, about 5 minutes, taking care not to burn. Transfer the *dal* to a fine mesh sieve and let water run through the *dal*. Rub the *dal* between your hands to remove the oil.

In a mini-food processor or blender, process the ginger, garlic and 1 to 2 teaspoons of water to a paste. In a large non-stick saucepan, put the *dal* and about 3 cups water. (The water level should be about 1 inch above the *dal*.) Bring to a boil and lower the heat to simmer. Add the ginger and garlic paste, red pepper powder, black salt, turmeric and salt. Stir. Cover with a tight-fitting lid. Gently simmer until the *dal* is thoroughly softened and tender, about 45 minutes to 1-1/2 hours. Stir the *dal* every 15 minutes, adding water if necessary to prevent burning.

Whisk the yogurt in a bowl. Add the yogurt to the *dal*, increase the heat to medium and cook, stirring, for 1 to 2 minutes until smooth and creamy. If it is too thick, add a little water and continue stirring. Whisk together the cream cheese and skim milk. Stir into the *dal* until completely combined.

TEMPERING: Heat the mustard oil to the smoking point in a small non-stick pan. Remove the pan from the heat and let the oil cool slightly. Add the dried red peppers and cook over low heat until lightly browned. Add the chopped garlic. Stir constantly until the garlic is golden brown. Add the tempered mixture to the *dal* and stir. Check for salt. Serve hot.

YIELD: 8 servings with other dishes.

ADVANCE PREPARATION: Cook the *dal* several days before serving. Refrigerate, covered. Temper the *dal* just before serving.

COOK'S TIPS:
1. Do not use a pressure cooker because this is a thick *dal* purée that tends to stick to the bottom of the pan and clog the vent in the lid.
2. If you wish a richer *dal*, substitute the cream cheese with 1/2 cup heavy cream.

163 Calories per serving:

11 G Protein	378 MG Sodium
2 G Fat	7 MG Cholesterol
25 G Carbohydrate	

Inspired by Master Chef Mohammed Imtiaz Qureshi, Dum Pukht Restaurant, Maurya Sheraton, New Delhi.

Fragrant Roasted Mung Dal

BHAJA MUNG DAL

❧❧❦

I first enjoyed this superb, healthy *dal* in Anna Sanyal's home. Her family's colorful recipe has a marvelous orchestration of flavors and textures, highlighted by the distinctive flavor of dry roasted mung beans, Indian spices and coconut. Anna serves the *dal* with rice and Indian bread for lunch or supper. The flavors taste even better when made a day ahead.

1 cup split *mung dal*
1 teaspoon ground turmeric
1–2 fresh green chilies, slit in half
   lengthwise
1/2 teaspoon salt, or to taste
1-1/2 tablespoons vegetable oil,
   preferably mustard oil
1/2 teaspoon cumin seeds
1 medium potato, peeled and cut
   into 1/4-inch cubes, soaked in
   cold water for 15 minutes and
   drained

1 cup cauliflower florets, cut into
   1/4-inch pieces
1/2 cup sliced green beans, cut in
   1/4-inch pieces
1 cup fresh ripe tomatoes, cut in
   1/4-inch pieces
2 tablespoons ground coconut
1/4 teaspoon *garam masala*
   (page 43)

GARNISH:

2 tablespoons chopped fresh
   coriander leaves

Pick over the *dal* but do not wash. Rub in a dry towel to get rid of loose dust. Heat a large non-stick skillet over moderate heat. Add the *dal* and stir until it turns golden brown. Transfer to a fine mesh sieve and rinse thoroughly with water. Drain.

In a heavy-bottomed saucepan, add the roasted *dal* and 8 cups of water. Bring to a boil, skimming away any surface scum. When water is clear add 3/4 teaspoon of the turmeric, the chilies and 1/2 teaspoon of salt. Simmer, covered, until the *dal* is very tender, about 35 to 45 minutes. Stir occasionally, adding a little water if the mixture sticks. (The *dal* is ready when it is tender to the bite and breaks easily when pressed between the thumb and index finger.) A thick purée will settle to the bottom, and the top will be thin and cloudy. During the last 15 minutes of cooking, turn the heat to very low to avoid sticking. Remove from the heat.

In a non-stick saucepan, heat the oil over moderate heat. Add the cumin seeds and cook until they pop, about 3 to 4 seconds. Add the potato, cauliflower and green beans. Stir for 3 minutes. Add the remaining turmeric. Stir-fry for 3 minutes. Add the tomatoes and cook until almost dry. Add the coconut and cook, stirring, for 2 minutes. Add the cooked *dal* with the cooking liquid. Bring the mixture to a boil and season to taste with salt. The *dal* should be a medium-thick soupy consistency. When serving, sprinkle with *garam masala* and garnish with chopped coriander. Spoon over rice or serve in small bowls with other dishes.

YIELD: 8 servings.

ADVANCE PREPARATION: Prepare 1 to 2 days ahead. Reheat. Add *garam masala* and garnish with coriander when serving.

155 Calories per serving:
- 2 G Protein   375 MG Sodium
- 4 G Fat   0 MG Cholesterol
- 23 G Carbohydrate

Inspired by Anna Sanyal, Darien, IL, formerly of Calcutta.

Chickpea Dal

KABULI CHANA DAL

❧

This marvelously textured *dal* with its combination of zesty and spicy flavors is extremely easy to prepare. It is a favorite in the Bangalore kitchen of Kitty Basith. In this recipe, puréed chickpeas are combined with coarsely chopped chickpeas. I find that good quality canned chickpeas are a time-saver and are almost as good as dried chickpeas.

This healthy dish can be prepared up to two days ahead of time. In fact, the flavor is improved. Serve with rice, Whole Wheat Bread (page 298) and a yogurt salad. For a special treat, try Piquant Lime Rice (page 226).

2 15-ounce cans chickpeas
2 teaspoons canola oil
1/2 teaspoon cumin seeds
1 small onion, minced
1 tablespoon minced fresh ginger
1 tablespoon minced garlic
1/2 teaspoon ground turmeric

1 tablespoon ground coriander
1/2–1 teaspoon red pepper
  powder
1-1/2 cups tomato sauce
1/2 teaspoon salt, or to taste
2 tablespoons fresh lime juice

Remove 1 cup chickpeas including the liquid from 1 can of chickpeas. Drain. Coarsely chop. In a food processor or blender, process the remaining chickpeas and the liquid to a purée. Set aside. Heat the oil in a non-stick saucepan over moderate heat. Add the cumin seeds and stir until they crackle, about 10 seconds. Add the onion, ginger and garlic. Stir until the onion is translucent. Add the turmeric, coriander and red pepper powder. Cook, stirring, for about 20 seconds, being careful not to burn. Add the tomato sauce. Bring to a boil, reduce the heat and let simmer for 1 minute. Add the chopped and puréed chickpeas. Cook, stirring, for 2 to 3 minutes to allow the flavors to blend. Add salt to taste. Remove from the heat. Add the lime juice and stir. Serve.

YIELD: 6 servings with other dishes.

ADVANCE PREPARATION: Prepare 1 to 2 days in advance. Refrigerate, covered. Reheat when serving.

176 Calories per serving:
- 7 G Protein
- 5 G Fat
- 29 G Carbohydrate
- 882 MG Sodium
- 0 MG Cholesterol

Inspired by Kitty Basith, Willowbrook, IL, formerly of Bangalore.

Whole Urad Dal

SABAT URAD DAL

∽∾

This is the most popular *dal* in north India. It is easily prepared and nourishing.

1 cup whole black gram beans,
  sabut urad
15 dried red kidney beans
1 teaspoon shredded fresh ginger
4 cloves garlic, crushed
Salt to taste

2 teaspoons olive oil
1/2 onion, sliced
1/2 teaspoon red pepper powder
1/2 teaspoon *garam masala*
  (page 43)

Sort, wash and drain the beans as described on page 55. Place the beans and 2 cups of water in a large heavy-bottomed saucepan and soak for at least 4 hours or overnight. Add 1-1/2 cups of water to the pan with the ginger, garlic and salt. Cover and bring to the boil over high heat. Reduce the heat to low and cook until the beans are soft and mushy, about 45 minutes, stirring occasionally. Remove from heat.

In a non-stick skillet, heat the oil over moderate heat. Add the onion and stir-fry for 2 minutes. Add 2 tablespoons of water. Reduce the heat and cook, stirring, until the onions are golden brown. Add the red pepper powder and *garam masala*. Stir for 20 seconds. Pour this mixture over the *dal* and serve.

YIELD: 4 servings with other dishes.

VARIATION: After browning the onion, add one medium diced tomato. Cook until the tomato is soft. Add the remaining ingredients and combine with the cooked *dal*.

226 Calories per serving:
9 G Protein   75 MG Sodium
3 G Fat   0 MG Cholesterol
42 G Carbohydrate

Inspired by Meena Mohindra, Burr Ridge, IL, formerly of New Delhi.

Hearty Five Dals

DAL PANCHRATAN

∾࿏ࢲ

Here is a nutritious, wholesome Rajasthani dish that combines five types of *dals* permeated with flavorsome spices, seasonings and tomatoes. Although Executive Chef Mohideen says the *dal* should be fiery, you may adjust the chilies and red pepper powder to your taste. Serve simply spooned over hot rice with bread as a light meal, or as one of several dishes for a more elaborate menu.

3 tablespoons split *chana dal*
3 tablespoons split *toor dal*
3 tablespoons split *urad dal*
3 tablespoons split *masoor dal*
3 tablespoons split *mung dal*
1 teaspoon ground turmeric
1-1/2 teaspoons shredded fresh
    ginger
5 cloves of garlic, cut into slivers
2 teaspoons seeded, minced fresh
    green chili
1/2 teaspoon red pepper powder

1/4 cup minced red onion
1/3 cup chopped ripe tomato
2 teaspoons canola oil
1 teaspoon cumin seeds
1 tablespoon chopped fresh
    coriander leaves
1/2 teaspoon salt
1/2 teaspoon freshly ground black
    pepper
1 tablespoon fresh lemon juice
1/2 teaspoon freshly grated
    nutmeg

Sort, wash and drain the *dals* as described on page 55. Combine the *dals* in a bowl, cover with hot water and allow to soak for 3 to 5 hours. Drain.

In a large, heavy-bottomed non-stick saucepan combine the *dals* with enough water to cover by 2 inches. Stir in the turmeric. Bring to the boil over high heat. Reduce the heat to moderately low and cover. Cook gently for 1-1/2 hours, or until soft, stirring occasionally. Remove the pan from the heat. Beat the *dal* with a wire whisk until creamy and smooth. Set aside.

In a small bowl combine the ginger, garlic, chili, red pepper powder, onion and tomato. Heat the oil in a large non-stick skillet over moderately high heat. Add the cumin seeds and stir until they turn brown. Add the tomato mixture to the oil. Cook, stirring, for about 2 minutes. Add to the *dal* and continue to cook over moderate heat for about 1 minute, stirring constantly. Add the chopped coriander. Continue cooking for 1 to 2 minutes more. Season with salt and pepper. Remove from heat, add the lemon juice and sprinkle the nutmeg over the *dal*.

YIELD: 6 servings with other dishes.

ADVANCE PREPARATION: Prepare 2 days ahead. Refigerate, covered. If the *dal* thickens, stir in a little water when reheating. Add lemon juice and nutmeg prior to serving.

139 Calories per serving:
   8 G Protein   222 MG Sodium
   2 G Fat   0 MG Cholesterol
  23 G Carbohydrate

Inspired by G. Sultan Mohideen, Executive Chef, Rajputana Palace, Jaipur.

Spiced Chickpeas in Sauce

MASALA KABULI CHANA

☙❧

This intriguing recipe is prepared from brown-skinned whole *kabuli chana*, a variety of chickpea popular in north Indian dishes, available in Indian and Middle Eastern grocery stores. It must be soaked for at least eight hours or until it becomes soft. Serve in individual small bowls as an interesting and healthy accompaniment to a meal or on rice with a flatbread. If the *kabuli chana* is cooked in less water, the consistency is drier and it can be served as an appetizer.

1-1/2 cups whole dried chickpeas, *kabuli chana*
2 teaspoons canola oil
1 teaspoon cumin seeds
1 teaspoon ground turmeric
Pinch of ground asafetida
1/2–1 teaspoon red pepper powder
Salt to taste

1 tablespoon plus 2 teaspoons chopped fresh ginger
1 fresh green chili, minced
1 small ripe tomato, chopped
3 tablespoons fresh lemon or lime juice
2 tablespoons chopped fresh coriander leaves

Sort, wash and drain the chickpeas as described on page 55. Place the chickpeas in a bowl. Add enough water to cover by 2 inches. Soak for 8 hours or overnight. Drain.

In a non-stick saucepan, heat the oil over moderate heat. Add the cumin seeds, turmeric, asafedtida, red pepper powder and salt. Stir until the cumin seeds crackle. Add the chickpeas and enough water to cover them by 2 inches. Add 1 tablespoon of the chopped ginger, the green chili and tomato. Bring to a boil. Cover and simmer for 1-1/2 to 2 hours or until the chickpeas are just tender to the bite, but not overcooked. (The length of cooking time depends upon the age and dryness of the chickpeas, and even the cooking water.) Remove from the heat. Sprinkle the lemon juice, remaining ginger and coriander over the *dal*. Serve.

YIELD: 4 to 6 servings.

ADVANCE PREPARATION: Prepare 1 to 2 days ahead or freeze. Defrost before reheating prior to serving. Garnish when serving.

314 Calories per serving:
  16 G Protein   48 MG Sodium
  7 G Fat   5 MG Cholesterol
  49 G Carbohydrate

Inspired by Prem Sharma, Burr Ridge, IL, formerly of New Delhi.

ᴛᴀɴɢʏ Chickpeas

GHUGHNI

Healthy and nutritious chickpeas absorb other flavors remarkably well. Here they combine the subtle, sour taste of tamarind with interestingly spiced *chat masal* and other spices. While canned chickpeas can be used, I have found they do not have the wonderful texture found in the Indian dried chickpeas. Although time-consuming to soak and cook, it is well worth the effort. Serve as a snack with an Indian flatbread or as an interesting part of any meal. Sudha Mehrotra topped the dish with crumbled chickpea noodles, giving the dish another texture.

1-1/2 cups whole dried chickpeas
1 tablespoon *chat masala* (page 44)
1 teaspoon dry roasted cumin
  seeds, ground
1/2 teaspoon black salt
1/4 teaspoon salt
1/2 teaspoon mango powder

1-1/2 teaspoons tamarind
  concentrate
2 fresh green chilies, seeded and
  quartered
1 tablespoon chopped fresh
  coriander leaves

Sort and wash the chickpeas as described on page 55. Place the chickpeas in a bowl. Add sufficient water to cover by 2 inches. Soak for 8 hours or overnight. Bring to a boil in the soaking water. Reduce the heat to low and simmer, covered, for about 1-1/2 hours or until tender to the bite, adding more water if the level falls below that of the chickpeas. In a non-stick saucepan, add the chickpeas, *chat masala*, cumin, black salt, salt, mango powder and 1/4 cup of water. Bring to a boil. Lower the heat and simmer, covered, for 10 minutes. Add the tamarind concentrate and cook, uncovered for 3 to 5 minutes, stirring, to allow the flavors to mellow. Garnish with green chilies and chopped coriander. Serve.

YIELD: 4 to 6 servings with other dishes.

VARIATION: Serve sprinkled with crumbled chickpea noodles. They are a snack food, eaten directly from the package, sold in Indian grocery stores.

ADVANCE PREPARATION: Prepare 1 to 2 days ahead. Reheat gently. Garnish with green chilies and coriander when serving.

284 Calories per serving:
16 G Protein   437 MG Sodium
4 G Fat   5 MG Cholesterol
46 G Carbohydrate

Inspired by Sudha Mehrotra, Calcutta.

Chickpeas with Zucchini

CHANA AUR TORRE

∽∾∽

Contrasting textures, tastes and colors are most appealing in this attractive, easily prepared *dal*.

1 cup split *chana dal*   2 teaspoons fresh lemon juice
1 teaspoon ground turmeric   1 tablespoon chopped fresh
1 medium zucchini, chopped   coriander leaves to garnish
Salt to taste

TEMPERING:

1 tablespoon olive oil
1 teaspoon cumin seeds
1 medium onion, thinly sliced

1/4–1/2 teaspoon red pepper
powder

GARNISH:
1 tablespoon chopped fresh
coriander leaves

Sort and wash the *chana dal* as described on page 55. Soak the *dal* in sufficient hot water to cover by 2 inches for about 5 hours. Drain.

In a saucepan, combine the *dal*, turmeric and sufficient water to cover by 2 inches. Bring to the boil, reduce the heat and simmer for 1 hour. Add the zucchini, stir and continue cooking for 30 minutes or until the *dal* is soft and tender, adding more water if necessary to prevent burning and sticking to the pan. The finished *dal* should have the consistency of a coarse purée. Add the salt and lemon juice.

TEMPERING: Heat the oil in a small non-stick skillet over moderate heat. Add the cumin seeds and stir until they crackle. Add the onion and cook, stirring, for about 2 minutes. Reduce heat to low. Add 2 tablespoons water. Cook, stirring occasionally, until the onions are golden brown, about 10 to 15 minutes. Pour over the cooked *dal* and zucchini. Serve sprinkled with chopped coriander leaves.

YIELD: 6 servings with other dishes.

ADVANCE PREPARATION: The dish may be prepared 1 to 2 days ahead. Reheat prior to serving. Prepare tempering and pour over the cooked dish prior to serving.

147 Calories per serving:
  9 G Protein   31 MG Sodium
  3 G Fat   0 MG Cholesterol
23 G Carbohydrate

Inspired by Suman Sood, Registered Dietitian; President, Club of Indian Women, Chicago, formerly of New Delhi.

Cabbage Dal

GOBHI DAL

∞ᢀᨆᢀᨆᢀ∞

A delicately spiced lentil dish.

1 cup split *chana dal*
1 tablespoon olive oil
1/2 teaspoon black mustard seeds
1 small onion, chopped
1/2–1 green chili, seeded and
   chopped

1/4 pound cabbage, shredded
1/4 teaspoon ground turmeric
Salt to taste
2 teaspoons ground coconut

Sort and wash the *dal* as described on page 55. Soak the *dal* in suffi-cient hot water to cover by 2 inches for 3 hours. Drain.

In a non-stick saucepan, combine the *dal* and sufficient water to cover by 2 inches. Bring to a boil. Reduce the heat, cover and simmer for approximately 45 minutes, stirring occasionally, until tender and soft. Drain.

In a large non-stick saucepan, heat the oil over moderate heat. Add mustard seeds and stir-fry until they crackle. Add the onion, chili and *dal*. Cook, stirring, for 1 minute. Add the cabbage, turmeric and salt. Toss to combine. Cook, stirring occasionally, until the cabbage is ten-der and the *dal* is the consistency of a coarse purée. Sprinkle with the coconut. Stir to combine. Serve hot.

YIELD: 6 servings with other dishes.

ADVANCE PREPARATION: Prepare ahead. Reheat. Sprinkle with the coconut and stir just before serving.

160 Calories per serving:
  3 G Protein   139 MG Sodium
  3 G Fat   0 MG Cholesterol
 31 G Carbohydrate

Spinach Dal, Bengali Style

SAAG DAL BENGALI

⤫⤬⤫

Brilliant green spinach is combined with yellow split *toor dal* in this easily prepared, interestingly spiced *dal* from Bengal. Serve hot with rice or Indian whole wheat bread, or as one of the dishes in a full Indian meal.

1 cup split *toor* or *mung dal*
2 cups packed, trimmed spinach
   leaves (about 1/3 pound)

1 teaspoon cumin seeds

TEMPERING:

1 tablespoon canola oil
1 teaspoon ground turmeric
Salt to taste

1/2–1 teaspoon red pepper powder
1/2 teaspoon cumin seeds
1-1/2 teaspoons ground coriander

Sort and wash the *dal* as described on page 55. Soak the *dal* in 2 cups of warm water for 3 hours. Drain.

Put *dal* and 3-1/2 cups of water in a large non-stick saucepan. Bring to the boil, stirring occasionally. Reduce the heat to low and cover with a tight-fitting lid. Simmer for about 30 minutes or until the *dal* is tender and plump. Stir occasionally, adding water if necessary to prevent burning. Each piece of *dal* should be tender and soft, but not mushy.

Meanwhile, wash, dry and tear the spinach into 2-inch pieces.

Dry roast 1 teaspoon of the cumin seeds for about 10 to 15 seconds until brown. Add the cumin seeds and the spinach to the *dal* and cook, stirring, for 2 to 3 minutes.

TEMPERING: Heat a small non-stick skillet over medium heat. Add the oil, red pepper powder, cumin seeds and coriander and cook for about 10 seconds, or until the cumin is lightly browned. Pour over the cooked *dal.* Serve immediately.

YIELD: 6 servings.

ADVANCE PREPARATION: Prepare the *dal* 1 day ahead. Temper the spices just before serving. Pour over the *dal*. Serve.

143 Calories per serving:
  9 G Protein   219 MG Sodium
  3 G Fat   0 MG Cholesterol
 22 G Carbohydrate

Inspired by Sudha Mehrotra, Calcutta.

Spinach Dal, Andrah Pradesh Style

PALAKOORA PAPPU ANDRAH

࿎ဝၔ

This southern *dal* from Andhra Pradesh contains a smooth and silky golden purée of pink lentils known as *masoor dal*. Combined with a hint of sourness from the tomatoes and heat from the chilies, the final flourish of fresh spinach creates a beautiful marbled effect. Serve with Tomato Rice (page 229), Pepper Chicken, Chettinad Style (page 129) and a yogurt salad.

2/3 cup *masoor dal*
1/4 teaspoon ground turmeric
1/8 teaspoon ground asafetida
2 teaspoons canola oil
2 dried red chilies, chopped
1/2 teaspoon black mustard
  seeds
1/2 teaspoon cumin seeds
2/3 cup chopped red onion
8 cloves garlic, cut into 1/4-inch
  slivers

6 fresh green chilies, halved and
  seeded
1 large ripe tomato, cut into 16
  wedges
2 cups packed, trimmed spinach
  leaves
Salt to taste
2 tablespoons minced fresh
  coriander leaves
1/8 teaspoon freshly grated
  nutmeg

Sort and wash the *dal* as described on page 55.

In a large non-stick saucepan, combine the *dal*, turmeric, asafetida and 2 cups of water. Bring to the boil, stirring often. Reduce the heat to low and simmer, partially covered, for 20 to 25 minutes, or until the *dal* is cooked and a thick purée. Stir occasionally to prevent sticking. Remove from the heat.

Heat the oil in non-stick wok or skillet. Add the dried red chilies and stir until they turn light brown in color. Add the mustard seeds and stir until they crackle. Add the cumin seeds. Stir. Add the onions and sauté until translucent, about 1 to 2 minutes. Add the garlic and green chilies and stir until the onion starts to turn light brown, about 2 to 3 minutes. Add the tomato. Stir until the skin of the tomato curls. Add the cooked *dal* and 1-1/2 cups water to the pan. Stir to combine. Bring to a boil and cook for about 4 to 5 minutes or until a medium-soupy consistency. Add the spinach and cook for 2 minutes, stirring. Add salt to taste. Sprinkle with the coriander and nutmeg.

YIELD: 4 servings with other dishes.

ADVANCE PREPARATION: Prepare up to the addition of the spinach several hours ahead. For best results, add the spinach and cook prior to serving. You may complete the whole dish, but some of the freshness of the flavor of the spinach will be lost.

COOK'S TIP: Swiss chard leaves may be used in place of the spinach.

205 Calories per serving:
- 12 G Protein
- 4 G Fat
- 33 G Carbohydrate
- 72 MG Sodium
- 0 MG Cholesterol

Inspired by Praveen Anand, Executive Chef, Dakshin Restaurant, Park Sheraton, Madras.

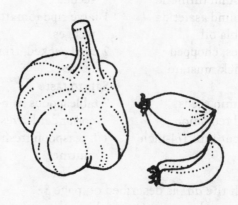

Spinach and Dal Purée, Chettinad Style

KEERAI MASSIAL

～～～

Here is a delicate vegetable dish from the Chettiar community of south India. Fresh spinach is enhanced by the subtle flavors of nutty *mung dal*, cumin, a touch of chili and tangy lime. Serve with Vegetable Pilaf (page 230), Grilled Swordfish, Chettinad Style (page 155) and Tomato and Yogurt Salad (page 269).

1/2 cup split *mung dal*
1 12-ounce bag fresh spinach,
　 trimmed, washed and chopped
2 teaspoons olive oil
1 teaspoon cumin seeds
1 large onion, chopped
4 cloves garlic, minced

1–2 green chilies, seeded and
　 minced
Salt to taste (optional)
1 teaspoon *garam masala* (page 43)
2 tablespoons fresh lime juice
1 tablespoon chopped fresh
　 coriander leaves (optional)

Sort and wash the *dal* as described on page 55. In a large non-stick saucepan, combine the *dal* and 2 cups of water. Bring to the boil. Reduce the heat to low and cover with a tight-fitting lid. Gently simmer for 20 to 30 minutes, or until the *dal* is tender and plump, stirring occasionally. Pat the spinach dry on paper towels.

In a large non-stick saucepan, heat the oil over moderate heat. Add the cumin seeds and stir until they are brown, about 10 seconds. Add the onion, garlic and chilies. Cook, stirring occasionally, until the onion is soft. Add the chopped spinach and cook over low heat until wilted. Add the cooked *dal* and mash all the ingredients together to create a coarse purée. Season with salt, if desired. Sprinkle with *garam masala*. Add the lime juice, stir and garnish with chopped coriander, if desired.

YIELD: 4 to 6 servings with other dishes.

ADVANCE PREPARATION: Prepare 1 day ahead. Refrigerate. Add *garam masala*, lime juice and chopped coriander prior to serving.

COOK'S TIP: Use 1 10-ounce package of frozen leaf spinach, thawed and drained, in place of fresh spinach. Press in a sieve to extract as much water as possible before adding the cooked *dal*.

147 Calories per serving:

9	G Protein	74	MG Sodium
3	G Fat	0	MG Cholesterol
23	G Carbohydrate		

Inspired by Praveen Anand, Executive Chef, Dakshin Restaurant, Park Sheraton, Madras.

Tomato Dal

TAMATAR PAPPU

ᴂᴂᴂ

Tender, plump lentils and red tomatoes punctuated with chilies and red pepper powder give this dish from Andrah Pradesh a lot of zing! If you prefer a milder *dal*, reduce the amount of red pepper powder. Serve with Indian bread for a light meal or as an accompaniment, with other dishes, as part of a more elaborate meal.

1/2 cup split *toor dal*
1/3 teaspoon ground turmeric
1 teaspoon canola oil
2 teaspoons black mustard seeds
2 teaspoons cumin seeds
1/4 cup chopped onion
3 fresh green chilies, cut in half
   lengthwise

2 teaspoons red pepper powder
12 fresh curry leaves (optional)
1 cup chopped ripe tomatoes
1/8 teaspoon salt
1-1/2 teaspoons fresh lime juice

GARNISH:
2 teaspoons chopped, fresh
   coriander leaves to garnish

Sort and wash the *dal* as described on page 55. Place the *dal*, 3/4 cup of water and a pinch of the turmeric in a large non-stick saucepan. Bring to a boil over moderate heat, stirring occasionally. Reduce the heat to moderately low. Cover with a tight-fitting lid. Gently simmer for 20 to 30 minutes, or until the *dal* is tender and plump. Stir occasionally. If necessary, add 1 to 2 tablespoons water to prevent *dal* from sticking. Remove from the heat and set aside.

Heat the oil over moderate heat in a non-stick skillet. Add the mustard seeds and cook until they crackle. Add the cumin seeds and stir until lightly browned, about 5 seconds. Add the onion and green chili and stir-fry until the onion is translucent. Add the remaining turmeric, red pepper powder and stir for 20 seconds. Add the curry leaves, if desired, tomatoes and 1/4 cup of water. Cook, stirring, until the tomatoes soften and most of the liquid has evaporated, about 3 minutes. Add the cooked *dal* and stir. Season with salt. Reduce the heat to low and cook briefly until the *dal* is a dry coarse purée. Add the lime juice. Garnish with chopped coriander leaves.

ADVANCE PREPARATION: Cook ahead completely. Add lime juice and chopped coriander prior to serving.

136 Calories per serving:
- 8 G Protein
- 2 G Fat
- 22 G Carbohydrate
- 188 MG Sodium
- 0 MG Cholesterol

Inspired by Chef C.S. Ramnath, Windsor Manor, Bangalore .

Spicy Vegetable and Lentil Stew

SAMBAR

∼≫ basi ∼

In south India, *Sambar*, a lentil and vegetable "stew," is a daily staple. It is always made with *toor dal* but can also include vegetables such as green beans, carrots, eggplant, parsnips, cauliflower, squash or okra. Traditionally, it is very hot. I have watched cooks add handfuls of dried red chilies to this stew, but you can decide how much heat to add. While traveling throughout south India, I sampled many variations of *sambar*, some of which brought tears to my eyes. One of my favorite breakfasts or luncheons is *Idlis* (page 70), steamed rice and urad *dal* dumplings, *sambar* and a chutney, possibly mango or mint and coriander. When mixed with rice or *idlis*, the *sambar* mellows and becomes a heartwarming vegetarian dish.

2/3 cup split *toor dal* or yellow split peas
1 teaspoon ground turmeric
1-inch ball of tamarind pulp
1 tablespoon olive oil
1 teaspoon black mustard seeds
1/2 teaspoon fenugreek seeds
1/2 teaspoon cumin seeds
6 dried red chilies
2–4 teaspoons seeded, minced fresh green chilies
6 fresh curry leaves
1/2 cup peeled shallots
1 tablespoon *Sambar Masala* (page 45)

1/4 teaspoon ground asafetida, *hing*
2 medium ripe tomatoes, cut into 1/2-inch wedges
1 medium eggplant, about 1/2 pound, cut into 1–1/2 inch cubes
1/2 pound okra, trimmed, cut into 1-1/2-inch pieces
1 cup tomatoes, puréed
1/2 teaspoon red pepper powder
Salt to taste
2 tablespoons chopped fresh coriander leaves

Sort and wash the *dal* as described on page 55. Place the *dal* in a bowl. Add sufficient warm water to cover by 1 inch. Soak for 3 to 5 hours. Drain.

In a large non-stick saucepan combine the *dal*, 6 cups of water and the turmeric. Bring to the boil over high heat. Reduce the heat to low, cover with a tigh-fitting lid and simmer for about 30 to 40 minutes, stirring occasionally. The *dal* should be very soft and broken down to a coarse purée. Remove from the heat. Strain the *dal*. Reserve the water for Spicy Tomato-Flavored Lentil Broth (page 95) or another dish. With a whisk, beat the *dal* to a smooth purée. Set aside.

Meanwhile, place the tamarind pulp in a bowl. Pour 1 cup of hot water over the pulp and soak for 20 minutes. Mash the pulp with a spoon or with your fingers. Pour the tamarind and liquid into a sieve and strain into a small bowl, squeezing out as much of the tamarind liquid as possible. Discard the fibers.

Heat the oil in a large non-stick saucepan over medium heat. Add the mustard seeds and stir until they crackle. Add the fenugreek and cumin seeds, red chilies, green chilies and curry leaves. Stir for 30 seconds. Add shallots and stir until soft and slightly browned. Add *sambar masala* and asafetida. Stir. Add the tomatoes and stir for 1 minute. Add the eggplant and okra. Stir for 3 to 4 minutes. Add the tamarind liquid, puréed tomatoes and red pepper powder. Partially cover and simmer until the vegetables are tender. Add the puréed *dal* and salt to taste. Simmer for 5 minutes, stirring occasionally. Sprinkle with chopped coriander. Serve in small bowls.

YIELD: 8 to 10 servings with *idlis*.

ADVANCE PREPARATION: Prepare 1 day ahead. Refrigerate. Reheat gently prior to serving.

129 Calories per serving:
  7 G Protein   36 MG Sodium
  3 G Fat   0 MG Cholesterol
 21 G Carbohydrate

Inspired by K. Natarajan, Executive Chef, Taj Coromandel Hotel, Madras.

Chickpea Dumplings in Yogurt Sauce, Punjabi Style

PUNJABI KADHI

∼≈⌢

One of many delights served to me in Inder and Aruna Sharma's New Delhi home was a dish of delicate chickpea flour dumplings floating in a flavorful, smooth, creamy yogurt sauce. This nutritious north Indian vegetarian specialty is often served as part of their Sunday luncheon. For a simple lunch or supper, serve it with *basmati* rice, a vegetable, such as spinach, and a crunchy salad.

In Aruna's original recipe the dumplings were deep-fried in oil. I have varied her recipe by cooking the dumplings in stock. I believe you will enjoy this light version.

DUMPLINGS:

1/4 cup nonfat plain yogurt
1/4 teaspoon red pepper powder
1/4 teaspoon salt
2 cups chickpea flour

Pinch of baking soda
8 cups unsalted vegetable or
  chicken stock

SAUCE:

2 cups nonfat plain yogurt
2/3 cup chickpea flour
1/2 teaspoon ground turmeric
1/2 teaspoon red pepper powder

1–2 minced, seeded fresh green
  chilies
1/2 teaspoon salt, or to taste

TEMPERING:

2 teaspoons canola oil
1/2 teaspoon black mustard seeds
1 teaspoon cumin seeds
1/4 teaspoon fenugreek seeds

1–2 dried red chilies
1 small onion, minced
2 fresh curry leaves (optional)

DUMPLINGS: Combine the yogurt, 1/2 cup warm water, red pepper powder and salt in a bowl. Put the flour in a food processor and process for 10 seconds. With the machine running, pour the yogurt mixture through the feed tube. The contents will have the consistency of a thick paste. Continue processing for about 3 to 4 minutes, turning the processor on and off every 15 seconds. The batter should become light and airy. When ready to cook the dumplings, add the baking soda and mix well. Bring the stock to a boil in a large saucepan. To test the consistency of the batter, drop a spoonful in boiling stock. If it stays at the bottom, the batter is too thick and needs further beating. Drop the paste mixture by the spoonful into the boiling stock using another spoon to push the batter. The dumplings should be about 3/4 inch in diameter. Do not worry if all the dumplings are not the same size and shape. Cook the dumplings in batches, for 4 to 5 minutes. Remove with a slotted spoon. Let drain on paper towels. Continue cooking the remaining dumplings in this manner. When all are cooked, let them cool slightly. Then cover tightly.

SAUCE: Place the yogurt in a large bowl and beat until smooth. Add 6 cups of water, the chickpea flour, turmeric, red pepper powder, green chilies and salt and whisk until smooth. This may be lightly processed in the food processor if desired.

TEMPERING: Heat the oil in a large saucepan over moderate heat. Add the mustard seeds and stir until they crackle. Add the cumin and fenugreek seeds, dried red chilies, onion and curry leaves, if desired. When the onions are translucent and the cumin and dried red chilies darken, add the sauce mixture and bring almost to a boil. Stir constantly to prevent the yogurt from separating and curdling. Add the dumplings and stir for 2 to 3 minutes. Reduce the heat to medium-low and cook gently, uncovered, for about 35 minutes. Stir often to prevent the sauce from sticking and burning. Add salt if desired. Serve immediately.

YIELD: 10 servings with other dishes.

252 Calories per serving:
16	G Protein	229	MG Sodium
4	G Fat	1	MG Cholesterol
43	G Carbohydrate		

Inspired by Inder Sharma, President, Pacific Asia Travel Association and Chairman, SITA World Travel, New Delhi.

Yogurt Salads Raita

≈≈≈

Spiced Yogurt Salad

BHURANNI

≈≈≈

Here is a splendid, spirited palate refresher that is equally welcome with rich Mughlai dishes as with a Western buffet or barbecue.

3 cups plus 2 tablespoons nonfat
  plain yogurt
1/8 teaspoon peeled, shredded
  fresh ginger
1/8 teaspoon slivered garlic
2 tablespoons nonfat cottage
  cheese

1/4–1/2 teaspoon red pepper
  powder
1/2 teaspoon roasted cumin seeds,
  ground
1 tablespoon chopped fresh coriander leaves
Salt to taste (optional)

Place the 3 cups of yogurt in a sieve over a bowl and let it drain for 3 hours in the refrigerator.

Meanwhile, place the ginger and garlic in a small bowl with 2 tablespoons of water. Let soak for 3 hours. Discard the garlic and ginger, keeping the soaking water. Discard the yogurt draining liquid.

In a food processor or blender, process the remaining 2 tablespoons of yogurt and the cottage cheese to a smooth, creamy consistency.

In a bowl, combine the drained yogurt and cottage cheese mixture, ginger and garlic liquid, red pepper powder, ground cumin and chopped coriander leaves. If desired, add salt to taste. Cover and chill in the refrigerator until ready to serve.

YIELD: 4 to 6 servings.

102 Calories per serving:
  12 G Protein   141 MG Sodium
   0 G Fat   5 MG Cholesterol
  15 G Carbohydrate

Inspired by Master Chef Imtiaz Qureshi, Dum Pukht Restaurant, Maurya Sheraton, New Delhi.

Spiced Eggplant, Tomato and Yogurt Salad

BAINGAN BHARTA RAITA

≈≈

This is a delectable and versatile dish that can be served as a yogurt salad or as a dip for vegetables.

1 recipe Roasted Eggplant Purée   1/2 cup nonfat plain yogurt,
  with Seasoned Yogurt   lightly beaten

Prepare eggplant purée according to recipe. Stir in yogurt until well blended. Chill. Serve.

YIELD: 4 to 6 servings.

116 Calories per serving:
  5 G Protein   336 MG Sodium
  4 G Fat   1 MG Cholesterol
  17 G Carbohydrate

Inspired by Mrs. Bachi Karkaria, Food Editor, Times of India, Bombay.

Green Pepper and Yogurt Salad

SIMLA MIRCH RAITA

∾⨀∿

In Madras, Saroja Subbaraman prepares this southern salad by stir-frying green peppers with mustard seeds and then combining them with the yogurt. I find it quite refreshing to blanch or steam the green peppers.

2 green peppers, halved and seeded
2 cups nonfat plain yogurt, drained
1 fresh green chili pepper, seeds
   removed and minced
2 teaspoons minced fresh
   coriander leaves

1/2 teaspoon salt (optional)
1 teaspoon extra-virgin olive oil
   (optional)
1 teaspoon black mustard seeds
   (optional)

Blanch the peppers in boiling water for 1 to 2 minutes. Drain and refresh in cold water. Cut the peppers into 1/4-inch cubes.

In a bowl whisk the yogurt. Stir in the green peppers, chili pepper, coriander leaves and salt, if desired.

YIELD: 4 to 6 servings.

VARIATION: Heat the oil in a small non-stick skillet. Add the mustard seeds and stir until they crackle. Let cool slightly. Add to the yogurt mixture and stir. Cover and chill in the refrigerator until ready to serve.

ADVANCE PREPARATION: Prepare 1 day ahead. Refrigerate. Serve.

77 Calories per serving:
 8 G Protein   82 MG Sodium
 0 G Fat   3 MG Cholesterol
12 G Carbohydrate

Inspired by Saroja Subbaraman, Madras.

Tomato and Yogurt Salad

TAMATAR RAITA

❧❧❦

The contrast between the brilliant red tomatoes and creamy white yogurt is vivid and appealing. Marble-size firm cherry tomatoes cut into quarters are also delectable.

3/4 cup nonfat plain yogurt
2 small ripe tomatoes,
  diced
1/2 cup minced onion

1 fresh green chili, finely minced
2 tablespoons chopped fresh
  coriander leaves

Place the yogurt in a bowl and whisk with a fork until creamy and smooth. Add the tomatoes, onion, chili and coriander and stir lightly to combine. Cover and chill in the refrigerator until ready to serve.

YIELD: 4 servings.

47 Calories per serving:
4 G Protein   128 MG Sodium
0 G Fat   1 MG Cholesterol
8 G Carbohydrate

Inspired by Kitty Basith, Willowbrook, IL, formerly of Bangalore.

Spinach and Yogurt Salad

PAALAK RAITA

∽✑

This simple salad combines spinach and yogurt with the refreshing touch of fresh coriander, the tartness of lemon juice and the zip of pepper. It is excellent served with any meal or as a dip with vegetables.

1/2 pound fresh spinach, trimmed, washed and chopped
2 cups nonfat plain yogurt
1/4 teaspoon ground white pepper
1/4 teaspoon red pepper powder (optional)

1 teaspoon roasted cumin seeds, ground
2 tablespoons minced fresh coriander leaves
2 teaspoons fresh lemon juice

Steam the spinach over boiling water for 2 to 3 minutes, or until wilted. Remove the spinach, cool slightly then squeeze out any moisture.

Place the yogurt in a bowl and whisk with a fork until creamy and smooth. Add the white pepper, red pepper powder, if desired, and cumin seeds. Mix well. Add the spinach, minced coriander and lemon juice. Cover and chill in the refrigerator until ready to serve.

YIELD: 6 servings

ADVANCE PREPARATION: Prepare 1 day ahead. Refrigerate, covered. Add lemon juice prior to serving.

51 Calories per serving:
  6 G Protein   84 MG Sodium
  0 G Fat   2 MG Cholesterol
  8 G Carbohydrate

Cucumber and Yogurt Salad

KACHUMBAR RAITA

∽◌∾

1 small cucumber, peeled and seeded	1 tablespoon chopped fresh mint or coriander leaves
1 small onion, minced	1 fresh green chili, seeded and finely sliced (optional)
2-1/2 cups nonfat plain yogurt	

Finely shred the cucumber into 1/2-inch lengths. Place in a bowl with the onion and yogurt. Stir to mix. Cover and chill in refrigerator until ready to serve. Garnish with mint and chili.

YIELD: 4 to 6 servings.

90 Calories per serving:
  9 G Protein   102 MG Sodium
  0 G Fat   3 MG Cholesterol
15 G Carbohydrate

Inspired by Sous Chef Kamal Kumar Channa, Tandoor Restaurant.

Pineapple and Yogurt Salad

ANANNAS RAITA

∽◌∾

Refreshingly simple, this is an inviting addition to a meal on a hot day.

1 cup low-fat plain yogurt	1 cup cubed fresh pineapple, cut into 1-inch cubes

Drain the yogurt in a sieve for 20 minutes. Discard the liquid. In a bowl, combine the yogurt and pineapple. Cover and chill in the refrigerator until ready to serve.

YIELD: 4 to 6 servings.

49 Calories per serving:
- 3 G Protein
- 0 G Fat
- 9 G Carbohydrate

- 40 MG Sodium
- 1 MG Cholesterol

Banana and Yogurt Salad

KEELA RAITA

࿇

Bananas combined with fresh mint, coconut, tart lime juice and yogurt are the perfect palate refresher during a meal or as a lovely fruit dessert. It's no wonder that bananas are an Indian favorite, as there are said to be about 400 varieties!

1-3/4 cups nonfat plain yogurt
2 tablespoons finely chopped fresh
   mint leaves
2 tablespoons ground coconut
1–2 fresh green chilies, seeded and
   finely shredded

1/8 teaspoon freshly grated
   nutmeg
2 teaspoons fresh lime juice
2 firm, ripe bananas, peeled and
   thinly sliced

Place the yogurt in a bowl and whisk with a fork until creamy and smooth. Add the mint, coconut, chilies, nutmeg and lime juice and stir lightly to combine. Add the bananas and stir well. Cover and chill in the refrigerator before serving.

YIELD: 4 to 6 servings.

ADVANCE PREPARATION: Prepare 1 day ahead. Serve chilled.

147 Calories per serving:
- 7 G Protein
- 3 G Fat
- 26 G Carbohydrates

- 90 MG Sodium
- 2 MG Cholesterol

Salads

∾

Indian Cottage Cheese Salad

PANEER SALAD

∾

A dieter's delight, this colorful salad is tossed with the most traditional of Indian dressings—lemon juice, orange juice, salt and crushed black peppercorns.

2 quarts 2 percent milk
4 tablespoons fresh lemon juice
1 green bell pepper, cut into
  1/4-inch strips

2 cups bean sprouts, blanched for
  30 seconds and drained
1 small ripe tomato, cut into
  1/4-inch strips

DRESSING:

2 tablespoons fresh lemon juice
2 tablespoons fresh orange juice

1/2–1 teaspoon black peppercorns,
  crushed
Salt to taste

Prepare the Indian "cottage cheese," *paneer.* Heat the milk slowly in a large non-stick saucepan over medium heat, stirring occasionally to prevent the milk from sticking to the bottom and a skin from forming on the top. When the milk comes to a boil, lower the heat slightly and stir for 1 minute. Stir in the 4 tablespoons of lemon juice to allow the milk to separate into soft, moist curds. This should take about 10 to 20 seconds. When the lumps of curd begin to form, stir the mixture very slowly and carefully to prevent the freshly formed curds from disintegrating into small pieces. Immediately remove from heat. Let stand for a few minutes to cool.

Line a strainer with several layers of cheese cloth. Pour the cheese mixture through the lined strainer into a bowl. Hold the cheese cloth under a medium stream of running water for 10 to 20 seconds to remove the lemon smell. Gather up the sides of the cheese cloth and secure the top by tying the cheese cloth together. Gently squeeze the cheese cloth to remove any excess moisture. Hang the cheese cloth over a bowl for about 1-1/2 hours. Place the cheese packet (still in the cheese cloth) on a flat surface and cover the entire top with a very heavy object, such as a cast-iron skillet. Let the cheese sit for 1 hour, or until it becomes firm and all the moisture has been extruded. The cheese must be firm enough to be cut into shreds. This yields 2 cups of *paneer.* Cut the *paneer* into shreds and place in a bowl with the green pepper, bean sprouts and tomato.

DRESSING: Combine the lemon and orange juice, crushed peppercorns and salt. Add the dressing to the *paneer* prior to serving and toss lightly. Cover and chill until ready to serve. Serve cold.

YIELD: 4 to 6 servings.

ADVANCE PREPARATION: Prepare the *paneer* 2 days ahead. Refrigerate. Cut into shreds several hours before serving. Prepare the dressing several days ahead. Refrigerate. Toss with salad when serving.

COOK'S TIP: If the curd does not form after adding all of the lemon juice, you may have to add more lemon juice gradually until lumps of curd form and the whey separates.

276 Calories per serving:

18 G Protein	307 MG Sodium
10 G Fat	36 MG Cholesterol
31 G Carbohydrate	

Inspired by Arvind Saraswat, Director, Food Production, Northern Region, Taj Mahal Group of Hotels, Bombay.

Fresh Mango Salad

AAM SALAD

꩜

When golden, aromatic mangoes are in season, this easily-prepared, tantalizing salad from the scenic Coorg area in the state of Karnataka is one of my favorite summer dishes.

1 teaspoon black mustard seeds
1–2 large ripe mangoes, about 1
  pound
1 cup nonfat plain yogurt
1 fresh green chili, seeded and
  minced

2 teaspoons ground coconut
1 teaspoon sugar
1 teaspoon extra-virgin olive oil
1–2 dried red chilies
1 small shallot, thinly sliced

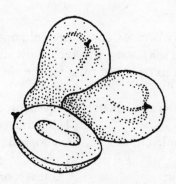

Grind 3/4 teaspoon of the black mustard seeds to a powder in a mini processor, blender or spice grinder. Peel the mangoes and cut the flesh into 1/2-inch cubes.

Place the yogurt in a bowl and whisk with a fork until smooth and creamy. Add the green chili, ground mustard seeds, coconut and sugar. Stir to combine. Add the mangoes and stir gently to combine.

In a small non-stick skillet, heat the oil over moderate heat. Add the remaining mustard seeds and stir until they crackle. Add the dried red chilies and cook until they turn a few shades darker. Add the shallot and stir-fry until slightly browned. Remove from the heat. Add to the mango mixture and stir. Check for sweetness. If mangoes are not fully ripe, more sugar may need to be added. Serve chilled or at room temperature.

YIELD: 4 to 6 servings.

ADVANCE PREPARATION: Prepare ahead. Cover and refrigerate. Serve.

130 Calories per serving:
  5 G Protein   46 MG Sodium
  2 G Fat   1 MG Cholesterol
 26 G Carbohydrate

Inspired by Chitra Moghul, Bangalore.

Shrimp-Stuffed Tomato Salad

JHINGA-TAMATAR

∾◌∾

Stuffed tomatoes are a most appealing cold appetizer, light luncheon or buffet dish. You may vary the recipe by substituting rice for the potato and flaked water-packed tuna for the shrimp.

8 firm, ripe plum tomatoes, about   1 teaspoon tomato purée
  2 pounds   1/2 pound cooked shrimp, coarsely
1 medium potato, boiled in the   chopped
  skin and cooled   1 teaspoon extra-virgin olive oil
3/4 cup minced onion   1/2 teaspoon salt, or to taste
1–2 green chilies, seeded and
  minced

GARNISH:

2 tablespoons chopped fresh   4–8 romaine lettuce leaves
  coriander leaves

Wash and dry the tomatoes. Cut each tomato in half lengthwise. Using a spoon or small knife, carefully scoop out the pulp. Mince finely and place in a bowl. Invert the tomato shells on a rack to drain for about 15 minutes. Dry the inside of the tomatoes with a paper towel.

Peel the potato and cut into 1/4-inch cubes. In a bowl combine the onion, potato, green chilies, tomato purée, shrimp, olive oil and salt to taste.

Distribute the filling equally among the tomato halves, about 2 tablespoons for each tomato, being careful not to pack the filling. Garnish the top of each tomato half with chopped coriander. Serve one tomato half on a lettuce leaf as an appetizer or two halves as a luncheon dish. Serve chilled or at room temperature.

YIELD: 4 servings as a luncheon dish or 8 servings as an appetizer.

COOK'S TIP: Cherry tomatoes may be substituted for the plum tomatoes. Proceed as in recipe. Serve as an appetizer.

ADVANCE PREPARATION: Prepare filling 1 day in advance. Store, covered, in the refrigerator. Stuff the tomatoes 3 to 4 hours prior to serving.

166 Calories per serving:
  15 G Protein   439 MG Sodium
   3 G Fat   111 MG Cholesterol
  22 G Carbohydrate

Cucumber and Tomato Salad

KACHUMBAR AUR TAMATAR SALAD

⌇⌇⌇

1 medium cucumber, peeled, seeded and cut into 1/4-inch cubes
1 medium onion, minced
1 medium tomato, diced into 1/4-inch cubes

2 teaspoons extra-virgin olive oil
1 tablespoon fresh lemon or lime juice
1/8 teaspoon salt, or to taste
Freshly ground black pepper

In a bowl combine the cucumber, onion, tomato, olive oil and lemon juice. Season to taste with salt and pepper. Cover and chill in the refrigerator until ready to serve.

YIELD: 4 servings.

49 Calories per serving:
- 1 G Protein
- 2 G Fat
- 7 G Carbohydrate
- 77 MG Sodium
- 0 MG Cholesterol

Onion and Tomato Salad, Parsi Style

PYAZ AUR TAMATAR PARSI

∽◡∾

This delectably crisp and spicy onion salad is from the Parsi community of Bombay. The dressing is a tart, sweet combination of brown sugar and tamarind. If you desire a less spirited version, remove the seeds from the chilies.

2 medium onions, halved and thinly sliced
2 teaspoons salt
1-inch ball of tamarind pulp
2-1/2 teaspoons brown or palm sugar

2 small ripe tomatoes, finely chopped
1 tablespoon shredded fresh ginger
1-2 hot green chilies, thinly sliced
2 tablespoons chopped fresh coriander leaves

Sprinkle the onions with salt and let stand for 1 hour.

Meanwhile, place the tamarind pulp in a bowl. Pour 1/4 cup of hot water over the pulp and soak for 20 minutes. Mash the pulp with a spoon or with your fingers. Pour the tamarind and the liquid through a sieve and strain into another bowl, squeezing out as much of the tamarind liquid as possible. Discard the fiber. Add the sugar to the tamarind liquid, stir to dissolve and set aside.

Drain the onions, squeezing out as much liquid as possible. Rinse under cold running water and drain well. In a bowl, combine the onions, tomatoes, ginger and chilies. Pour the tamarind mixture over the salad and toss to mix. Sprinkle the coriander leaves on top. Cover and chill in the refrigerator before serving.

YIELD: 4 servings with other dishes.

57 Calories per serving:
  2 G Protein   153 MG Sodium
  0 G Fat   0 MG Cholesterol
 13 G Carbohydrate

Inspired by the chefs of the Parsi Ratan Tata Institute, Bombay.

Onion Salad, Parsi Style

PYAZ SALAD PARSI

Easily prepared, this salad is refreshing with any meal.

1 medium onion, finely chopped   Pinch of salt
2 teaspoons minced fresh   1 fresh green chili, seeded and
  coriander leaves   finely chopped (optional)
2 teaspoons rice vinegar   4 teaspoons finely chopped tomato

In a bowl combine the onion, coriander leaves, vinegar, salt, chili and tomato. Cover and allow to stand for 1 hour for the flavors to develop.

YIELD: 4 servings.

13 Calories per serving:
  0 G Protein   44 MG Sodium
  0 G Fat   0 MG Cholesterol
  3 G Carbohydrate

Tomato and Green Pepper Salad, New Delhi Style

TAMATAR AUR SIMLA MIRCH

⌇∾⌇

This colorful salad, delicately spiced with cumin, appears almost daily on New Delhi tables.

2–3 tomatoes, about 10 ounces, cut into 1/3-inch dice
1 green bell pepper, about 6 ounces, cut into 1/3-inch dice
1/2 teaspoon salt

1 tablespoon lime juice
1 teaspoon roasted cumin seeds, ground to a powder
Freshly ground pepper to taste

Combine all of the ingredients in a bowl. Chill. Serve.

YIELD: 6 to 8 servings.

17 Calories per serving:
1 G Protein
0 G Fat
4 G Carbohydrate

197 MG Sodium
0 MG Cholesterol

Southern Mixed Vegetable Salad

THAKKALI-VELLARIKKAI-CARROT KOSUMALLI

⌇∾⌇

Here is a versatile hot and flavorful salad that might possibly be called the south Indian version of salsa. The vegetables are chopped fine to enable the natural juices to emerge. Serve it as a refreshing accompaniment to any meal, to top broiled fish or as a dip with chips or raw vegetables. In this classic preparation from Mangalore on the west coast, local cooks would use four times as many green chilies!

1 carrot, peeled and chopped
1 cucumber, peeled, seeded and
   chopped
1 medium, ripe tomato, chopped

1 fresh green chili, minced
1/4 cup chopped fresh coriander
   leaves

DRESSING:

2 teaspoons canola oil
1 teaspoon black mustard seeds
1 teaspoon cumin seeds
1 teaspoon split *urad dal*
1 dried red chili, halved and
   seeded

1/2 teaspoon ground asafetida,
   hing
8 fresh curry leaves
2 tablespoons fresh lime juice
1/2 teaspoon salt

In a bowl combine the carrot, cucumber, tomato, chili and coriander leaves.

DRESSING: Heat the oil in a small non-stick skillet over moderate heat. Add the mustard and cumin seeds and stir-fry until the mustard seeds crackle. Add the *dal*, dried red chili, asafetida and curry leaves. Cook, stirring, until the *dal* is golden brown. Remove from heat. Let cool slightly. Add the lime juice to the dressing and mix well. Season with salt. Serve at room temperature or cover and chill in the refrigerator until ready to serve.

YIELD: 4 servings.

65 Calories per serving:
2 G Protein
3 G Fat
9 G Carbohydrate

301 MG Sodium
0 MG Cholesterol

Inspired by Executive Chef P. N. Raman, Head, Department Food & Beverage, Welcomgroup Graduate School for Hotel Administration, Manipal.

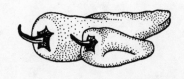

Mixed Fruit and Vegetable Salad

PHAL KI CHAT

∽◡∽

1 medium, ripe tomato, cut into
  1/4-inch cubes
1 large apple, peeled, cored and cut
  into 1/4-inch cubes
1 large pear, peeled, cored and cut
  into 1/4-inch cubes
1 orange, peeled, sectioned and cut
  into 1/4-inch cubes

1 cucumber, peeled, seeded and
  cut into 1/4-inch cubes
1 carrot, peeled and cut into
  1/4-inch pieces
8 radishes, cut into quarters and
  diced into 1/4-inch cubes
Salt and pepper to taste

In a bowl combine the tomato, apple, pear, orange, cucumber, carrot and radishes. Season with salt and pepper to taste. Cover and chill in the refrigerator before serving.

YIELD: 4 servings

ADVANCE PREPARATION: Prepare 2 hours in advance.

65 Calories per serving:
  1 G Protein   41 MG Sodium
  1 G Fat   0 MG Cholesterol
 16 G Carbohydrates

Inspired by Prem Sharma, Burr Ridge, IL, formerly of New Delhi.

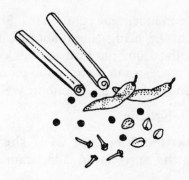

Chutneys, Pickles
Chatneys, Achars

୨୦୯୨

Carrot Chutney

GAAJAR CHATNEY

୨୦୯୨

This outstanding chutney is an excellent accompaniment to any meal.

1 tablespoon olive oil
3 medium carrots, peeled and
  thinly sliced
1/2 cup thinly sliced onion
1 large clove garlic, chopped
1-1/2 teaspoons chopped fresh
  ginger

2–3 dried red chilies
1 tablespoon ground coriander
1/4 teaspoon cumin seed
Salt to taste
2 tablespoons fresh lemon or lime
  juice

Heat the oil in a non-stick skillet over moderate heat. Add the carrots and stir-fry for 2 to 3 minutes. Add the onions, garlic, ginger, dried red chilies, coriander and cumin seed. Stir-fry until the onions are soft and translucent, being careful not to brown.

Remove the skillet from the heat and let cool slightly. Place the mixture in a food processor or blender and process to a smooth purée. Add salt to taste and lemon juice. Combine well.

YIELD: approximately 1 cup.

ADVANCE PREPARATION: Prepare 1 week ahead. Store in a tightly sealed glass jar in the refrigerator. Add lemon or lime juice prior to serving.

78 Calories per serving:
  2 G Protein   57 MG Sodium
  4 G Fat   0 MG Cholesterol
10 G Carbohydrate

Fresh Coriander Chutney

DHANIA CHATNEY

∽◡◠∾

This chutney is made fresh daily in Indian homes. Its refreshingly perky taste is delightful as dipping sauce for snacks and highly seasoned dishes. It is also very rich in Vitamins A and C.

2 cups tightly packed fresh
coriander leaves
1/2 teaspoon cumin seeds, roasted
and ground
1/2–1 green chili, seeds removed,
coarsely chopped

1-1/2 tablespoon fresh lemon
juice
1/2 teaspoon salt, or to taste
Freshly ground black pepper

In a food processor or blender combine the coriander, cumin, chili and lemon juice. Process to a paste, pushing down the ingredients several times during processing. Season with the salt and black pepper. Serve in a nonmetallic bowl.

YIELD: approximately 1 cup.

ADVANCE PREPARATION: The chutney will keep refrigerated for up to 1 week in a tightly covered glass bowl.

VARIATION: Add 2 to 3 tablespoons plain nonfat yogurt for a more mellow chutney. This will keep several days refrigerated.

2 Calories per serving:
0 G Protein
0 G Fat
0 G Carbohydrate

37 MG Sodium
0 MG Cholesterol

Mint-Coriander Chutney

PUDINA CHATNEY

∽つ◡ぐ∾

Refreshingly sharp and bracing, Mint-Coriander Chutney is the perfect accompaniment to both savory and spicy dishes. It is also a delectable dipping sauce for vegetables.

Because there are many varieties of mint, you may want to add some nonfat plain yogurt to the chutney to temper the sharpness. Since this chutney will keep for up to one week, refrigerated, you may want to double or triple the recipe if you are serving Indian food often.

1/4 cup tightly packed fresh mint leaves	8 green onions, chopped
3/4 cup tightly packed fresh coriander leaves	1-2 fresh green chilies, seeded and chopped
1 tablespoon chopped fresh ginger	1 tablespoon fresh lemon juice
	1/8 teaspoon salt, or to taste

In a food processor or blender, process the mint, coriander, ginger, green onions and green chilies to a coarse paste. Add the lemon juice and salt and gently process to a creamy relish. Transfer to a glass container. Cover tightly. Chill in the refrigerator until ready to serve.

YIELD: approximately 1 cup.

ADVANCE PREPARATION: Prepare up to 1 week in advance. Store in a tightly covered glass container in refrigerator.

VARIATION: Add 2 tablespoons nonfat plain yogurt prior to serving.

23 Calories per serving:
2 G Protein   38 MG Sodium
0 G Fat   0 MG Cholesterol
3 G Carbohydrate

Inspired by Suman Sood, Registered Dietitician; President, Club of Indian Women, Chicago, formerly of New Delhi.

Tamarind Chutney

GOR AMLI NI CHATNEY

∽ɔɕ∼

This delectable chutney combining tangy, sweet and fruity flavors is one of my preferred accompaniments. If you plan to prepare many Indian meals, you may want to double or triple the recipe, as it keeps refrigerated for at least one month.

4 tablespoons tamarind paste, soaked in 1 cup of hot water for 20 minutes
1/4–1/2 teaspoon red pepper powder

2 tablespoons brown sugar, or to taste
1/2 teaspoon salt
1 tablespoon *garam masala* (page 43)

Strain the soaked tamarind pulp, forcing it against the sides of the sieve to extract all the juices. Reserve the liquid. Discard the pulp.

In a small saucepan, combine the red pepper powder, brown sugar, salt, *garam masala* and tamarind liquid. Simmer over low heat, stirring constantly, until slightly thickened. Cool. Refrigerate in a covered glass jar.

YIELD: 1 cup.

ADVANCE PREPARATION: Prepare 1 month ahead. Keep tightly covered in a glass jar in the refrigerator.

16 Calories per serving:
  0 G Protein   238 MG Sodium
  0 G Fat   0 MG Cholesterol
  4 G Carbohydrate

Inspired by Suman Sood, Registered Dietitian; President, Club of Indian Women, Chicago, formerly of New Delhi.

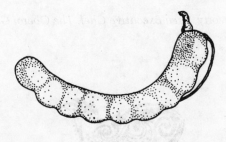

Tomato Chutney

TAMATAR CHATNEY

∞∽∾

Try this refreshing relish with any Indian or Western meal.

2 large ripe tomatoes, peeled and
  chopped
1–2 fresh green chilies, minced
2 teaspoons minced fresh ginger
1/2 teaspoon minced garlic
2 teaspoons minced, fresh
  coriander leaves

Salt to taste
2 teaspoons olive oil
1/2 teaspoon mustard seeds
3 small dried red chilies, crushed
5 fresh curry leaves (optional)

In a bowl, combine the tomatoes, green chilies, ginger, garlic and coriander leaves. Heat the olive oil over moderate heat in a small nonstick skillet. Add the mustard seeds and stir until they crackle. Add the dried red chilies, and curry leaves if desired. Stir until the red chilies darken slightly. Pour over the tomato mixture. Season to taste with salt. Serve.

YIELD: 2 cups

7 Calories per serving:
0 G Protein
0 G Fat
1 G Carbohydrate

6 MG Sodium
0 MG Cholesterol

Inspired by S. Charavorty, Area Executive Chef, The Oberoi Grand Hotels, Bombay.

Sweet, Hot and Sour Mango Chutney

MAANGAI VELLA PACHCHADI

∽∾∾

During the mango season, this popular, sweet, hot and sour version of chutney from the Chettiar community in Tamil Nadu will usually appear during every elaborate banana leaf banquet and wedding. The intricate flavors are apparent when the chutney is made one week ahead. Choose a mango that is half to three-quarters ripe.

2 tablespoons split *mung dal*
1 medium unpeeled green mango, cut into 1-inch pieces
1/2 teaspoon salt

6 tablespoons brown sugar
1/2–3/4 teaspoon red pepper powder

TEMPERING:

2 teaspoons canola oil
1/2 teaspoon black mustard seeds
1/2 teaspoon *urad dal*

1–2 dried red chilies, halved
1/8 teaspoon ground asafetida, *hing* (optional)

In a large non-stick saucepan, combine the *mung dal* and 3 cups of water. Bring to the boil, reduce the heat and simmer, covered, for about 10 minutes, or until the *dal* is tender but not mushy. Add the mango pieces and salt. Cook for 5 more minutes. (The mango should remain firm.) Add the brown sugar and red pepper powder. Stir well to dissolve the sugar. Remove from heat.

TEMPERING: Heat oil in a small non-stick skillet. Add the black mustard seeds and stir until they crackle. Add the *urad dal*, red chilies and asafetida. Cook until the *dal* and chilies have darkened. Pour over the cooked mango mixture.

YIELD: approximately 1-1/2 cups.

ADVANCE PREPARATION: Prepare 1 week ahead. Cover. Refrigerate.

18 Calories per serving:
  0 G Protein   49 MG Sodium
  0 G Fat   0 MG Cholesterol
  3 G Carbohydrate

Inspired by chefs of the Park Sheraton Hotel, Madras.

Southern Tomato Chutney

TAKKALI THOVIYAL

~~~

Here is a tangy tomato chutney from Madras.

2 teaspoons olive oil
2 tablespoons split *chana dal*
2/3 cup chopped onions
2–3 dried red chilies

1/2 teaspoon ground turmeric
Salt to taste
1 cup ripe tomatoes, roughly
  chopped

TEMPERING:
2 teaspoons olive oil
1–2 dried red chilies

3/4 teaspoon black mustard seeds
6 fresh curry leaves (optional)

Heat the oil in a large non-stick skillet over moderate heat. Add the *chana dal* and stir until light golden brown. Add the onions and cook, stirring, until translucent. Add the dried red chilies, turmeric and salt to taste. Stir for 30 seconds. Add the tomatoes and cook, mashing, until the tomatoes are crushed. Remove from the heat. Let cool. Place the mixture in a food processor or blender. Add 6 tablespoons of water and process to a coarse mixture. Transfer to a glass bowl.

TEMPERING: Heat the oil in a small, non-stick pan over moderate heat. Add the red chilies and stir until they are lightly browned, about 10 to 20 seconds. Add the mustard seeds, and curry leaves if desired, and stir until the mustard seeds crackle. Pour the tempering over the tomato mixture. Mix well. Serve at room temperature.

YIELD: approximately 2 cups.

ADVANCE PREPARATION: Prepare 1 day ahead. Refrigerate. Prepare tempering and add to the chutney several hours prior to serving. Serve at room temperature.

12 Calories per serving:
  0 G Protein   17 MG Sodium
  1 G Fat   0 MG Cholesterol
  1 G Carbohydrate

Inspired by Mrs. A. Mullens, Principal, Institute of Hotel Management Catering Technology & Applied Nutrition, Madras.

Carrot Pickle

GAAJAR ACHAR

∽⌇◡◠

These spiced carrots are a specialty of the Parsis of Bombay. For best flavor, use juicy sweet carrots.

1 pound carrots, peeled and cut
    into 2-1/2-inch strips
6 cloves garlic, minced
1-1/2 tablespoons red pepper
    powder, or to taste
1 teaspoon crushed cumin seeds

1/3 teaspoon ground turmeric
2 teaspoons black mustard seeds
1/3 cup fresh lemon juice
1 teaspoon canola oil
1 teaspoon salt

In a glass bowl, combine the carrots, garlic, red pepper powder, cumin seeds, turmeric, mustard seeds and salt. Toss well.

Heat the oil in a non-stick skillet over moderate heat. Add the carrots and spices. Stir-fry for 1 minute. Add the lemon juice and cook for 2 minutes more, or until the carrots are tender to the bite.

Remove from the heat.

Transfer the mixture to a sterilized jar and fill it tightly. Cover it with a nonmetallic lid. Shake the jar. Store in the refrigerator for three days.

YIELD: 1 pint.

ADVANCE PREPARATION: Prepare 1 week ahead. Serve at room temperature.

22 Calories per serving:
1 G Protein   161 MG Sodium
1 G Fat   0 MG Cholesterol
4 G Carbohydrate

Inspired by Gev Desai, Executive Chef, Maurya Sheraton, New Delhi.

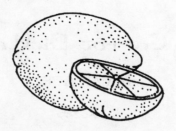

Sour Lemon or Lime Pickle

NIMBU ACHAR

৵৹৻

One of the most popular pickles is lemon or lime and this is one of the simplest. Pickles are traditionally made in the summer so that they may mature in the intense Indian sun. During their first three to four weeks of maturation, the pickles are set out daily to age in the sun. The sunlight provides an antiseptic reaction, plus it helps to speed the fermentation. Each evening, the jars are brought into the house and set out in the sun again in the morning.

It is important to choose good quality, smooth thin-skinned small lemons or limes that are free of any blemishes or soft spots. You may serve them in a month however, they taste better after three months and even better after six months; or one year. Prem Sharma says the longer a pickle matures, the better it tastes. She has a cherished jar of pickles that belonged to her late mother which is about 70 years old! It has now crystallized and she uses it for medicinal purposes to soothe stomach problems.

10 small smooth-skinned lemons or limes
2-1/2 teaspoons red pepper powder
1 teaspoon black pepper

Pinch ground asafetida, *hing*
1/2 teaspoon crushed red pepper flakes
5 tablespoons plus 1 teaspoon salt

Wash and thoroughly dry the lemons or limes. Set them in the sun or air-dry them in a warm oven for 5 minutes. Cut each one in half. Cut each half into 8 wedges. Save any juice. Let the wedges air dry for one day.

Combine the red pepper powder, black pepper, asafetida, crushed dried red pepper flakes, salt and any juice in a bowl and mix well. Squeeze the wedges slightly while combining with the mixture in the bowl.

Pack the mixture into a sterilized, 1-quart jar.

Set the jar in the sun every day for 3 weeks, bringing the jar in at night. Shake the jar two to three times a day. After the third week, the pickles do not have to be set in the sun, but must be shaken two to three times a day for another week. Let the pickles mature for at least one month. Once the pickles have been opened, they must be refrigerated.

YIELD: makes enough to fill a 1-quart jar.

8 Calories per serving:
0 G Protein   1149 MG Sodium
0 G Fat   0 MG Cholesterol
4 G Carbohydrate

Inspired by Prem Sharma, Burr Ridge, IL, formerly of New Delhi.

BREADS

$\mathcal{T}$he range of Indian breads is formidable. In the north you will find bread served at every meal, while in the south, breads often make way for rice. Breads are generally made from whole wheat flour and in most cases are flat, unleavened discs about four to six inches in diameter. *Naan* bread is baked in the *tandoor* oven. *Chapatis* or *Rotis* are grilled. *Parathas* are shallow-fried. *Puris* are deep-fried. Breads can also be stuffed with potatoes, *dals* or other vegetables.

For purposes of light cooking, I have included recipes that are griddle-baked and shallow-fried, plus Steamed Chickpea Bread, *Khaman Dhokla* (page 298), which is also considered to be a snack food.

Steamed Chickpea Bread KHAMAN DHOKLA
Griddle-Baked Whole Wheat Bread CHAPATI YA ROTI
Layered Whole Wheat Bread PARATHA
Potato-Stuffed Bread ALOO PARATHA

Steamed Chickpea Bread

KHAMAN DHOKLA

~~~

This version of succulent golden bread is a specialty of Gujarat. The bread is steamed and colorfully garnished with chopped fresh coriander, mustard seeds and often with coconut flakes. It is served warm or at room temperature as a snack or with a complete meal. Serve with Mint-Coriander Chutney (page 285).

1-1/2 cups sifted chickpea flour (measure after sifting)
1/4 teaspoon ground turmeric
1/4 teaspoon salt
1/8 teaspoon ground asafetida
1 teaspoon brown sugar, dissolved in 2 teaspoons hot water

2/3 cup nonfat plain yogurt
1/2 teaspoon baking soda
1/2 teaspoon baking powder
Canola spray

GARNISH:

1 tablespoon canola oil
2 teaspoons black mustard seeds
3–5 green chilies, cut into 1/4-inch slices

3 tablespoons chopped fresh coriander leaves
1/3 cup unsweetened coconut flakes (optional)

In a bowl, combine chickpea flour, turmeric, salt, asafetida, dissolved brown sugar, yogurt and 3 tablespoons water. Stir to combine thoroughly. Cover and set aside in a warm place for 8 hours or overnight.

Prepare a steamer. Set a trivet inside a 6-quart pot large enough to hold an 8-inch round cake pan while leaving a 1-1/2-inch space between the cake pan and the steamer pot edge to allow the steam to circulate properly. The trivet should allow the cake pan to be suspended at least two inches above the water so that no water will touch the steaming pan base. Add boiling water to the pan to a level of about 1-1/2 inches. Cover. Lightly mist an 8-inch round cake pan with canola oil.

When you are ready to steam the bread, sprinkle the baking soda and baking powder into the chickpea flour mixture. Stir to mix. Add 3 tablespoons warm water. With a gentle hand, stir in one direction

3 tablespoons warm water. With a gentle hand, stir in one direction until the batter begins to froth. Immediately pour the batter into a prepared pan and place it in the steamer. Place the lid on the steamer. Tie the ends of the tea towel or fold them up securely to prevent the towel from touching the steamed *Dhokla*. This is to prevent condensation that might collect on the lid from dripping on the steaming *Dhokla*. Steam for about 8 to 12 minutes or until a toothpick inserted in the bread comes out clean. If not, steam a few more minutes. Remove the bread from the steamer and set aside, loosely covered, for about 10 minutes. When steaming, check the water to make sure it has not boiled away.

GARNISH: In a small non-stick pan, heat 1 tablespoon canola oil over moderate heat. Add the mustard seeds and cook until they crackle. Add the green chilies and stir for 15 seconds. Add 1/3 cup water and stir to combine, about 30 seconds. Remove from heat. Let cool to room temperature.

Turn the bread out on a cutting board and cut into 1-1/2-inch squares. Arrange the bread in a single layer on a serving tray. Sprinkle coriander leaves and coconut flakes over the top. Pour the cooled chili mixture over the bread, covering the entire top, taking care to allow the mixture to drizzle into the cut portions of the *Dhokla*. Serve warm or at room temperature.

YIELD: 24 pieces.

63 Calories per piece
4 G Protein	58 MG Sodium
2 G Fat	0 MG Cholesterol
10 G Carbohydrate	

Inspired by Mrs. Rajendra Shah, Oak Brook, IL, formerly of Rajkot, Gujarat.

Griddle-Baked
Whole Wheat Bread

CHAPATI YA ROTI

∾∾

This basic whole wheat bread is called *Roti* in the north and *Chapati* in other parts of India. It is one of the most popular of the north Indian breads and is served with most meals. It can be made with *chapati* flour, available in Indian grocery stores, but I find you can also make an excellent version using sifted whole wheat and white flours.

The bread is traditionally cooked on a *tava*, a slightly concave cast-iron pan, but can be made successfully in a heavy cast-iron skillet or on a non-stick griddle.

Chapati dough should be quite soft. It is difficult to tell the exact amount of water necessary, as this depends upon the type of flour and the humidity in the air. Try the amount of water suggested, but don't hesitate to add more or less to produce a soft dough. The dough can be kneaded by hand or in a food processor, which I prefer. After kneading, it must rest for at least half an hour.

1-3/4 cup sifted whole wheat flour, plus extra for dusting
3/4 cup unbleached all-purpose flour

Salt to taste
3/4 cup warm water (110–120°F.)

Combine the whole wheat and all-purpose flours and salt in a large bowl. Add about 1/2 cup of the water to moisten the flour and allow it to adhere in a mass. Gradually add about another 1/4 cup of water, until a dough is formed and can be kneaded.

Place the dough on a work surface and knead the dough for 6 to 8 minutes until it is smooth. Put the dough in a bowl. Cover with a damp cloth and let the dough rest for 30 minutes to 3 hours at about 65°F.–75°F. If you want to leave it longer, you can refrigerate it, well covered, for up to 24 hours. Let the dough come to room temperature before rolling it out.

To make the dough in a food processor: Using the steel cutting blade, process the flours together for about 5 seconds. With the machine running, gradually add about 1/2 cup warm water through the feed tube in a steady stream until the mixture begins to hold together. As the flour begins to form a mass, add the remaining 1/4 cup of water in dribbles until the dough forms a ball. Process for 40 to 50 seconds more to knead the dough. It should be smooth and elastic to the touch. Let the dough rest in the bowl for 1 to 2 minutes. Rub your hands with flour and carefully remove the dough.

Put the dough in a bowl. Cover with a damp cloth and let the dough rest for 30 minutes to 3 hours as described above.

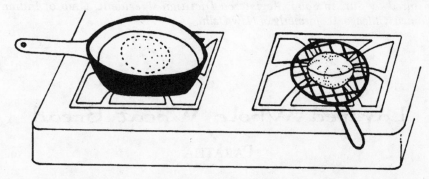

Place a cast-iron skillet or non-stick griddle over medium heat for 3 to 5 minutes. Meanwhile, knead the dough again. Divide it into 14 parts. Because the dough will be very sticky, rub your hands with a little flour while handling it. Roll each piece into a smooth ball. Flour the work surface and roll the ball in it. Press the ball to make a 2-inch patty. Roll the patty out evenly with a rolling pin, lightly dusting it frequently with flour, until it is 5-1/2 to 6 inches round. (Do not use excess flour as it will make the *Chapati* brittle.)

When the skillet is hot, pick up the *Chapati* and pat it with your hands to shake off any excess flour. Slap it onto the hot skillet. Let it cook on low heat for approximately 1 minute. When small bubbles begin to form, turn the *Chapati* over and cook for about 30 seconds. Turn on another burner with a high flame. Put the *Chapati* on a metal cake rack and hold it about 2 inches over the burner. In seconds, the *Chapati* will puff up. Continue to cook, turning it once, until small black flecks appear. The bread will burn easily if it is not constantly moved about over the heat.

Put the *Chapati* in a large napkin to keep warm. Repeat the process until all are cooked. If desired, brush one side with melted butter or *ghee.*

ADVANCE PREPARATION: Ideally, *Chapatis* should be eaten as soon as they are prepared. If you wish to eat them later, wrap the whole stack in aluminum foil and either refrigerate for a day or freeze. The *Chapatis* may be reheated in the foil in a 425°F. oven for 15 to 20 minutes.

83 Calories per serving:

3 G Protein	11 MG Sodium
0 G Fat	0 MG Cholesterol
18 G Carbohydrate	

Inspired by Suman Sood, Registered Dietitian; President, Club of Indian Women, Chicago, IL, formerly of New Delhi.

Layered Whole Wheat Bread

PARATHA

ᘛᘚ

Paratha dough is similar to *Chapati* dough except that less water is used, creating a stiffer dough. The bread is fully cooked on the *tava* and does not puff up like a *Chapati*. The dough is rolled, folded and then rolled again, creating a multitude of layers similar to puff pastry. Parathas are usually basted with *ghee* to make them crisp and rich. I have modified the recipe by substituting olive oil.

1-3/4 cups sifted whole wheat flour	1/4 teaspoon salt
1-3/4 cups all-purpose flour, plus extra for dusting	1 tablespoon plus 1/2 teaspoon extra-virgin olive oil
	1 cup warm water

In a bowl, combine the whole wheat and all-purpose flours and salt. Drizzle 2 teaspoons of the oil over the top. Rub the oil in with your fingertips until the mixture has the consistency of coarse oatmeal. Add about 1/2 cup of the water, slowly mixing it with the flour until it adheres to the mixture in a rough mass. Then dribble the remaining

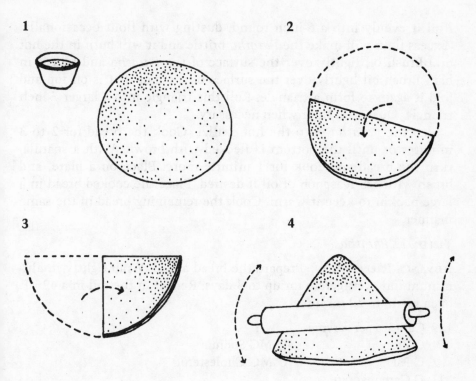

1

2

3

4

1/2 cup of water, mixing until it forms a medium-stiff dough. Knead the dough on a work surface, dusting occasionally with the extra flour to keep it from sticking, until it becomes silky, smooth and no longer sticky, about 10 minutes. Shape the dough into a ball, rub it with the remaining 1 teaspoon of oil and put it in a plastic bag. Let the dough rest for 30 minutes. You may leave it unrefrigerated for up to 3 hours. If you wish to leave it longer, cover and refrigerate it for up to 1 day. Let it come to room temperature before rolling it out.

TO MAKE DOUGH IN THE FOOD PROCESSOR: With the metal chopping blade in place, put the flours in the food-processor bowl. With the machine running, gradually add the 1 cup of water through the feed tube just until the mixture forms a ball. With the machine running, add 2 teaspoons of the oil. Process for 45 seconds. Carefully remove the dough to a lightly floured surface. Spread the remaining 1 teaspoon of oil over the top and knead for 30 seconds. Let the dough rest as above.

Heat a large cast-iron skillet or non-stick griddle on medium-low heat. Meanwhile, knead the dough again and form into 12 equal balls. Take one of the balls. Cover the remaining dough. Flatten the ball into a 2-inch patty. Dust both sides lightly with all-purpose flour.

Roll it evenly into a 6-inch round, dusting with flour occasionally. (Excess flour will make the *Paratha* brittle and it will burn in the hot oil.) Brush oil lightly over the surface of the *Paratha* and fold it in half. Brush oil lightly over the surface of the half that is on top and fold it again to form a triangle. Roll this triangle into a larger 7-inch triangle. Dust with flour when necessary.

Slap the *Paratha* onto the hot skillet. Cook the bread for 2 to 3 minutes or until the bottom is flecked with brown. With a spatula, turn the bread and cook for 1 minute more. Place on a plate, and brush with 1/8 teaspoon of oil if desired. Place the cooked bread in a large napkin to keep it warm. Cook the remaining bread in the same manner.

YIELD: 12 *Parathas.*

ADVANCE PREPARATION: Prepare the bread ahead. Wrap tightly in aluminum foil. Refrigerate for up to 3 days. Reheat in the foil in a 425°F. oven for 15 to 20 minutes.

139 Calories per serving:
4	G Protein	49 MG Sodium
2	G Fat	0 MG Cholesterol
27	G Carbohydrate	

Inspired by Suman Sood, Registered Dietitian; President, Club of Indian Women, Chicago.

Potato-Stuffed Bread

ALOO PARATHA

࿔

Tasty, potato-stuffed bread is a delicacy savored by many Indians for breakfast, as a snack or as a light lunch. Serve with Mint-Coriander Chutney (page 285) and a yogurt salad of your choice. These are best hot, but can be served at room temperature as well.

Double recipe *Paratha* dough recipe (page 302).

2 teaspoons olive oil
1-1/2 teaspoons minced garlic
1-1/2 teaspoons peeled, minced
   fresh ginger
1-1/2 teaspoon cumin seeds
2-3/4 cups warm mashed potatoes
1-1/2 teaspoon ground coriander

1/4 teaspoon red pepper powder
1/4 teaspoon ground turmeric
Salt to taste
1 tablespoon fresh lime juice
2 teaspoons brown sugar
2-1/2 tablespoons minced fresh
   coriander leaves

Heat the oil in a large non-stick skillet over moderate heat. Add the garlic, ginger and cumin seeds and stir until the cumin turns brown. Add the mashed potatoes, coriander, red pepper powder, turmeric, salt to taste, lime juice, brown sugar and coriander leaves. Stir to mix. Continue cooking and stirring for about 1 to 2 minutes to allow flavors to blend. Remove from heat. Divide into 12 portions and allow to cool.

Prepare the *Paratha* dough and roll in balls. Roll the dough balls into 6-inch rounds. Place a portion of the potato filling in the center of one round, leaving a border of about 1-1/2-inches around the edge. Using a pastry brush, moisten the edge with water. Place another round on top of the potato filling. Gently press the edges together to seal in the filling, removing any air bubbles that may have formed. As you shape the breads, place them, well spaced, on foil- or waxed-paper–lined cookie sheets. Cover with a clean dish towel.

Heat a cast-iron skillet or non-stick griddle for about 2 minutes over moderately high heat. Cook the breads, 1 or more at a time without crowding, for 2 to 3 minutes, or until the bottom is flecked with brown. Turn the bread over and cook for 2 minutes more, or until both sides of the bread are golden brown. Keep covered in a warm oven. If desired, the filled *Parathas* may be served at room temperature.

YIELD: 12 stuffed *Parathas*

ADVANCE PREPARATION: Cook the *parathas* ahead. Refrigerate for 1 to 2 days. Reheat in a 425°F. oven for 15 to 20 minutes or until heated throughout.

329 Calories per serving:
  10 G Protein   257 MG Sodium
   5 G Fat   1 MG Cholesterol
  63 G Carbohydrate

Inspired by Suman Sood, Registered Dietitian; President, Club of Indian Women, Chicago, IL.

SWEETS

Indians have an intense sweet tooth. For the most part, Indian sweets are extremely rich and are prepared primarily with dried fruits and nuts, milk, cream or yogurt. Sweet dumplings may be soaked in sugar syrups, while other sweets are similar to marzipan. There is always a fantastic abundance of sweets served during any festive occasion. Traditionally, desserts such as rice pudding are served along with the savory dishes to be eaten at any time during the meal.

I have selected some of my favorites but omitted many of the better-known classic recipes, as they do not fit in with the concept of light Indian food. And, of course, the refreshing and perfect conclusion to a spicy Indian meal is fresh fruit. Select mangoes, pineapples, oranges, melons, or bananas, or whatever fruit is in season. Serve them alone or combined.

Creamy Cheese Balls SANDESH
Sweet Yogurt Custard MISHTI DOI
Yogurt with Saffron SHRIKHAND
Semolina Halva with Golden Raisins SOOJI HALVA
Toasted Vermicelli Milk Pudding, Muslim Bohri Style
SHEER KORMA
Rice and Saffron Pudding KESARI KHEER
Saffron-Flavored Rice Pudding PHIRNEE
Rice Pudding PAYASAM
Urad Dal Rice Cakes with Custard and Melba Sauces
AL HAMDU
Vanilla Custard Brandy Sauce I
Vanilla Custard Brandy Sauce II
Melba Sauce
Easy Nonfat Mango Ice Cream AAM KULFI
Mangoes with Saffron-Flavored Yogurt AAM DAHI
Mangoes with Kewra-Flavored Yogurt AAM DAHI
Oranges with Saffron-Flavored Yogurt NARINGA DAHI
Sweet Apricot Sauce QUBANI KA MEETHA
Fresh Fruit Compote PHAL CHAT

Creamy Cheese Balls

SANDESH

∾ᘓᘔ∾

Bengalis love *Sandesh*, a delicately sweetened, soft-textured treat. It is usually made from fresh *paneer*, a cheese prepared from milk (see page 50), but Prem Sharma has devised a delicious, time-saving variation using ricotta cheese. Often the *Sandesh* is molded into various shapes such as a fish, fruit or flower, which you may do if you have the small molds. It can be served as a sweet at any time during the meal or at the end of a meal with Sweet Yogurt Custard (page 311) or fresh fruits.

1 pound low-fat ricotta cheese	24 golden raisins or thinly slivered
1/4 cup sugar	pistachio nuts
1 teaspoon minced orange zest	

Put the ricotta in a sieve. Press out as much moisture as possible. In a blender or food processor, process the ricotta until smooth. Remove the ricotta from the processor and knead on the work surface for 2 minutes.

Place the ricotta in a non-stick heavy-based saucepan over very low heat. Stir constantly with a wooden spoon until it begins to look dry and forms a solid mass, about 10 to 15 minutes. Remove from the heat and cool slightly. (It will be a little loose to begin with but will continue to thicken as it cools.) Add the sugar and orange zest and mix with the ricotta.

Press the mixture into a flat cake and allow to cool. When cool enough to handle, roll the mixture into 1-inch round balls. Place a raisin or pistachio slivers on top of each ball. Allow to cool completely and then store in layers, separated with waxed paper, in an airtight container. Refrigerated, they may be kept for up to 4 days.

YIELD: approximately 3/4 pound.

59 Calories per serving:
4 G Protein	14 MG Sodium
1 G Fat	0 MG Cholesterol
6 G Carbohydrate	

Inspired by Prem Sharma, Burr Ridge, IL, formerly of New Delhi.

Sweet Yogurt Custard

MISHTI DOI

∾∾

This delicious dessert, traditionally sweetened with date syrup, is often the finale to a Bengali meal. I was first served *Mishti Doi* during dinner in the home of Amar Mehrotra in Calcutta and later in New Delhi in the home of Inder Sharma. Inder explained that this is definitely a Bengali taste and said there is only one shop in New Delhi that sells it. The recipe has been modified by using 2 percent milk and nonfat dry milk instead of the usual whole milk.

4 cups 2 percent milk	3 tablespoons nonfat dry milk
3 tablespoons sugar	1 cup nonfat plain yogurt

Lightly oil the bottom and sides of a large heavy-bottomed non-stick saucepan with an oiled paper towel. Add the milk and bring to a boil over medium-high heat, stirring constantly until rising and foaming subside. Lower the heat to medium. Add the dry milk gradually, stirring, to prevent lumps from forming. Add the sugar and cook, stirring often to prevent sticking or burning, until the milk is reduced by half, about 20 minutes. The mixture should have a whipping-cream consistency. Remove the pan from the heat. Let stand until lukewarm.

Preheat the oven to 200 °F. Arrange 6 custard cups in a baking pan.

Pour the mixture into a medium-size bowl. In a small bowl, lightly beat the yogurt until smooth and creamy. Add about 3 tablespoons of the thickened milk mixture to the yogurt. Whisk lightly until smooth. (A hand-held blender is wonderful for whisking.) Pour the yogurt mixture into the thickened milk and whisk lightly until well blended. Divide the mixture between the custard cups. Pour hot water into the pan around the cups to a depth of approximately 1–2 inches. Bake for 20 minutes. The custard will still be soft. Let cool. Cover with plastic wrap and chill in the refrigerator until the custard is completely set. Serve chilled.

YIELD: 6 servings.

ADVANCE PREPARATION: Prepare 1 day ahead. Chill, covered, in refrigerator. Serve.

132 Calories per serving:
  8 G Protein   120 MG Sodium
  3 G Fat   13 MG Cholesterol
 18 G Carbohydrate

Inspired by Sudha Mehrotra, Calcutta.

Yogurt with Saffron

SHRIKHAND

∽ჟ∾

This classic yogurt dessert of the Gujarati Jains is often served at weddings and other special occasions. The original version calls for yogurt cheese, heavy cream and milk. I have substituted nonfat yogurt for a less rich, but delightful, refreshing dessert. Served in individual bowls and garnished with pistachio nuts, it is luscious when topped with fresh mango slices, pineapple, bananas or any other fruit in season.

1 quart nonfat plain yogurt
1/3 cup confectioners' sugar
1/8 teaspoon saffron threads,
   rubbed to a powder with the
   fingertips and soaked in
   1 tablespoon warm skim milk
   for 20 minutes

1/2 teaspoon cardamom seeds,
   ground
1/4 teaspoon freshly grated
   nutmeg
2 tablespoons slivered pistachio
   nuts

Line a strainer with cheesecloth. Put the yogurt in the cheesecloth and let it drain for about 6 hours. Discard the liquid.

In a bowl, combine the drained yogurt, sugar, saffron and soaking liquid, ground cardamom and nutmeg. Beat with a fork until light and fluffy. The *shrikhand* should have the consistency of a thick custard and a sweet and tangy flavor. If it tastes sour, add more sugar. Spoon into individual serving dishes. Garnish with pistachio nuts. Serve chilled.

YIELD: 4 servings.

ADVANCE PREPARATION: Prepare 1 day in advance.

COOK'S TIP: If the saffron is not dry enough to powder with your fingers, heat it over low heat until brittle, being careful not to burn the saffron. Powder the saffron between your fingers or in a mortar and pestle. Add the hot milk and stir.

VARIATION: Substitute 3 to 4 drops rose essence for the saffron.

254 Calories per serving:
  14 G Protein   163 MG Sodium
   2 G Fat   5 MG Cholesterol
  48 G Carbohydrate

Semolina Halva with Golden Raisins

SOOJI HALVA

∽∾∾

In India, *halva* is one of the most popular desserts and snack foods and is served during weddings and banquets, as well as for everyday enjoyment. It may be made from grains, vegetables such as carrots, or legumes. This recipe is made from semolina, which is extremely nourishing and was served to me in Meena Mohindra's home as a late morning brunch dish with toast and milk.

Halva is at its best when served hot or at least room temperature. It is usually loaded with clarified butter, *ghee*, but I have substituted corn oil margarine and corn oil with good results.

3/4 cup sugar
1/4 teaspoon freshly grated
  nutmeg
1/4 teaspoon ground cinnamon
1/4 teaspoon ground cloves
3/4 teaspoon cardamom seeds,
  ground

1/4 teaspoon saffron threads
4 tablespoons corn oil margarine
3 tablespoons corn oil
1 cup fine-grained semolina
1/4 cup sliced pistachio nuts

In a large heavy-bottomed saucepan, combine the sugar, ground spices, cardamom seeds, saffron and 4 cups of water over low heat. Stir until the sugar is dissolved. Increase the heat and bring to a gentle boil for a few minutes, stirring. Set aside.

Meanwhile, melt the margarine and corn oil in a large, heavy nonstick saucepan over low heat. Add the semolina and stir constantly until the grains swell and darken to a light golden color, about 10 minutes. Remove the pan from the heat. Gradually pour the spiced syrup into the semolina, stirring constantly. Be very careful because at first the grains may boil up in the pan. This will stop as all the liquid is absorbed. Return the pan to the heat and increase the heat to high. Whisk the semolina mixture for about 3 to 4 minutes or until thick and smooth. (The mixture will thicken as it cools.) Garnish with sliced pistachio nuts. Serve warm.

YIELD: 6 to 8 servings

ADVANCE PREPARATION: The *halva* may be made ahead. When it cools the texture may be no longer light. Reheat the mixture in a double boiler, whisking, until warm. Serve.

VARIATION: For a rich *halva*, forget the calories, substitute unsalted butter and top it with whipped cream!

356 Calories per serving:
  5 G Protein   90 MG Sodium
 17 G Fat   0 MG Cholesterol
 47 G Carbohydrate

Inspired by Meena Mohindra, Burr Ridge, IL, formerly of New Delhi.

Toasted Vermicelli Milk Pudding, Muslim Bohri Style

SHEER KORMA

~~~

In this popular north Indian pudding, very fine Indian vermicelli, called *sevian*, is cooked in milk with cardamom and dates. There are many variations to this pudding. This one is from Rashida Anees, a Muslim Bohri. Since the Bohra came from Arab countries and settled in Bombay, Rashida's version combines the culinary tastes of both cultures.

This sweet is a must for the Muslim religious festival called *Eid*, which is celebrated at the end of Ramadan, the annual month of fasting. During *Eid*, most Muslim homes make large quantities of the pudding and leave it in the center of the table in a large punch bowl. Both the family and the many guests who stop by to celebrate the festival enjoy *Sheer Korma* throughout the day, as it can be served at room temperature or chilled.

In India, the pudding is also served as the customary sweet starter for a meal, as well as for dessert.

2 teaspoons canola oil
3 ounces Indian vermicelli broken
   into 1-1/2-inch pieces
1 quart skim milk
1/4 cup nonfat dry milk
2 tablespoons sugar
1/2 teaspoon cardamom seeds,
   crushed

3 pitted dates, chopped
1 tablespoon golden raisins
2 teaspoons sliced almonds
2 teaspoons unsalted, blanched
   pistachio nuts, sliced
1 tablespoon toasted charoli seeds
   (optional)

Heat the oil in a large non-stick saucepan over moderate heat. Add the vermicelli and stir until golden brown. (Be very careful not to burn the vermicelli as it will turn golden brown very quickly.) Add the milk and milk and dry milk. Bring to a rolling boil, stirring constantly, until the mixture is the consistency of light cream, about 10 to 15 minutes. Do not let the milk stick to the pan and burn. Add the sugar, cardamom, dates and raisins. Continue cooking at a rolling boil, stirring constantly, for about 30 to 40 minutes. When the mixture starts to thicken and is the consistency of a thin pudding, remove from the heat. Stir in the almonds and pistachio nuts. Pour into a large bowl or individual goblets. Garnish with toasted *charoli* seeds, if desired. Serve at room temperature or chilled.

YIELD: 4 servings.

ADVANCE PREPARATION: Prepare 1 to 2 days ahead. Refrigerate, covered with plastic wrap.

VARIATION: If *charoli* seeds are not available, do not add pistachio nuts to the pudding when cooking. Garnish with toasted pistachio nuts instead.

242 Calories per serving:

12 G Protein	154 MG Sodium
4 G Fat	8 MG Cholesterol
38 G Carbohydrate	

Inspired by Rashida Anees, Bombay.

Rice and Saffron Pudding

KESARI KHEER

~~~

This traditional rice pudding flavored with saffron and garnished with golden raisins and almonds is a specialty of Handi Restaurant, Taj Palace Inter-Continental, New Delhi.

India has many rice puddings prepared from milk that has been condensed by reducing during cooking. The most popular one is *Kheer*, although in other parts of India variations of rice pudding are known as *Phirnee* (page 318) and *Payasam* (page 319).

Indian rice puddings are thinner than American ones and are made by reducing milk to a semi-thick consistency. Therefore, it is important to use a heavy, non-stick pan to reduce the milk to prevent scorching and sticking during cooking.

1 tablespoon canola oil
1/2 cup *basmati* or other long-
  grained rice, washed and soaked
  in water for 20 minutes, drained
  and air-dried
6 cups skim milk
1/4 cup nonfat dry milk
1/2 cup sugar

1/2 teaspoon ground cardamom
1 teaspoon saffron, soaked in
  2 tablespoons warm skim milk
  for 20 minutes
5 teaspoons golden raisins
3 tablespoons toasted, slivered
  almonds

Heat oil in a large, heavy-bottomed non-stick saucepan over moderate heat. Add the rice and stir until it darkens one or two shades. Add the milk and dry milk. Bring to a rolling boil. Cook, stirring, for about 10 to 15 minutes, to insure the rice does not stick to the pan. Be careful to keep the rice grains whole. At the end of cooking, the milk should have the consistency of light cream. Add the cardamom and sugar. Continue cooking, stirring constantly, until it is reduced to about one-third of its original volume and has a thin custardlike consistency, about 40 to 50 minutes. Be very careful to avoid scorching in final stages of cooking. Rub the saffron and milk mixture between your fingers to extract the flavor of the saffron. Stir the saffron liquid and the raisins into the milk. Stir for 1 minute. Cool to room temperature. The pudding will continue to thicken as it cools. Pour into a large serving bowl or individual dishes. Garnish with almonds. Serve hot, room temperature or chilled.

YIELD: 8 servings.

ADVANCE PREPARATION: Prepare 1 to 2 days ahead. Refrigerate, covered with plastic wrap. Serve chilled or at room temperature.

164 Calories per serving:
- 7 G Protein
- 3 G Fat
- 27 G Carbohydrate

- 87 MG Sodium
- 3 MG Cholesterol

Inspired by Chef Arvind Saraswat, Director of Food Production, Northern Region, Taj Mahal Group of Hotels.

Saffron-Flavored Rice Pudding

PHIRNEE

~~~

According to Executive Chef Mohideen, *Phirnee* is always made at the Royal Palace in Jaipur during *Sharad Purnima*. During this festival, which is celebrated in October on a brilliant moonlight night, there is a dinner party accompanied by lots of dancing and singing. *Phirnee* is put in earthenware bowls and then placed outside the palace in the moonlight. It is covered with a net and left until the next morning, as it is believed that the moonbeams can turn it into a nectar. When decorated with silver leaf and served for breakfast during the festival, it is considered a special treat, especially for the children.

Although not typically Indian, *Phirnee* is delightful when topped with fresh fruit, such as raspberries, orange sections or peaches.

2 cups 2 percent milk
1 cup rice flour
2 cups water
1/2 teaspoon saffron threads,
  soaked in 2 tablespoons warm
  skim milk for 20 minutes

2 tablespoons nonfat dry milk
1/2 cup sugar
1/2 teaspoon ground cardamom
2 to 3 drops *kewra* essence
12 dry roasted pistachio nuts,
  slivered

In a bowl, combine the rice flour and the water. Rub the saffron between your fingers in the milk to extract the flavor. Bring the milk just to a boil in a non-stick saucepan. Add the rice flour mixture to the milk gradually, whisking constantly. Over modreate heat, cook at a gentle boil for about 10 to 15 minutes, whisking constantly until the mixture has the consistency of a thick paste. (The mixture must be cooked at least 10 minutes to cook the flour.) Add the sugar, cardamom, *kewra* and three-quarters of the saffron liquid, reserving some for garnish. Continue to cook until the sugar has dissolved, stirring often to prevent the mixture from sticking and burning. Remove from heat. If there are any lumps, force them through a sieve while still hot. Cool the pudding, stirring occasionally to prevent a skin from forming on the surface. When the pudding has reached room temperature, pour into individual serving dishes or traditional Indian earthenware bowls. Sprinkle with the pistachio nuts and the reserved saffron liquid. Cover with plastic wrap. Refrigerate until well chilled. Serve chilled or at room temperature.

YIELD: 4 to 6 servings.

ADVANCE PREPARATION: Prepare 1 day in advance. Refrigerate, covered with plastic wrap. Serve chilled or at room temperature.

VARIATION: Substitute 6 drops rose water for *kewra* essence.

315 Calories per serving:
8 G Protein	74 MG Sodium
3 G Fat	9 MG Cholesterol
65 G Carbohydrate	

Inspired by G. Sultan Mohideen, Executive Chef, Rajputana Palace, Jaipur.

Rice Pudding

PAYASAM

∾꒰ꕥ꒱∾

Rice pudding flavored with cardamom is loved by all Indians and served at weddings and special occasions. Saroja Subbaraman's pudding from Madras has the consistency of a light cream soup and is usually served warm.

The unique flavor of this rice pudding comes from the slow cooking of the milk, which when boiled down has magnificent changes in texture, flavor and color, plus a beautifully perfumed aroma.

Saroja Subbaraman started her banana leaf lunch with *Payasam* because, as she explained, in the south a meal usually starts with a sweet. She uses whole milk in her pudding, but I have combined skim milk with nonfat dry milk powder to produce good results. For additional flavor, top the pudding with raspberries, strawberries, bananas or any fresh fruit in season.

1/2 cup *basmati* or other long-grained rice, washed, drained and air dried
8 cups (2 quarts) skim milk
1/2 cup nonfat dry milk

1/4 teaspoon ground cardamom
1/2 cup sugar
2 tablespoons raisins
2 tablespoons toasted sliced almonds or pistachio nuts

Heat a large heavy-bottomed non-stick saucepan over moderate heat. Add the rice and stir until the rice is one or two shades darker and has a nice aroma. Add the milk and the dry milk. Bring to a rolling boil. Stir gently for about 10 to 15 minutes to prevent the rice from sticking to the pan while trying to keep the rice grains whole. At the end of this time, the mixture should have the consistency of light cream. Add the cardamom and sugar. Continue cooking at a rolling boil, stirring constantly to prevent it from sticking to the bottom of the pan and burning. When it has reached about one-third its original volume and is thickened to a thin pudding consistency, about 30 to 40 minutes, add the raisins and cook, stirring, for about 1 minute. Remove from the heat and cool to room temperature. The pudding will continue to thicken as it cools. Pour the pudding into a large shallow serving dish or into individual serving dishes. The pudding may be served at room temperature or chilled. Serve garnished with toasted sliced almonds or pistachio nuts. If serving chilled, cover with plastic wrap and chill in the refrigerator. Serve.

YIELD: 6 servings.

ADVANCE PREPARATION: Prepare 1 to 2 days ahead. Refrigerate, covered with plastic wrap. Serve.

COOK'S TIP: If the pudding gets too thick, add a little skim milk.

283 Calories per serving:
15 G Protein
6 G Fat
51 G Carbohydrate
200 MG Sodium
6 MG Cholesterol

Inspired by Saroja Subbaraman, Madras.

Urad Dal Rice Cakes with Custard and Melba Sauces

AL HAMDU

⟿⟾

This dessert looks and tastes so elegant you will be surprised that it is so low in calories! Golden *Idlis* float on a bed of brandy-flavored custard and are topped with a raspberry melba sauce. Executive Chef Mohideen's creation may be cross-cultural, but it is one he serves often in the Rajputana Palace, Jaipur.

1 recipe for *Urad Dal* and Rice
    Dumplings, *Idli* (page 70)

1 recipe Vanilla Custard Brandy
    Sauce (page 322 or 323)
1 recipe Melba Sauce (page 324)

Prepare *Idlis* as directed on page 70. Cut *Idlis* in half and lightly brown in a non-stick skillet. Remove.

Meanwhile prepare the Vanilla Custard Brandy Sauce and Melba Sauce. To serve, pour a little custard brandy sauce on a plate. Place 2 *Idli* halves in the center of the plate on top of the sauce. Top the *Idlis* with melba sauce. Serve.

YIELD: 8 servings.

ADVANCE PREPARATION: Steam *Idlis* and cook custard brandy sauce and melba sauce ahead. Brown *Idlis* just prior to serving so they will be warm when serving.

220 Calories per serving:
  9 G Protein   170 MG Sodium
  2 G Fat   28 MG Cholesterol
 43 G Carbohydrate

Inspired by G. Sultan Mohideen, Executive Chef, Rajputana Palace, Jaipur.

Vanilla Custard Brandy Sauce 1

Here is a superb sauce for the purist who prefers using a vanilla bean. It is time-consuming, but well worth the effort.

2 cups skim milk
1/4 cup powdered milk
1 vanilla bean, about 2-1/2 inches
1 tablespoon cornstarch

1/4 cup sugar
1 large egg, beaten
1 tablespoon brandy

In a small saucepan, combine 1 cup of the milk, powdered milk and vanilla bean. Heat over medium-low heat until small bubbles form around the edge of the pan. Remove the pan from the heat. Set aside for about 30 minutes, or until cool. Remove the vanilla bean pod. Split the vanilla bean and scrape out the seeds. Add the seeds to the pan and set aside. Discard the pod.

Fill the bottom of a double boiler with just enough water so that the top will not touch it when the pan is inserted. Bring the water to a rolling boil. In a bowl, combine the remaining 1 cup of milk and the cornstarch. Stir until smooth. Add the milk mixture to the top pan of the double boiler. Add the sugar and whisk until well blended. Add the reserved vanilla-seasoned milk to the pan and cook until small bubbles form, whisking constantly. Do not let the mixture come to a boil. Remove the pan from the heat. Remove 1/4 cup of the hot milk mixture and stir gradually into the beaten egg. Add the egg and milk mixture gradually to the milk mixture in the pan, stirring constantly. Return the pan to the top of the double boiler. Cook over low heat, stirring constantly, until the mixture is just thick enough to coat a spoon. Remove from the heat and strain into a bowl. As the custard cools, beat occasionally to release the steam. Let cool. Stir the brandy into the custard. Cover with plastic wrap and chill in the refrigerator for at least 3 hours.

YIELD: 8 servings or about 1-3/4 cups.

ADVANCE PREPARATION: Prepare 1 to 2 days in advance. Refrigerate, covered.

VARIATION: Substitute 1/8 teaspoon crumbled saffron threads, soaked for 20 minutes in 2 tablespoons of warm skim milk, for the vanilla.

71 Calories per serving:
  4 G Protein   51 MG Sodium
  1 G Fat   28 MG Cholesterol
 11 G Carbohydrate

Inspired by G. Sultan Mohideen, Executive Chef, Rajputana Palace, Jaipur.

Vanilla Custard Brandy Sauce II

A tasty, quick alternative when you don't have time to be a purist.

2 cups skim milk
1-1/2 teaspoons cornstarch
1/3 cup confectioners' sugar
1/4 cup powdered milk

1/2 cup egg substitute
1 teaspoon vanilla extract
1 tablespoon brandy

Fill the bottom of a double boiler with just enough water so that the top will not touch it when the pan is inserted. Bring the water to a rolling boil. In a bowl, combine 1 cup of the cold milk with the cornstarch. Stir until there are no longer any lumps. Add the sugar and whisk until well blended. Set aside. Place the remaining 1 cup of milk and the powdered milk in the top pan of the double boiler. Cook, stirring, until small bubbles form around the edge of the pan. Stir in the cornstarch mixture gradually and cook until the sugar is dissolved and small bubbles form, whisking constantly. Do not let the mixture come to a boil. Place the egg substitute in a large bowl. Remove 1/4 cup of the hot milk mixture and stir gradually into the egg substitute. Slowly add the remaining milk mixture, stirring constantly. Return to the double boiler. Cook, stirring constantly, until the mixture is just thick enough to coat a spoon. Remove the pan from the heat and strain into a bowl. As the custard cools, beat occasionally to release the steam. Stir in the vanilla and brandy. Chill for at least 3 hours.

YIELD: 8 servings or about 1-3/4 cups.

ADVANCE PREPARATION: Prepare 1 to 2 days ahead. Refrigerate.

71 Calories per serving:
  4 G Protein   51 MG Sodium
  1 G Fat   5 MG Cholesterol
11 G Carbohydrate

Melba Sauce

2 cups fresh or frozen unsweet-   2 tablespoons sugar-free raspberry
  ened raspberries   preserves
                            1 teaspoon cornstarch

Combine the raspberries, preserves, cornstarch and 1/3 cup water in a blender or food processor. Purée until smooth. Fill the bottom of a double boiler with just enough water so that the top will not touch it when the top pan is inserted. Bring the water to a boil. Place the puréed mixture in the top pan of the double boiler. Cook until the sauce is thick and clear. Let cool. Strain the purée to remove the seeds. Chill, covered, in the refrigerator.

YIELD: 6 to 8 servings.

ADVANCE PREPARATION: Prepare several days ahead. Refrigerate, covered.

VARIATION: Substitute strawberries or peaches and unsweetened preserves for raspberries or use any fruit of your choice.

30 Calories per serving:
  0 G Protein   6 MG Sodium
  0 G Fat   0 MG Cholesterol
  7 G Carbohydrate

Inspired by G. Sultan Mohideen, Executive Chef, Rajputana Palace, Jaipur.

Easy Nonfat Mango Ice Cream

AAM KULFI

～∽∾

Here is a simplified version of Indian ice cream, *kulfi*. Mango pulp made from the Alphonso mango, a cherished south Indian variety, is available in Indian or Mexican grocery stores. If you prefer less intense mango flavor, use less pulp.

1/2 gallon nonfat, frozen vanilla yogurt

1-pound-14-ounce can mango pulp

In a food processor or blender, combine the frozen yogurt and mango pulp. Pour the mixture into a container suitable for freezing. Cover securely with foil and place in the freezer for 30 to 45 minutes, or until 1/2 inch of the mixture is frozen around the sides. Whisk for 2 minutes, or whip with an electric hand blender, until the mixture has doubled in volume. Cover and return to the freezer for a further 20 to 25 minutes. Whisk or whip with electric hand blender again until the mixture is doubled in volume. Pour into one large or individual ice cream containers. Cover and return the mixture to the freezer. Serve when completely frozen.

YIELD: 12 to 14 servings.

ADVANCE PREPARATION: Prepare 1 week in advance. Freeze.

VARIATION: Substitute strawberry, raspberry or any fruit pulp for the mango pulp.

193 Calories per serving:
- 4 G Protein
- 0 G Fat
- 44 G Carbohydrate
- 75 MG Sodium
- 0 MG Cholesterol

Inspired by Prem Sharma, Burr Ridge, IL, formerly of New Delhi.

Mangoes with Saffron-Flavored Yogurt

AAM DAHI

೨ಲ೧

Luscious, juicy mangoes served with golden saffron-flavored yogurt are absolutely sumptuous!

1/8 teaspoon saffron threads, crushed

1–2 large ripe mangoes, about 1 pound, peeled and cut into 1/2-inch cubes

2 cups nonfat plain yogurt

2 teaspoons fresh lime juice

Pour 1/3 cup warm water over the saffron. Let stand for 20 minutes.

In a bowl, whisk the yogurt and lime juice until smooth and creamy. Strain the saffron liquid into the yogurt and mix well. Add the mango cubes and combine. Chill in the refrigerator.

YIELD: 4 servings.

COOK'S TIP: If mangoes are not sweet, add sugar to taste.

128 Calories per serving:
   7 G Protein
   0 G Fat
   27 G Carbohydrate

82 MG Sodium
3 MG Cholesterol

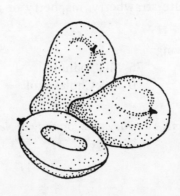

Mangoes with Kewra-Flavored Yogurt

AAM DAHI

~∽~

When succulent mangoes are in season, I try to serve them as often as possible. They are plentiful and much loved in India. Here, *kewra* essence highlights their splendid flavor. *Kewra* essence may be purchased in Indian grocery stores.

2 cups nonfat plain yogurt
2–3 drops *kewra* essence
4 teaspoons minced fresh mint
  leaves
1/4 cup sugar, or to taste

2 teaspoons fresh lemon juice
1–2 large, ripe mangoes, about
  1 pound, peeled and cut into
  1/2-inch cubes

In a bowl, whisk the yogurt, *kewra*, mint leaves, sugar and lemon juice together. Add the mango cubes and combine. Chill in the refrigerator.

YIELD: 6 servings.

COOK'S TIP: *Kewra* essence is quite potent. Be careful not to add too much!

118 Calories per serving:
  5 G Protein
  0 G Fat
 26 G Carbohydrate
    55 MG Sodium
     2 MG Cholesterol

Oranges with Saffron-Flavored Yogurt

NARINGA DAHI

❧∼❧

A unique light dessert, typical of Indian cooking, and quick to make.

1/4 teaspoon saffron threads,
  crushed
2 cups nonfat plain yogurt

1/4 cup sugar
2 teaspoons fresh lime juice
2 oranges, peeled and sectioned

Rub the saffron between your fingers. Pour 1/2 cup warm water over the saffron. Let stand for 20 minutes.

In a bowl, whisk the yogurt, sugar and lime juice until smooth and creamy. Strain in the saffron liquid and mix well. Add the orange sections and combine with the yogurt mixture. Chill in the refrigerator.

YIELD: 4 servings.

129 Calories per serving:
  7 G Protein
  0 G Fat
  27 G Carbohydrate

80 MG Sodium
3 MG Cholesterol

Sweet Apricot Sauce

QUBANI KA MEETHA

❧∼❧

During a delightful visit to southern Hydrabad, I savored this divine apricot sauce. As we enjoyed the cool summer breezes on the lovely flower-laden verandah of the Krishna Oberoi Hotel, Chef Talwar topped a freshly made vanilla ice cream with the apricot sauce. You may also serve the sauce over frozen vanilla yogurt or any fresh fruit of your choice. When added to the yogurt drink, *Meetha Lassi* (page 337), it becomes a luscious, cool, refreshing apricot-flavored "milk-shake."

1 pound dried apricots	1/2 cup sugar
2-1/2 cups water	1 tablespoon fresh lemon juice

In a saucepan combine the apricots and water. Cook over medium heat for 15 to 20 minutes, or until tender. Stir in the sugar and lemon juice. Pour the apricot mixture into a food processor or blender and process to a smooth purée. Use immediately or refrigerate.

YIELD: 6–8 servings as a topping.

ADVANCE PREPARATION: Prepare ahead. The sauce will keep for up to 4 weeks, covered in the refrigerator.

129 Calories per serving:
   1 G Protein   3 MG Sodium
   0 G Fat   0 MG Cholesterol
  33 G Carbohydrate

Inspired by G.S. Talwar, Executive Chef, The Krishna Oberoi, Hyderabad.

Fresh Fruit Compote

PHAL CHAT

༺༢༺

A splendid ending to an Indian feast!

1 ripe pineapple, peeled, cored and
  cut into 1/2-inch wedges
1 pint strawberries, hulled
1 pint blueberries
2 apples, peeled, cored and sliced
  into 1/2-inch wedges
2 oranges, peeled and sectioned
1 small cantaloupe, cut into balls

2 bananas, sliced
2 peaches, peeled, pitted and sliced
1/3 cup strained fresh lime juice
1/3 cup strained fresh orange juice
3 tablespoons honey (optional)
2 tablespoons minced fresh mint
  leaves

In a bowl, combine the above ingredients. Chill. Serve.

YIELD: 20 servings

VARIATION: Combine any fresh fruits in season.

74 Calories per serving:
 1 G Protein
 0 G Fat
18 G Carbohydrate
11 MG Sodium
 0 MG Cholesterol

Inspired by Prem Sharma, Burr Ridge, IL, formerly of New Delhi.

BEVERAGES

Delicious, cool beverages are a necessity in India's hot climate. Nothing is better on a sultry day than a refreshingly spiced lime drink or *lassi*, a yogurt drink that ranks as one of the most popular refreshments throughout India. It is nutritious, filling and delectable.

India is one of the world's largest producers of tea, which grows in the foothills of the Himalayas in the north and the Nilgiri Mountains in the south. Tea is usually offered to guests and is always enjoyed by Indians throughout the day.

∿◠∿◠∿◠∿◠∿◠∿◠∿◠∿◠∿◠∿◠∿◠∿

Orange-Pineapple Refresher   BAHAR-E-CHAMAN
Cocum Refresher   KOKAM SHARBAT
Limeade with Ginger and Mint   NIMBU ADRAK PUDINA
Spiced Lime-Ginger Refresher   ADRAK SHARBAT
Indian Summer Punch   THANDAI
Rose-Flavored Yogurt Drink   MEETHA LASSI
Salted Yogurt Drink   KHATTA LASSI
Mango-Flavored Yogurt Drink   LASSI AAMWALI
Mango Refresher   AAM KA PHOOL
Spiced Tea   MASALA CHAI
Cardamom Tea   ELAICHI MASALA CHAI
Iced Mint Tea   PUDINA CHAI

∿◠∿◠∿◠∿◠∿◠∿◠∿◠∿◠∿◠∿◠∿◠∿

Orange-Pineapple Refresher

BAHAR-E-CHAMAN

~~~

Orange and pineapple juice unite with mint, Indian black salt and ground cumin in this exotic drink from Agra. Literally translated, *Bahar-e-Chaman* means "king of the orchard." You may choose any combination of fruit juices for this thirstquencher.

If you wish, freeze the beverage to a "slush" in an ice cream machine and serve it as a palate refresher between courses.

3 cups fresh orange juice
1 cup pineapple juice
1 tablespoon fresh lime juice, or to
    taste
1/4 teaspoon dry roasted cumin
    seeds, ground to a powder

1/8 teaspoon black salt, *kala
    namak*
Crushed ice

GARNISH:
4 mint sprigs   4 lime slices

In a blender, combine the orange, pineapple, lime juice, cumin and black salt. Refrigerate until well chilled. Stir and serve in chilled glasses with crushed ice. Garnish with mint sprigs and lime slices.

YIELD: 4 servings.

120 Calories per serving:
  2 G Protein   74 MG Sodium
  0 G Fat   0 MG Cholesterol
 28 G Carbohydrate

Inspired by Anil Misri, Executive Chef, Mughal Sheraton, Agra.

Cocum Refresher

KOKAM SHARBAT

While at the Institute of Hotel Management, Bombay, I was served this exotic drink. The unusual combination of *cocum*, a local tart fruit, tangy black salt and nutty cumin, sweetened with sugar is believed to be excellent for cooling the system on hot summer days. *Cocum* is available at Indian grocery stores.

1/3 cup plus 2 tablespoons *cocum*
1/3 cup plus 1 tablespoon sugar
1/8 teaspoon black salt

1 tablespoon dry roasted cumin
    seeds, ground
Salt to taste

Soak the *cocum* in cold water for 2 hours or boil in 1 cup of water for 5 minutes. Let cool slightly. Strain through a sieve, squeezing out all excess liquid. Reserve the liquid and discard the *cocum*.

Heat 4 cups of water and the *cocum* liquid in a saucepan. Add the sugar, black salt and cumin. Stir until the sugar dissolves. Remove from heat. Add salt to taste. Chill in the refrigerator.

YIELD: 4 servings.

82 Calories per serving:
 0 G Protein   109 MG Sodium
 0 G Fat   0 MG Cholesterol
20 G Carbohydrate

Inspired by I. Gomes, Head of Food & Beverage, Institute of Hotel Management, Catering & Technology, Bombay.

Limeade with Ginger and Mint

NIMBU ADRAK PUDINA

∽✍∿

This invigorating version of limeade is most welcome on a hot day.

1 cup fresh lime juice, about 6–8
   thin-skinned limes
1/2 teaspoon peeled, grated fresh
   ginger
14 fresh mint leaves

1/3 cup sugar, or to taste
Ice cubes
Mint sprigs to garnish

Carefully peel the skin from 3 of the limes using a vegetable peeler or lime zester. Be careful not to include any of the bitter, underlying white pith.

In a mortar or heavy bowl, combine the lime zest, grated ginger, mint leaves and sugar. Crush with a pestle or a small round object to release the aromatics.

Combine the crushed mixture with lime juice. Add 1 cup of water. Whisk or blend in blender until the sugar dissolves. Add 3 more cups of water and additional sugar if desired. Let the mixture chill for at least 30 minutes. To serve, add ice cubes to a glass. Strain the beverage into the glasses. Garnish each drink with a mint sprig.

YIELD: 4 servings.

ADVANCE PREPARATION: Prepare several days ahead. Keep chilled and covered in refrigerator.

123　Calories per serving:
  2　G Protein
  2　G Fat`
 28　G Carbohydrate

101　MG Sodium
  5　MG Cholesterol

Spiced Lime-Ginger Refresher

ADRAK SHARBAT

~~~

Here is a refreshing thirst quencher for a blistering day.

3 tablespoons peeled, chopped
    fresh ginger
1 teaspoon whole black pepper-
    corns (optional)
2-1/4 cups sugar

2 cups fresh lime juice, about 12
    thin-skinned limes
Ice cubes
Lime slices to garnish

In a mini food processor or blender, process the ginger and 2 table-spoons of water to a paste. In a saucepan, combine the paste, pepper-corns, if desired, and 2 cups of water. Bring to a boil over moderate heat. Reduce the heat and simmer for about 5 minutes. Add the sugar and cook, stirring, until the sugar has dissolved. Strain the mixture into a large pitcher. Add the lime juice and mix well. Chill. When serving, add 4 cups of cold water or carbonated water to the concentrate. Serve over ice cubes. Garnish with a lime slice.

YIELD: 10 servings.

ADVANCE PREPARATION: Prepare several days ahead. Add additional water or carbonated water to the concentrate when serving.

187 Calories per serving:
  0 G Protein   1 MG Sodium
  0 G Fat   0 MG Cholesterol
 49 G Carbohydrate

Indian Summer Punch

THANDAI

⤳⤶

This is a memorable drink for me because it was the first beverage I tried upon my arrival in India during *holi*, the festival of colors. I enjoyed it so much I want to share it with you.

2 tablespoons fennel seeds
1/2 teaspoon cardamom seeds
5 whole cloves
1/3 cup raisins
1/2 cup blanched almonds
1/4 cup pistachio nuts
1 cup dried fruit seeds, melon, sunflower, papaya or pumpkin
1 tablespoon sugar
1/4 teaspoon saffron, rubbed to a powder between your fingers and soaked in 2 tablespoons warm skim milk for 20 minutes (optional)
1/4 cup nonfat dry milk
1 quart skim milk
Cracked ice

In a spice or coffee grinder, grind the fennel and cardamom seeds and the cloves to a fine powder.

In a saucepan, soak the raisins, almonds, pistachio nuts and fruit seeds in 2 cups of boiling water for 1 hour. Bring the mixture to a boil. Carefully pour the mixture into a food processor or blender and process to a smooth paste. Add the spice powder and sugar. Blend until the sugar has dissolved completely. Pour the mixture into a large pitcher. Add 2 cups of water and the dry milk to the processor. Process to combine and remove all the remaining paste mixture. Add to the mixture in the pitcher. Strain the liquid through a fine sieve pressing to extract as much of the mixture as possible. Return the mixture to the pitcher with the saffron liquid and stir. Chill. Stir before serving. Serve over cracked ice.

YIELD: 10 to 12 servings.

VARIATION: For an easy *Thandai*, purchase prepared canned *Thandai* concentrate in an Indian grocery store. Follow directions on can.

197 Calories per serving:
   10 G Protein   62 MG Sodium
   12 G Fat   2 MG Cholesterol
   15 G Carbohydrate

Inspired by Gev Desai, Executive Chef, Maurya Sheraton, New Delhi.

Rose-Flavored Yogurt Drink

MEETHA LASSI

Lassi is a popular summertime drink that is often served with lunch. At the many street stalls, *lassi* is poured from one glass to another sometimes held at a height of two to three feet, giving it the all-important froth. It is very easily made at home, and an electric hand-held blender is excellent for creating the froth.

1 cup nonfat plain yogurt   2–3 drops rose or *kewra* essence
1 cup iced water or skim milk   Crushed ice
3–4 tablespoons sugar, or to taste

Whisk all the ingredients in a blender, or in a bowl using an electric hand-held blender, until frothy. Serve immediately over crushed ice.

YIELD: 2 to 3 servings.

132 Calories per serving:
  7 G Protein   80 MG Sodium
  0 G Fat   3 MG Cholesterol
 28 G Carbohydrates

Inspired by Meena Mohindra, Burr Ridge, IL, formerly of New Delhi.

Salted Yogurt Drink

KHATTA LASSI

∾⌇⌇∾

Prepare *lassi* on page 337, but omit the sugar and add a pinch of salt.

YIELD: 2 to 3 servings.

60 Calories per serving:
  7 G Protein   149 MG Sodium
  0 G Fat   3 MG Cholesterol
  9 G Carbohydrate

Mango-Flavored Yogurt Drink

LASSI AAMWALI

∾⌇⌇∾

Mango pulp offers a flavorsome variation to *lassi*. If fresh mangoes are in season, prepare your own pulp in the food processor or blender. Canned Alphonso mango pulp is available in Indian grocery stores. If using canned pulp, reduce the amount of sugar to taste.

1 cup nonfat plain yogurt	3 tablespoons sugar
1-1/2 cups iced water	3 to 4 drops rose or *kewra* essence
6 tablespoons mango pulp	Crushed ice

Whisk all the ingredients in a blender, or in a bowl and use an electric hand-held blender, to whip until frothy. Serve immediately over crushed ice.

YIELD: 4 servings.

COOK's TIP: When using a hand-held blender, add the milk to the bowl. Whip, keeping the blade in the bottom of the bowl for 15 seconds. Continue whipping with a gentle up-and-down motion, lifting the beaters almost to the top of the liquid, until the *lassi* triples in volume, about 60 seconds.

50 Calories per serving:
  0 G Protein   1 MG Sodium
  0 G Fat   0 MG Cholesterol
 13 G Carbohydrate

Inspired by Meena Mohindra, Burr Ridge, IL, formerly of New Delhi.

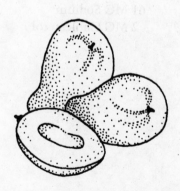

Mango Refresher

AAM KA PHOOL

❦

Prepared from green mangoes, this is an intriguing thirstquencher.

1 large firm green mango, about 1-
   1/2 pounds
8–10 tablespoons sugar
1 pint nonfat milk

2 teaspoons powdered milk
   (optional)
1/4 teaspoon crushed fennel seeds

In a saucepan, place the mango and water to cover. Bring to the boil, reduce the heat and cook until soft, about 30 minutes. Cool to room temperature. Peel and seed the mango. Place the pulp in a blender or food processor and process to a smooth purée. Add the sugar, milk and powdered milk and process until well combined. Line a sieve with a double layer of cheesecloth. Strain the mixture, pressing down with the back of a spoon. Chill well. Stir to mix before serving. Sprinkle crushed fennel seeds over the top of each drink.

YIELD: 4 servings.

ADVANCE PREPARATION: Prepare 1 day ahead. Chill. Serve.

203 Calories per serving:
   4 G Protein
   1 G Fat
   48 G Carbohydrate
           61 MG Sodium
           2 MG Cholesterol

Spiced Tea

MASALA CHAI

Spiced tea is a cherished beverage throughout India, served at any time of the day.

1 2-inch piece cinnamon
3 green cardamom pods
2 cloves
2 tablespoons sugar, or to taste

3 heaped teaspoons orange pekoe tea or 4 tea bags
1/4 cup skim milk

Bring 3 cups of water to a boil in a small saucepan. Add the spices, sugar and tea. Stir. Remove from the heat. Cover and let stand for about 10 minutes. Add the milk and return to the heat. Bring just to a boil, stirring. Strain the tea into cups and serve hot, with extra sugar if desired.

YIELD: 4 servings.

VARIATION: The milk and sugar may be omitted. Reduce the tea leaves to 1-1/2 heaped teaspoons or 2 bags.

29 Calories per serving:
 1 G Protein
 0 G Fat
 7 G Carbohydrate

 8 MG Sodium
 0 MG Cholesterol

Inspired by Kiran Vohra, Oak Brook, IL, formerly of Bombay.

Cardamom Tea

ELAICHI MASALA CHAI

༄

Here is a delightfully spiced cardamom tea.

6 green cardamom pods
3 heaped teaspoons orange pekoe
  tea or 4 tea bags

1/4 cup skim milk, or to taste
Sugar to taste

   In a small saucepan bring 3 cups of water, the cardamom pods and tea to the boil. Reduce heat to simmer and simmer for 6 minutes. Add the milk. Bring just to the boil. Strain the tea into cups and serve with sugar, if desired.

YIELD: 4 servings.

VARIATION: Substitute cinnamon or cloves for the cardamom.

5 Calories per serving:
1 G Protein   8 MG Sodium
0 G Fat   0 MG Cholesterol
1 G Carbohydrate

Inspired by Meena Mohindra, Burr Ridge, IL, formerly of New Delhi.

Iced Mint Tea

PUDINA CHAI

∽◡∾

Fresh sun-brewed mint tea is superb!

6 orange pekoe tea bags
1/4 cup fresh mint leaves
3 tablespoons fresh lemon or lime-
  juice

Sugar to taste
Ice cubes

Put the tea bags, mint leaves, lemon juice and 4 quarts of water in a large glass container. Add sugar to taste and set in the sun for 2 to 3 hours. Serve in glasses over ice cubes.

YIELD: 16 to 18 servings.

3 Calories per serving:
0 G Protein
0 G Fat
1 G Carbohydrate

7 MG Sodium
1 MG Cholesterol

Inspired by Prem Sharma, Burr Ridge, IL, formerly of New Delhi.

Menus

❦

The following menus, while Indian, are geared to American tastes and manners of dining. Many of the dishes can be made in advance and reheated at time of serving. This is explained in "Advance Preparation" accompanying individual recipes.

The menus vary from an easily prepared dinner to an elaborate buffet. Traditional Indian meals, which I savored during my travels, are also included. You may be interested in knowing more about Saroja Subbaraman, Amar Mehrotra and the Parsis of Bombay. Detailed information about their lifestyle, customs and traditions are included in the **Welcome to India** chapter beginning on page 5.

A simple Indian meal consists of one main vegetable, meat or poultry dish served with a rice dish; a *dal*; probably an accompanying vegetable dish; a yogurt salad, *raita*; and, in the north, bread. In addition, the meal might also include a chutney of some sort and possibly some lentil wafers, *Pappadums*. All of the dishes are served at the same time. As the meal gets more elaborate or more people are being served, more main course dishes and accompaniments would be carried to the table.

Keep in mind that the recipes in the book can be doubled or tripled, depending on the number of people you are serving. Unless otherwise specified, a single recipe should suffice for the following menus.

Simple Dinner for 4

Vegetable Pilaf   *Tehari Pullao*
Spiced Green Beans   *Masala Sem*
Chicken Kebabs   *Murgh Tikka*
Spinach and Yogurt Salad   *Paalak Raita*
Mint-Coriander Chutney   *Pudina Chatney*
Lentil Wafers   *Pappadums*
Fruit

Elegant Dinner for 6

Spiced Chicken Soup   *Jehangiri Shorba*
Lamb Biryani, Dum Pukht Style   *Kachchi Gosht Biryani*
Eggplant Topped with Tomato and Coriander-Flavored Yogurt Sauce
   Badal Jaam
Dal Qureshi
Spiced Yogurt Salad   *Bhuranni*
Griddle-Baked Whole Wheat Bread   *Roti or Chapati*
Toasted Vermicelli Milk Pudding, Muslim Bohri Style   *Sheer Korma*

Sumptuous Holiday Buffet for 10

Lamb Braised in Spiced Yogurt   *Gosht Pasanda*
Spiced Chicken Breast   *Khuroos-e-Tursh*
Potatoes, Green Peas and Tomatoes   *Aloo Matar Tamatar*
Plantain Poria   *Vashakkai Porial*
Chickpeas with Zucchini   *Chana aur Torre*
Fragrant Lemon Rice   *Elumichampazham Sadam*
Tomato and Green Pepper Salad, New Delhi Style   *Tamatar aur Simli Mirch*
Pineapple Sesame   *Anannas Sasme*
Mint-Coriander Chutney   *Pudina Chatney* (triple the recipe)
Tamarind Chutney   *Gor Amli ni Chatney* (triple the recipe)
Fresh Fruit Compote   *Phal Chat* (double the recipe)

Summer Barbecue for 8

Potatoes with Green Onions   *Aloo Pyaz ka Sabzi*
Curried Potatoes, Carrots and Green Beans, Bangalore Style   *Sabzi
    Porial Bangalore*
Barbecued Ginger Shrimp   *Jhinga Adraki*
Spiced Grilled Lamb Kebabs   *Boti Kababs*
Chickpea *Dal   Kabuli Chana Dal*
Fresh Mango Salad   *Aam Salad*
Southern Style Mixed Vegetable Salad   *Thakkali-Vellarikkai-Gaajar
    Kosumalli*
Coriander-Mint Chutney   *Pudina Chatney* (double the recipe)
Fresh Fruit

Spirited South Indian Fare for 4

Carrot and Green Pea Porial   *Gaajar Matar Porial*
Spiced Potatoes Coondapur   *Batate Masala Coondapur*
Andhra Chili Chicken   *Mirpukai Kodi*
Tomato Dal   *Tamatar Pappu*
Cucumber and Yogurt Salad   *Kachumbar Raita*
Coriander-Mint Chutney   *Pudina Chatney*
Fresh Fruit

Madras-Style Vegetarian Brunch for 6
[based on a meal served at Saroja Subbaraman's Home, see page 23]

Mixed Vegetables in Yogurt Sauce   *Avial*
Fiery Potatoes Smothered with Onions   *Aloo Pyaz*
Yogurt Rice   *Masuru Anna*
Green Pepper and Yogurt Salad   *Simla Mirch Raita*
Lentil Wafers   *Pappadums*
Rice Pudding, *Payasam* or fruit

Calcutta-Style Dinner for 6 [based on a meal served at Amar Mehrotra's Home, see page 11]

Cumin-Flavored Potatoes   *Jeera Aloo*
Fenugreek Chicken, Bengali Style   *Methi Murgh Bengali*
Tangy Chickpeas   *Ghughini*
Spinach *Dal*, Bengali Style   *Saag Dal Bengali*
Tomato and Yogurt Salad   *Tamatar Raita*
Basmati Rice   *Chawal*
Lentil Wafers   *Pappadums*
Easy Mango Ice Cream   *Aam Kulfi*

A Parsi Wedding Feast for 10

The Parsis are a small religious sect who first came to India in the seventh century, fleeing religious persecution in their native Persia. Over the centuries they embraced many of the ways of their adopted country, and their cooking evolved into an exotic blend of the flavors of Persia and those of India.

Gev Desai, a Parsi, Executive Chef of the Maurya Sheraton, New Delhi, shared the following Parsi wedding feast, *Langan nu Bhonu*, which is cooked by special *babarchis* cooks. In deference to my request for more health-conscious food, he altered the original Parsi recipes.

He explaines that the guests are seated in lines (about 20 to 30 people each) on one side of long tables. As on all special feasts, the guests eat on banana leaves. All service is done by two people, one holding a huge hot platter of the dish being served and the other spooning the food onto individual banana leaves.

The feast is accompanied by aerated water flavored with raspberry, pineapple or orange. Executive Chef Desai says, "Of course, the true Parsi asks for club soda and out comes a half bottle of whiskey from his pocket, which is quickly poured into the glass." Before the feast commences, the host or the bride and groom exclaim *jumbo jee!* Eat well!

Fish in Tomato Sauce, Parsi Style   *Saas ni Macchi*
and
Spiced Rice with Lentils, Parsi Style   *Kichri Parsi*
or
Parsi Fish Parcels   *Patri ni Macchi*
plus
Baby Lamb Stew, Parsi Style   *Kid nu Gosht*
Lamb Biryani, Parsi Style   *Aloo Dar*
Onion and Tomato Salad, Parsi Style   *Pyaz aur Tamatar* Parsi
Griddle-Baked Whole Wheat Bread   *Roti* or *Chapati*
Lentil Wafers   *Pappadums*
Indian Ice Cream   *Kulfi**

*This can be purchased in an Indian store or iced nonfat yogurt may be substituted.

Glossary

~∂∂~

Asafetida *hing:* A dried gum resin that comes from Kashmir, asafetida is sold as a pale-yellow powder. Its flavor resembles garlic or shallot, and the powder is supposed to aid digestion. When sprinkled over spices during cooking, its flavor disappears, leaving behind a subtle, delicate aroma.

Black Cumin Seed or Royal Cumin *shahi jeera:* A thin black seed that is a close relative of cumin, this is used mainly in north Indian dishes and is grown in Kashmir, Punjab and Uttar Pradesh. The flavor is aromatic and peppery, quite unlike regular cumin seeds.

Black Salt *kala namak:* This reddish-gray salt has a distinctive earthy flavor. It is the primary ingredient in the spice blend *chat masala*, which is used for sprinkling on snack foods such as *chats*. There is no substitute.

Cardamom *elaichi:* There are two types of cardamom pods, green and white. Inside each are small brownish-black seeds, which turn creamy-white when bleached in the sun, but are soft green when air-dried. Green pods are preferred because the volatile oils in the seeds are more potent. For subtle flavoring, whole pods are added to dishes such as rice pilafs. When the seeds are removed from the pod, crushed and powdered, they are most often used in sweets. Green cardamom, cardamom seeds and ground cardamom are available in Indian and Middle Eastern grocery stores.

Carom *ajwain:* Piquant-flavored seeds that look like celery seeds, carom's flavor is similar to thyme. It is used to season vegetables, snacks and pickles.

Cayenne: See red pepper powder.

Chana Dal: This split and husked relative of the chickpea is one of the most popular *dals* in India. For complete information see page 55.

Charoli Seed *chironji:* This is a small, round nutlike seed with a distinctive flavor, used to garnish sweets. If unavailable, pistachios may be substituted as a garnish for sweets, although the flavor and texture are quite dissimilar.

Chat Masala: A sand-colored powder containing many ingredients, this is predominately flavored with mango powder, black salt and asafetida. It is sprinkled over fruit snacks, called *chat,* and on other dishes. A prepared *chat masala* is available from Indian grocery stores, but there is a recipe for it on page 43.

Chenna *cheese:* This is an unripened fresh cheese that is simple to make. The directions for making *chenna* appears on page 43.

Chickpeas *kabuli chana:* Dried chickpeas are available in most grocery stores. Before use, they must be soaked. Not to be confused with *kala chana,* a smaller dark brown *dal.* The two are not interchangeable. For more information on chickpeas, see page 56.

Chickpea Flour *besan:* A finely-ground flour made from roasted *chana dal* and used extensively in vegetable fritters and batters. Chickpea flour may be purchased in grocery stores. It can be found in health food stores where often it has not been roasted before being ground and has a raw taste. If using this, roast it lightly in a dry pan prior to use.

Chilies, Green *hari mirch:* Fresh chilies are a rich source of Vitamin A and C, and are used extensively in Indian cooking. As there are many varieties of chilies, it takes a little experimenting to ascertain their "heat." Usually, the smaller the chili, the hotter the taste.

In India, the chili seeds are not removed in many preparations. Because most of the heat of the chili is in the seeds and the veins, these can easily be removed to leave the rich flavor of the chilies without all of the heat.

Choose fresh green serrano, japaleno or other hot green chilies with skins that are brightly colored and have no brown spots.

One note of caution: when handling fresh chilies, you may want to wear gloves. When cutting them, be sure not to touch your eyes or lips, and to wash your hands thoroughly with soap and water when finished. Before preparing other foods, wash your knife and chopping block.

Chilies may be stored loosely wrapped in a paper towel inside a plastic bag in the refrigerator.

Chilies, Dried Red *lal mirch:* These are sun-dried pods of the capsicum plant. Most of the heat of the dried chilies is concentrated in the seeds. If you wish a milder dish, remove them. As a rule, crushed chilies are hotter than whole chilies because the seeds are mixed in with the skin. Often, they are soaked in water to reduce the heat.

Coriander Leaves, Fresh (Cilantro, Chinese Parsley) *hari dhania:* Widely used in India, Southeast Asia and other warm climates, coriander has a warm-bodied, pungent and agreeable flavor. It is an important ingredient in cooking as well as in garnishing. To store, wash, dry, and put the fresh herb in a container of water with the root ends down. Cover the top of the leaves with a plastic bag. The coriander will keep for 1 to 2 weeks, refrigerated.

Coriander Seed *dhania:* Coriander seeds are sold both whole and ground. They have an entirely different flavor from fresh coriander leaves and cannot be used as a substitute.

Curry Leaves, Fresh *meetha neem:* Thin, highly aromatic leaves, which look almost like lemon leaves, these are used daily in the south Indian kitchen to flavor almost everything from *dals* to yogurt. Fresh curry leaves are available at Indian grocery stores. To store, keep in an airtight container, refrigerated. They will keep for about 2 weeks. Dry curry leaves are available, but are usually stale and lack flavor. They are not worth purchasing.

Curry Powder *masala:* Curry powder purchased in American markets is virtually unknown in India. Indians blend their own regional spice mixtures, which are known as *masalas*. South India has its own special blend of curry powder (*sambar masala,* page 45). It has no resemblance to our store-bought curry powder, which is unacceptable because it is laden with the flavor of raw turmeric and other spices. Madras Indian curry powder purchased in Indian grocery stores is acceptable.

Dal: In India, dried beans, peas and lentils are called *dals*. A complete explanation of *dals* can be found on page 55.

Essences *ruh:* These are concentrated flavorings extracted from spices and herbs. The most commonly used ones are *ruh kewra*, extracted from the root of the screw pine plant, and *ruh gulab*, extracted from scented rose petals.

Fenugreek Leaf *methi sak:* These edible green leaves with a strong bitter taste are sold during the summer at Indian grocery stores.

Fenugreek Seed *methi:* This rusty-brown rectangular seed is used both whole and ground. Light, dry roasting brings out its best flavor.

Garam Masala: A mixture of aromatic dry-roasted and ground spices, which varies in each region of India, *garam masala* is usually added toward the end of cooking to give the finishing touch to a dish. It is easily made (page 43), and is preferable to the *garam masala* purchased in Indian grocery stores, which tends to be stale and lack fragrance.

Ginger, Fresh *adrak:* This aromatic rhizome of the ginger plant provides a sharp, pungent flavor and pleasing aroma. Indians believe it has digestive properties and a cleansing effect on the body.

Kala Chana Dal: Known in English as bengal gram, this is a small variety of the chickpea. For complete description of *dals* see page 55.

Kalongi *nigella:* This is a round black seed with a peppery taste.

Kewra Essence *ruh kewra:* A strong, perfumed essence from the screwpine plant, it is used to flavor sweets. Use sparingly. It is available in Indian grocery stores.

Mango, Green *aam:* The green or unripe mango is used in the preparation of chutneys and desserts.

Mango *aam:* Mangoes are so highly prized in India that they are called the "king of fruit." During the summer months when mangoes are in season, they are used frequently as an eating fruit, in salads and in beverages. Nothing is better than a luscious, sensuous mango! Some say the best mangoes come from the south and are known as the Alphonso mango. Alphonso mango pulp may be purchased canned in Indian grocery stores.

Mango Powder *aamchoor:* Peeled unripe green mangoes are cut into thin strips, dried in the sun and then ground into a fine powder, which is very sour but has a pleasant tang. It is used to give a piquant flavor to vegetables, salads, chutneys and other dishes. A dash of lime juice may be used as a substitute when the powder is used as a flavoring.

Masala: A mixture of spice, herb and seasoning combinations, *masalas* can contain from 2 to 25 or more ingredients.

Mung Dal *moong dal:* Known as green *gram dal*, this split bean has a delicate flavor. See page 55 for complete *dal* information.

Mustard Oil *sarson ka tel:* This intensely pungent mustard oil is used in Bengali cooking. To reduce its pungency and give it a more mellow flavor, mustard oil should be heated until the smoking point before cooking. Purchase only pure mustard oil in Indian grocery stores.

Mustard Seeds, Black *rai:* In the south, these tiny brown-black seeds are the most frequently used spice seed. When they are chopped into hot oil, they crackle and pop and develop a unique nutty flavor.

Paneer Cheese *paneer:* This unripened fresh cheese with the consistency of *tofu* cannot be purchased and must be made at home from milk. A recipe for *paneer* appears on page 50.

Poppy Seeds, White *khus khus:*   These tiny ripe seeds of the poppy plant are much smaller than the black seeds known in America, but they have a similar flavor.

Red Pepper Powder *puissi lal mirch:*   This fiery red powder is made from sun-dried red chili peppers, which are often dry roasted before being ground to a powder. All recipes in this book have been tested with red pepper powder purchased in Asian grocery stores. Cayenne pepper may be substituted. Chili powder, often used in Mexican cooking, should not be used, as it is prepared from a combination of spices unlike red pepper powder and will ruin the taste of the dish.

Rose Essence *ruh gulab:*   This is a diluted essence prepared from rose petals.

Saffron Threads *kesar:*   The world's most expensive spice, saffron is the dried stigma of the saffron crocus and is grown in the northern state of Kashmir and in Spain. The threadlike strands are dark orange and give food a bright yellow color with a distinctive aroma and taste. The threads are soaked in warm water or milk and then crumbled to allow them to infuse before they are added to a dish. Beware of inexpensive saffron or saffron powder, as it is probably inferior.

***Sambar Masala*:**   A delicate, aromatic spice mixture often used in south Indian cooking, this may be purchased in Indian grocery stores. A recipe for *Sambar Masala* appears on page 45.

***Sevian or Seviya*:**   Very thin threadlike vermicelli prepared from durum wheat, *sevian* is also available in roasted form. Be sure to purchase the type called for in the recipe.

Silver Leaf *vark:*   These are very thin sheets of edible pure silver or gold used as an opulent garnish for sweets and other dishes.

Tamarind *imli:*   This beanlike fruit of the tamarind tree has a tart citrus flavor. The fruit is mashed into a pulp and is sold in packages in Asian grocery stores. (See recipe for preparing Tamarind Liquid on page 54.) If unavailable, lime juice may be substituted.

***Toor Dal toovar or arhar dal*:**   This is a split lentil with a slightly sweet flavor. For complete information see page 57.

***Urad Dal*:**   This is a split dried bean that is a close relative of the mung bean. Southerners use *urad dal* in a multitude of dishes, even using it as a seasoning. For complete information see page 57.

***Vark*:**   See silver leaf.

U.S. AND METRIC CONVERSION TABLE

Symbol	When you know:	Multiply by:	To find:
VOLUME			
tsp	teaspoons	5.0	milliliters
tbsp	tablespoons	15.0	milliliters
fl oz	fluid ounces	29.57	milliliters
c	cups	0.24	liters
pt	pints	0.47	liters
qt	quarts	0.95	liters
gal	gallons	3.8	liters
ml	milliliters	0.034	fluid ounces
MASS **(Weight)**			
oz	ounces	28.35	grams
lb	pounds	0.45	kilograms
g	grams	0.035	ounces
kg	kilograms	2.2	pounds
TEMPERATURE			
F	Fahrenheit	5/9 (after subtracting 32)	Celcius
LENGTH			
in	inches	2.5	centimeters

QUICK ROUNDED MEASUREMENTS FOR EASY REFERENCE

VOLUME

1/4 tsp	= 1/24 oz	= 1 ml
1/2 tsp	= 1/12 oz	= 2 ml
1 tsp	= 1/6 oz	= 5 ml
1 tbsp	= 1/2 oz	= 15 ml
1 c	= 8 oz	= 250 ml
4 c (1 qt)	= 32 oz	= 1 liter

MASS (WEIGHT)

1 oz		= 30 g
4 oz		= 115 g
8 oz		= 225 g
16 oz	= 1lb	= 450 g
32 oz	= 2 lb	= 900 g
36 oz	= 2-1/4 lb	= 1,000 g (1 kg)

Bibliography

≈≈≈

Dalal, Tarla. *The Joys of Vegetarian Cooking.* Vakils, Feffer and Simons, Ltd., Bombay, 1989.

Devi, Yamuna. *The Art of Indian Cookery.* Bala Books, 1987.

Husain, Shehzad. *Entertaining Indian Style.* Treasure Press, Great Britain, 1985.

Jaffrey, Madhur. *An Invitation to Indian Cooking.* Vintage Books, 1975.

Jaffrey, Madhur. *A Taste of India.* Atheneum: New York. 1986.

Kalra, J. Inder Singh. *Cooking with Indian Masters.* Allied Publishers Limited: New Delhi. 1986.

Mehta, Jeroo. *Enjoyable Parsi Cooking.* Vakils, Feffer and Simmons, Ltd.: Bombay. 1992.

Padmanabhan, Chandra Padman. *Dakshin Vegetarian Delicacies from South India.* Indus Publishing: New Delhi. 1992.

Patil, Vilma. *Entertaining Indian Style.* UBS Publishers: New Delhi. 1992.

Patil, Vilma.. *Food Heritage of India.* Vakils, Feffer and Simons, Ltd.: Bombay. 1990.

Ray, Sumona. *Indian Regional Cooking.* Quill Publishing Co.: London. 1986.

Sahni, Julie. *Classic Indian Cooking.* William Morrow and Company, Inc., New York: 1980.

Sahni, Julie. *Classic Indian Vegetarian and Grain Cooking.* William Morrow and Company, Inc., New York. 1985.

Shenoy, Jaya. *Dakshin Bharat Cookbook.* Manipal Power Press: Manipal. 1989.

Singh, Digvijaya. *Cooking Delights of the Maharajas.* Vakils, Feffer & Simons, Ltd.: Bombay, 1982.

Singh, Manju. *A Taste of Palace Life.* Royal Indian Cookery, Windward: London. 1977.

Taneja, Meera. *New Indian Cookery.* Fontana Paperbacks: Great Britain. 1983.

Foods of the World; The Cooking of India. Time-Life Books: New York. 1969.

Index